BEING BOILED

Being Boiled

First Edition [2016]

Copyright © Thomas Scott 2018 All Rights Reserved

The rights of Thomas Scott to be identified as the author of this work have been asserted in accordance with the Copyright, Designs and Patents Act 1988

All rights reserved. No part of this publication may be reproduced, stored in a retrieval system, or transmitted, in any form or by any means electronic, mechanical, photocopying, recording or otherwise, without the prior written consent of the publisher. Any person who does any unauthorized act in relation to this publication may be liable to criminal prosecution and civil claims for damages.
This book is sold subject to the condition that it shall not, by way of trade or otherwise, be lent, re-sold, hired out or otherwise circulated without the publisher's prior written consent in any form of binding or cover other than which it is published and without a similar condition including this condition being imposed on the subsequent purchaser.

Spiderwize
Remus House
Coltsfoot Drive
Woodston
Peterborough
PE2 9BF

www.spiderwize.com

A CIP catalogue record for this book is available from the British Library.
The views expressed in this work are solely those of the author and do not necessarily reflect the views of the publisher, and the publisher hereby disclaims any responsibility for them.

This is a work of fiction. Names, characters, businesses, places, events and incidents are either the products of the author's imagination or used in a fictitious manner. Any resemblance to actual persons, living or dead, or actual events is purely coincidental. I have tried to recreate events, locales and conversations from my memories of them. In order to maintain their anonymity in some instances I have changed the names of individuals and places, I may have changed some identifying characteristics and details such as physical properties, occupations and places of residence.

ISBN: 978-1-912694-15-0
ebook ISBN: 978-1-912694-17-4

BEING BOILED

T. R. SCOTT

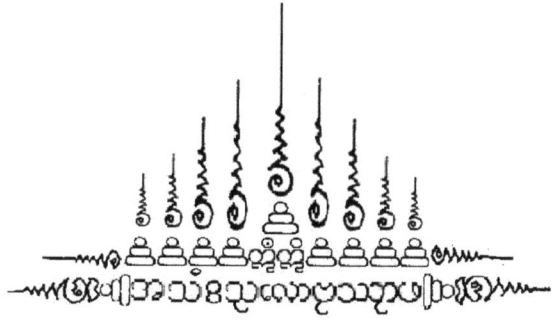

Listen to the voice of Buddha

SPIDERWIZE
Peterborough UK
2018

Acknowledgements

Lilias
Harry (The Hat)
Jack Blade
All my nieces and nephews
David, Harry and Wendy
Jim McKenna
Clare
Diane Scott
Ann-Marie
Shaz & Trood
Britt Romanos
Billy Sloan
Jonn Harton
Christina
Derek Fairlie
John Healey
Tokyo and Sarai
John McIver
Noi
Aunty Betty & Uncle Danny
Uncle David
All my colleagues
Mandip Kaur

Contents

Foreword By The Author 1

CHAPTER ONE
Empire State Human 5

CHAPTER TWO
Crying At The Discotheque 19

CHAPTER THREE
I Wonder Why? (He's The Greatest Dancer) 29

CHAPTER FOUR
Life In A Northern Town............................. 49

CHAPTER FIVE
Save A Prayer.. 63

CHAPTER SIX
Space Oddity... 79

CHAPTER SEVEN
One Night In Bangkok 99

CHAPTER EIGHT
Complex... 125

CHAPTER NINE
Are Friends Electric? 147

CHAPTER TEN
Tinsel Town In The Rain 177

CHAPTER ELEVEN
I Dream To Sleep 203

CHAPTER TWELVE
Being Boiled 225

CHAPTER THIRTEEN
Computer Love 253

CHAPTER FOURTEEN
Timeless Flight.. 273

CHAPTER FIFTEEN
Ghosts 293

CHAPTER SIXTEEN
Starburst 309

For Tucker...

Foreword by the Author

I woke up one day a few months ago and said to myself, I think I'm going to write a book! About what my head asked? Hmm, how about just 'My Life - so far', with alternating episodes and flashbacks of teenage years in Glasgow, failed marriages (two of them - the third one is still stable for now, but becoming hard work ha-ha), shit jobs, being in a band(s), sleeping in the streets, also countries I have either travelled to or worked in - locales such as Thailand and the Philippines, Los Angeles, Hong Kong, New York, Boston, Chicago, Las Vegas, Germany, Sweden, Finland, France, and a few other places.

I will also mention and write about all the nice ladies and all the bitches I have been with. I'm not really misogynistic although I do tend to agree on some points that Milo Yiannopoulos makes on behalf of down trodden males that the feminist movement seem to denigrate more and more lately, but I don't really care if I get called sexist as we all are to some point a bit sexist but that's normal for Men and Women, I'm not too sure how to address the Non- Binaries until Science discovers a new gender!

I will also talk about, or slate, and praise people I have met, have had sex with, perhaps some people I have loathed or even hated. My fascination with fast cars, weird parties in Los Angeles, experience with Ayhuasca (more commonly called DMT or Dimethyl Tryptamine), love of cats, my affair with synthesisers, and generally what I think of the world's politics, religion, and a whole bunch of crap that's going on around the planet at the moment.

The book's called 'Being Boiled' some of you will be thinking (and quite rightly so) that I borrowed this from 'The Human League' song of the same name, and of course you would be right - but, hey, we all live vicariously as someone else and no one is original, in my opinion, we are just the recycled products of a generation before us or the one to come.

To be clear, I'm no expert on anything, I am just a guy with a mouth and half a brain that dragged myself out of the gutters of Glasgow tenement life and managed to educate myself to a degree where I can walk and chew gum at the same time.

Foreword By The Author

So this book, or whatever you want to call it, is for anyone who has had a crap life, no money, waste of space girlfriends and wives, or who have been screwed by relatives (not literally, unless you have, it's just that I haven't). It may as well be called a sort of diary of events and semi-autobiographical in the loosest sense of the word.

Okay, so I may blurt out expletives along the way, as we all do from time to time, and I will sort of come across as knowledgeable and perhaps even wise (yeah, right). I know some nice, big words and others I will have to look up to make sure I don't sound like a meat-head - but, hey, it's my book and it's about getting your own life together and seeing life for what it is and doing the best you can in a rapacious society (woo hoo, big word already!).

The film, 'Fight Club', always reminds me that the dreams you have for life do not exist - for us, the profane, the 'sheople', there is no fortune for you unless you fit in with someone's agenda. There is no fame for you, unless you subscribe to a certain faith, there is nothing you can do that will elevate you to being at the top. The odds are stacked against all of us, except the bastards who are in control, of course, Estonians, Illuminati, Masons, you know who I mean, The Mystery Schools (and all roads lead to Rome, right?), in my opinion, are to blame for a lot of the world's woes and may well lead us into oblivion soon.

Okay, if you do pick this up to read (assuming you have it in your hands and you can read), then it may well resonate with your own experiences of life and loves, or the ups and downs. If it makes you laugh or reflect on things gone by, even only slightly, then for fuck's sake write your own book - it's just a bunch of words! Leave something of yourself behind in this world! Everyone has something to say about the world that we live in and the life that you have led or are currently leading, it's a great thing to be able to chronicle it all down for your own satisfaction or perhaps enjoyment. Some people have led a gifted life, some have led a charmed life, and some have led a very privileged life, indeed, we all have tales to tell and I recommend that everyone should at least attempt to write a book about all the things they have come across in their short existence and leave a legacy for others to read, ponder and perhaps even learn something from your own past experiences - it may never sell or it may just become a self-published book of your own selfish thoughts, but no one can deny the immortality of it and it's right to be a part of your existence that you leave behind when you are dust.

I am not going to apologise for any words or opinions that people may get upset with or think that perhaps I swear a bit too much, it's okay - I'm the one typing the words, I'm the one that's going to hell assuming one exists... you were only reading it!

CHAPTER ONE

EMPIRE STATE HUMAN

Thanks, Mum, I don't know what to say. She has just signed a finance contract with 'McCormack's Music' shop in Glasgow for a Mini Moog Synthesiser, and this incidentally is the shop where all the Glasgow bands went for their music gear, bands such as H20, Wet Wet Wet, Del Amitri, Altered Images, Orange Juice, Alex Harvey, to name drop but a few.

I never really understood that name (Wet Wet Wet), but I think we called them Wet Drip Splash! So annoying and yet so typical that they got where they did, what most bands dream about, and managed to fuck it all up as it inevitably happens when your have minimal brain cells.

I think it was a drug habit someone had succumbed to, classic tale of too much money and not knowing what to do with it - oh, too much money... lets help the poor - no, let's do drugs instead and fuck my life up...well done, guys, I know it was not all of you, but a certain individual. Let's hope you got some money out of your career before it all went to shit. As with all things, you never really get to hear or know the truth behind everything that went on before the self-destruction of something that was seemingly good on the surface but was eating itself from the inside out - yuk, sounds disgusting !

So, now I am the proud owner of a second hand Mini Moog. I remember getting strange looks from the rest of the passengers on the number 45 bus back to Springburn, sitting with this thing on my lap and my Mum sitting just across from me, wondering what the fuck she had just signed for.

I have often wondered who had owned it before me, had it been used in a well-known band and been on TV? I liked to think it belonged to, perhaps, 'Tubeway Army' and they had hocked it down south, only for it to turn up in Scotland and be taken home by me!

The next few weeks I was making the Moog create all these wonderful, weird noises that only a Moog can produce (and my Mum's ears were now wishing she had not signed for it). It was a mind opener and a zillion miles from the 'Bontempi Organ', which was sort of loaned to me from a 'mate' in 1978 who lived next door to me at that time, so thanks to Alan West, the red headed geek who had no friends and was known as 'The Halitosis Kid' to the rest of the street - I mean, this guy's breath could turn milk sour just by being in the same room, but he did help to kick-start my love affair with all things synth.

I would hook it up to my 'pride and joy' stereo system, which I bought from a catalogue at £6 a month, I think it was 'Littlewood's' or 'Kay's', or something like that. Anyway, the Moog was an integral part of my hi-fi system now, blasting through the speakers, which unfortunately did not last long - one night there was a curious rumbling sound and the speakers popped very loudly as the cones burst! I later learned that the Moog's filters had gone into 'self-oscillation' and, as the frequencies rose, the fate of my speakers was sealed. Fuck it! I needed more money to buy a decent 'Carlsboro' keyboard amp/speaker. I can't remember how I got the money together for this, but, bloody hell, it was worth it. It was so loud at two hundred true watts, had a fifteen inch speaker, and I could hear and feel every nuance the synth pumped out. I was in Synth Nirvana.

The Moog now sounded even better, the basses were big and fucking obnoxious and the lead lines were absolute sonic kisses to your eardrums. The Moog could only play one note at a time (monophonic), and there was so much in the sound due to the oscillators being split, the filters detuned and modulated, the ADSR (Attack, Decay, Sustain, Release) were calibrated to their longest setting, and the note I pressed was so organic that it changed tone and was just fucking beautiful. The deck was set to 'max' and the sound would take about eight to ten minutes to dissipate into oblivion, only for me to press the note once more, where it went through the cycle again, but subtly different every time.

Diane, my long time and suffering girlfriend of that era, was always huffing and puffing about how we never went out any more and how I loved my Moog more than her. We had a crappy fight over it one night and she left, leaving me to masturbate, or perhaps even fuck my faithful synth (shit, was she right?). I mean, what's the fucking problem with some women? They talk bollocks mostly, every second line, but do we try to change them? I just wish that some of the women I had been with and spent a considerable part of my life being around had some sort of world view or personal plan to make their lives or other people's lives better, but sadly, no - most of the women I ended up with were very basic people and very basic in their needs out of life, generally quite happy to be a drone or a mother with too many kids to feed, or a lush, druggie or alcoholic. I don't blame them for being like that at all, but in retrospect, I suppose I should have had the foresight to be looking for likeminded ladies that I could connect with.

We parted company around 1985 and I had never

seen her since, but strangely in the summer of 2006 I was driving through Charing Cross (Glasgow, not London) when I saw this woman walking along the pavement and thought it looked a bit like Diane. So I drove past her about seven times like some desperate kerb crawler, as I wanted to make sure it was her - after all, it had been years since I last saw her. Anyway, I parked up, got out of my car and, as she was walking towards me, I said softly, "Diane?" She stared at me for a bit and then the light came on and she smiled at me. In my head there was 'The Human League's song playing 'Louise', and the line "as if they were still lovers" was replaying itself over and over. It just seemed as though it were yesterday that we had last seen each other, she was still as pretty as ever, perhaps even more so, and I felt instant regret at losing her so long ago - seeing her there standing in front of me made me think of all the good times we had, the memories of something really good, something truly real, that you never find again.

She told me she had two kids who were all grown up now and that her life was good and she had been happy for a long time. I felt a slight pang of jealousy, could I say the same thing? I knew I had long ago married the wrong person, and it was just to escape from a violent household, but the marriage was wrong from the start - she was not my type in any way, shape, or form. She was lazy, drank too much, had an even crazier family than mine, and was sexually retarded as most catholic girls were at that time in the world. She was lewd and sometimes offensive, with a bad attitude, and I was glad it only lasted less than a year, but I knew I should have made things up with Diane and not wimped out. Back then, I thought it was too late to reconcile, you know the 'fix it' limit has gone after six months of not being in contact - I guess it was simply meant to be and I was happy at least that she had met someone she wanted kids with, because that was never part of my plan.

Of all the things I wanted to say to her - to say sorry about this and that, for being a fucktard, or to say 'I missed you' - I blurted out, "I should have married you!", to which she smiled at me again. We chatted about old times and how bald I was now (thanks, Diane). I watched her walk away and part of me wanted to time travel back to '79 and not buy the Moog - where's Doctor Who when you need him? Hey, Pete Capaldi anyone? If only I could have zipped back to when things were good with Diane and maybe married her, and had a better life or at least a happier one. Today I have no idea if my life was better because of the synth and the bands, but I like to think I did okay.

"Yes, yes, yes," I'm screaming at the top of my lungs, elated and excited that I have just nailed the exact sounds and learned to play 'Are Friends Electric' by Tubeway Army (yes, Gary Numan). That's it, I said to myself, I feel I'm ready to join a real fucking band, because now I could play anything from Kraftwerk or any synth based band that was knocking around at that time. I remember when I first got the synth, I would take some piano lessons and improve my understanding of chords and chord structures, so I hooked up with some guy from Motherwell, whose name is on a dusty shelf in my mind (If I remember, I will mention his name later in the book). We had some great ideas - he was more synth pop on the bass lines and I was more Kraftwerk on the lead lines and melodies, but it seemed to work in a hybrid fashion, creating catchy little tunes with some great, thumping dance beats - how could we fail?

We learnt from our mistakes, moved on and up, and just got better and better at writing tunes. For about two years we were learning and practicing our craft, gigging in working men's clubs (oh, joy), and then in early '81 something coalesced. I had written a song called 'The Park' I had 'borrowed' the drum track from 'The Human League's 'Open Your Heart' and it sounded like chart material until one of us tried to sing it... then it was clear that neither of us, despite our attempts at singing, were going to make it any better. We agreed it needed a woman's touch, so we got this red hot girl called Michelle, a gorgeous blonde, from Motherwell too! And, man, could she sing.

She was so hot my cock was always pointing north in salute to her beauty. The trouble was the other guy in the band was saluting her too, funny how we both had to hide the lumps in our trousers at the same time whenever she was in the same room (my lump was bigger, by the way). She had model looks, was tall, fucking sexy as hell, lovely face and arse, and a smooth, sexy voice made for singing. She was such tease without even trying and I always thought about maybe getting it on with her, but decided to not mix business with pleasure as it always works out badly in the end, right?

We booked some studio time (our first experience!) in, to be fair, a cheap '8 Track' Studio and got to laying down the track, which by now was sounding like a No.1 hit (don't they all, huh?). You know the kind of studio, piss stained, oddly cut carpets, vanilla paint on damp walls, and a coffee machine that looked like it had seen better days - there was always something odd floating in this one and I never had the courage to ask what the hell it was! The studio was somewhere near Motherwell, the studio guy seemed to be in tune with our sound, had taken an instant liking to Michelle, and was more interested in her than the track - what a fucking douche! Just mix the track, you sleazy cunt!

The band started out named as 'TransAtlantic', not as pretentious as it sounds, as we were thinking big from the start - America, here we come! Watch out, world. I had all these crazy ideas for visuals and art work, and at the same time I started wearing makeup and dyeing my hair - my family freaked! Now, let me explain, this is Glasgow in the late '70s, it was considered "gay" to fucking comb your hair, never mind dye it and wear makeup... how I never ended up beaten, stabbed, or laying on a slab in the morgue, I will never know. I have to point out, as some of you might be thinking it already - no! I am definitely not gay, (nothing wrong with gays, I'm just not one of them). The makeup was just for the band and crafting an image that would hurl us into stardom, or so I thought. I always loved Kenneth Williams from the 'Carry On' movies, who actually was gay, but never really admitted it - he would say things like, "I'm not gay, I just help them out when they are busy" ...ha-ha, brilliant!

The guy I was in the band with (still have no idea of his name), along with Michelle, wanted to try some more pop oriented songs and I was more or less agreeing as synth pop was just taking off in the UK, although not so much in Scotland, so we thought we could get on the bandwagon and beat anyone to it who had the same idea - hence the name change to 'DanceVision'.

Well, Michelle dropped a clanger shortly afterwards and said she could not do the band anymore as she was, wait for it - Pregnant! And guess who by? Yes, correct, the nameless fucker in the band! So, two years of sweat, blood, and tears were all about to go down the pan because they wanted to bump uglies (I was not jealous and I bet their eventual kid was not cute at all :-(fact!)

Being Boiled

I had grossly miscalculated the effect of dyeing my hair and wearing makeup could have, and how this would eventually help me fear for my life and look for another job. I worked in a bakery called 'Scars', owned by Serbs or Slovakians, I never really knew for sure where they came from, I just knew they were not indigenous to the UK. The pay was really shit and the work was hard, but at least I managed to feed myself and stay alive at a time when things were just as bleak then as they are becoming today. Anyway, the bakery was in a part of Glasgow that was named 'The Jungle', and most of the people who worked in this factory were from that area and were part animal, football hooligans and religious fuck heads - when they saw the colour of my hair go from dirty fair to black overnight, they were soon having a go at me. I should have realised that these 'NEDS' would not take to kindly to me changing my appearance.

I have no idea what I was thinking, but at the time it seemed a great image for the band and we knew, even then, that the music was not enough - we needed an image, a thing, something identifiable that was so off the wall that they had to notice us. Fuck, all the bands were doing something, long hair, make up, brightly coloured suits, two tone hair, high heels, anything goes and I guess we all owe this to David Bowie and 'Ziggy Stardust'... what a fucking genius! But, sadly, no longer with us, in flesh and blood, but always in our hearts and minds.

Unfortunately, the place where I worked was full

of retarded head bangers that only knew how to drink, smoke, do drugs, and attend tribal ball games where they shout abuse at others just like them! I was in the wrong place at the wrong time in my life and I was going to pay for my individuality with a few beatings sometime soon!

"Hey, you a fucking poof?" they would jibe at me. Some would throw hard, heavy things at me while my back was turned, I tried to explain the reason, but it was like explaining quantum physics to a bunch of bananas. The Bakery boss called me up to his office once to discuss my "individual looks" and would no doubt be having a go at me in some sort of managerial capacity. His name was Bill (who, now I think about it, looked like that dickhead PM, Cameron), he sat me down and looked right at me and said "What's with the black hair and nail varnish and eyeliner?" Oops! Oh, yes, I had become careless and was getting to work after gigs with no time to clean it all off properly, and to be fair he sort of understood what I was trying to do and, to give him credit, he was cool about it - but he did say he could not help if the wankers who worked here had a go at me which I sort of got and was highly worried about.

It was about this time that the real nastiness started - punches to my face in the changing room and kicks up my arse by these guys in their fifties as I was walking by became too much. I had worked here for years alongside most of them, and all because of my hair colour they were they were treating me like a fucking leper - maybe their brains would just not accept the changes that were happening in the world around them right now... some of the older guys were from the '40s and '50s, so their music view and world view were miles apart from '70s youths.

I decided to look for another job and get away from these vicious bastards as soon as I could and, as luck would have it, I found job in a 'Safeway' supermarket on Byres Road in the West End. My life was about to get better.

Glasgow –Old Springburn 1975

My Dad was kicking the shit out of my Mum after coming back from drinking all day. This had been going on for years, but tonight was different. Something was about to change forever, something inside my older brother suddenly snapped, screaming and crying he jumped on my Dad, trying to drag him off of my frightened Mum, whose nose was bleeding badly at this point. It was then that I, my younger sister, and brother all grew up on the same night, at the same moment. We all jumped up to help our older brother get this maniac off our Mum, the woman who had done her best throughout our lives - occasionally failing, but for the most part, she managed to somehow feed us, clothe us and keep us together.

We all kicked and pulled on our Dad's hair and punched him as hard as we could until he eventually let my Mum go. His face was full of anger and shock at what had just happened and, at that moment, we knew and he knew that this would be the last time that he would dare lift a hand to her or us!

On reflection, I know it's why I never had or wanted kids - what if I turned out to be a monster like him? How could I put anyone through that sort of life? This scared me so much I would lose sleep and worry about the future and how it would affect me being with anyone. I just hoped that deep down I was nothing like him and the violence was not transferable through a tragically inferior gene pool from somewhere down the tree.

I did not know it then, but one day very soon I would leave Glasgow and my woeful life behind and never ever look back.

CHAPTER TWO

CRYING AT THE DISCOTHEQUE

Tiffany's Dance Hall, Glasgow - October 1978

Fucking bitches!

It's a Thursday night, October 1978, and I'm lying on the floor, crying my eyes out like a dumped bride-to-be in 'Tiffany's' Dance Hall on Glasgow's Sauchiehall Street. I manage to get up, run past the bar and then to the main entrance, I make it to the street and flag down a passing black cab. I stumble in and spit my address at him through gritted teeth and the pain I can now feel on the inside of my legs. "Fucking! Fuck! Fuck! Fuck!" I remember saying to myself, as the cab sped away into the cold and wet night.

A week earlier I had went to an audition for 'Dancers' they were hiring at 'Tiffany's' - oh, yes, before I got into Bands and the music stuff, I was a bit of a disco dancer and a really good one at that! I had some 'street cred' on the local dance scene, notably 'Shuffles Discothèque' just a few doors away from 'Tiffany's' where myself and a few others were setting the trend in new dance moves and winning competitions.

There were two dance floors in 'Shuffles', upstairs was called 'Heaven' and downstairs was called 'Hell'. The upstairs arena was strangely named as it's where the Non-Poseurs went to dance to rock and roll, and other shitty music that was not disco, so the Poseurs (people who looked cool, wore drainpipe trousers, winkle picker, patent leather shoes and granddad collar shirts - before they became trendy and homogenised by all the crappy chain stores) I went to dance downstairs in 'Hell'. All the best-looking women went downstairs, it was strangely, fucking paradoxically, Heaven.

I had women queuing up, asking me to teach them how to dance and they were very grateful indeed! I never had a promiscuous bone in my body until I started going there. I would have sex in the ladies toilets, in the cloakrooms, and up alleyways with willing and very sexy ladies - the only thing I hated was the 'nookie badge' some of them insisted on giving me.

(A 'nookie badge' was a 'hickie' or a 'love-bite', a badge of honour during sex - a vampiric bite on the neck that left a considerable bruise and were fucking filthy looking things that took the best part of a week to get rid of!)

I had a disturbing experience one time with a lovely woman called 'Jan' (you know who you are). We were canoodling behind a concrete pillar in the alcove of the 'Royal Bank of Scotland'! I had her skirt up and was having a great time, pounding away, when I noticed that the full-length glass window behind her had an outline behind it. I'm thinking to myself, its 2am, there's no one in the bank at this time, surely? Still pumping away and nearly up to the nice, tickly bit, the shape moves closer and I can now see through the opaqueness of the glass, a pervy looking, old, security guard with his dick out, wanking himself off to me having sex with this girl who is unaware of what I can see - and, to my eternal shame, I carried on until I felt my gonads shudder with delight as my man juice said hello to her inner thigh (no condom available, so I pulled the little fella out just before lift-off), gave her a hug and then walked her to the late night buses queuing in George Square. There was no way I was going to tell her what was going on behind her back, but my older brother, however, found this story hilarious!

My sister, Wendy, told me that Tiffany's Dancehall were looking for warm up disco dancers and, as

I was interested in the money and the chance to dance in such a big place that had a huge dance floor, balconies, and it all looked so fucking posh, I went along. So, I pass the audition and I'm picked to dance on Thursday nights and instructed to team up with some random girl that was picked for that night as well. However, on the night... well, fuck me, she does not show up and probably got cold feet or something. So, here I am at 10pm, waiting to dance in front of approximately forty nurses and some other freaky looking women (nurses night as it turned out - the Western Infirmary Hospital was just around the corner!).

So, the manager says, "No dance partner, tonight?"

I said, "Aye, but it's ok - I don't need one... I can warm the crowd up and get them in the mood for dancing!"

And so, I get the chance to do my somersaults, spins and generally show off my flash moves to a bunch of semi-sexy nurses... he-he.

I am wearing my best poseur gear, it is a white 'Bowie' suit (short, waiter type jacket and pleated trousers) - I think they called it that and I bought it from some punk/new wave record store place in Queen Street for £15. I also had white, dance shoes; you know the ones that 'Pineapple' started selling years later, as a fashion accessory. So, here I am, I looked the part and I had just finished my first dance - "Fucking brilliant!" the manager says to me, he looks a lot like Paul Nicholas with a soft blonde perm in his hair (I remember thinking he was perhaps gay and made a mental note to assert my masculinity so he did not say or do anything he might regret) ...I'm not homophobic, I'm not afraid of my house!

I needed to take a leak, so I go to the men's room to shake the snake and he follows me in...

"For fucks sake," I say under my breath, "don't be gay, don't be gay, please don't be fucking gay!"

The fucker stands right beside me and is peeing merrily away when he then strikes up a conversation that nearly made me knuckle him out.

He says, "Err, do you strip?"

I said "Eh?"

He says it again a bit louder, "Do you strip?"

I said, "Fucking what?"

He said, "I'll double your money if you strip for the nurses next time you get up to dance."

Huge sigh of relief! He is essentially saying if I strip, he will give me an extra £20 - hell, yes! I am saving up for a Moog Synthesiser, so it would help - but I said, "I'll only take my jacket and shirt off!"

"Okay - deal!" he says and leaves the gents, while I am sighing with relief that I did not have to knock him out after all.

I have to admit, dancing in front of all those nurses does a lot for your mojo, I felt horny, sexed up and loving the attention, I was getting from them all.

They were all sitting around the dance floor at tables, eating and drinking - they were all

a lot older than me and some were definitely in their late forties and fifties... but, hey, I'm young and cocky, I'm up for it! So, I dance and then take my jacket off and throw it around. I now have the Nurses full attention and they think I am going to go the whole hog and strip down to my thong - no fucking chance, because they are not pretty enough to see my porridge gun. Now, I am stripping bit by bit, off comes my shirt and I dance and prance around on the floor making suggestive hip movements to them all, seeing they are all purring with approval and seemingly seriously disappointed I am not taking my trousers off!

Paul Nicholas then mouths across to me to dance in-between the tables while I have my shirt off, and I acknowledge him and mouth back 'okay' ...and this is when it all went wrong! I had no sooner got in-between the first set of tables when two big nurses grab me, I mean they made Hattie Jacques look like Twiggy, they could kick start jumbo jets with those legs and probably punch nails in with those fucking hands of theirs

"Get him! Grab the bastard!"

They pulled me down to the floor and one sat on my chest as the other one and a few other nurses all grabbed my trousers and pulled them down. I put up a brave struggle, but there were just too many hands pulling at my pants and cock. I could feel their nails digging into my inner thighs and scrotes, I was screaming like a lobster that was being boiled. I had a two ton arse in my face and about eight sets of hands making sure I was naked. I wanted to fucking die!

"What a bunch of witches", I am thinking, "I should have known Glasgow women were just like the men, perhaps even worse" I wanted to punch them all in their twats and bite their ugly nipples off, there is no way these were anywhere close to the nurses that we all dream about in sexy suspenders and cute uniforms! No fucking way - these were fully paid up members of the 'Sisters of Satan' club!

I remember eventually somehow getting up and running, clothes in hand as they all enjoyed the predicament I was in, bleeding from my inner thighs and just about crying with my nine inches swinging around (alright, seven inches - it's my fucking story, okay:-p). I get to the front door, got my trousers on and I'm out in the street flagging a taxi down - what a fucking night! Put me right off nurses and Carry On films for years.

The funny thing was I got a call the following Thursday from Mr Perm and he says, "It's 10pm, where the fuck are you?"

I said, "Did you not fucking get it? I quit last week, you thick cunt, go and fuck yourself!"

Sometimes I like to think that somewhere in time a nurse still has my black, satin, man-thong - complete with blood, sweat and tears. Ha-ha!

I remember one Hogmany in 'Shuffles Disco', I kissed one hundred ladies as a bet after 'The Bells' and I could not feel my lips for an hour, as they were numbed with all the action! Great night and good times that I thought would never come again... or so I thought!

STV Studios Glasgow 1978:

I entered some UK, regional Disco Dance thing in '78 that was aired on live TV (STV - Scottish Television) and I managed to fuck it up by falling over a few times. See, I had bought new shoes, so the soles were still a bit slippery and the floor was highly polished (thanks a lot, STV). I tried to score my shoes with some stones I found outside, but it was clearly not enough - I was slipping and sliding all over the place like some demented bovine with the falling-over disease. Some fucker called Grant Santino went on to win - I think the prize was a trip to 'Studio 54' in New York and some cash. I knew I was the better dancer, but fucked it all up by buying new shoes - what a fucking disaster! You can still find the clip on 'YouTube' and even see me fall over as I enter! What a maroon, right?

A very young Arlene Philips (but could also have been the lady who was in Saturday Night Fever) was on the judging panel and was drooling all over Grant, tongue in his mouth and gagging for it - I never had a chance. Yeah, sure, he could shake his arse a bit, but that was it, as far as I could see, and I have no idea what the hanky thing hanging out his back pocket was supposed to do unless it was a gay pride symbol from San Francisco, as some people have said to me. This was a bit like wearing the earring in the right ear instead of the left. I confused people by wearing one in each ear (no - it does not mean I am bi-sexual), and this got me a full week's suspension from school once... when the Headmaster asked me why I was wearing earrings - my answer? "To hide the holes, sir!"

CHAPTER THREE

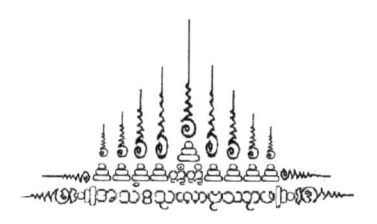

I WONDER WHY?
(HE'S THE GREATEST DANCER)

I had a variety of dancing jobs at the weekends for a year or so, and I used to take Diane (my sweet girlfriend of that era) with me - usually out of Glasgow City to small places in the country with the DJ who was employing me as a warm up dancer to get the crowd going at functions and local discos. The funny thing about youngsters in those days, as opposed to these days, was that in the '70s and '80s, most of the kids were shy and did not want to be the first ones up to dance on an empty dance floor for fear of embarrassment and ridicule of their dancing techniques (or lack of). So, to counteract this, they had people like me - show-offs, competition winners and the like to get the night in the right mood so everyone supposedly enjoyed themselves. Back then, guys did NOT dance with guys and had to ask a local girl if she was 'dancing'. This was usually initiated with a tap on said girl's shoulder while she was dancing around her own or a collection of her friend's handbags strewn around the floor.

This was not a great time for guys, I must admit, being between that age of knowing what your cock was for and having nothing to do with it except to use it as a 'DIY', stress relief tool. The sheer pressure and lack of social skills for interacting with the opposite sex was in itself a chasm to jump across - for fuck's sake, it was hard enough admitting to other guys you were going to a fucking Disco, but we all knew in reality it was the only focal point we would be able to get close to hot lassies and be able to 'get a bird' or start 'winching' (which was a colloquial term derived from 'Wenching', I believe).

I'm no historian, and my research may be sloppy, but this is how I honestly remember it. Mental note; oh, remember 'Wenches Bar', next to Queen Street station? All those scantily clad waitresses? Those were the days; - a bit like 'Centre Court', opposite Tiffany's... waitresses in tennis gear (remember that, Jonn?). I must admit, I did enjoy going there - a drink and testament to what you will do for money at the end of the week. Hey... wear a geeky outfit, yes sir! I have never prostituted myself in fancy dress

I Wonder Why? (he's The Greatest Dancer)

for a wage at the end of the week - yet! Anyway, to offset this embarrassing period before anyone wanted to get up and dance, they had 'moi' as one of the show-offs. I'd get up and start dancing, spinning and somersaulting, dropping down to my knees - I mean, John Travolta can fuck off! I could dance rings around that ugly fuck anytime and I did not need to be in 'Studio 54', New York to do it! Tony Manero - Attica! Attica! Attica! Well, he can kiss my hairy Scottish arse! Ha-ha!

Stonehaven could not be further away from 'Studio 54', and so this little town in Scotland was the venue for the Saturday night disco for the locals (too far for teens to get to Glasgow and back with no bus fare). The place looked okay, whilst the town looked quiet and ordinarily boring. As for me, I am all fired up and ready to enjoy myself. The place had about two hundred teens in attendance already with the lassies on one side and the guys on the other - all standing up like meerkats whenever one of the lassies walked by them.

Oh, I could pick up on the sexual tensions in this place... so many virgin guys and so many 'NEDS' (I should have explained this term before - this is Scottish slang for Non-Educated Delinquents) that had zero to no chance at all of getting a dance with any of the local girls. I mean, some of these guys were right out of the Stone Age as far as social skills were involved. I remember saying under my breath, "Fuck me, what a bunch of Troglodytes," and sniggering

Being Boiled

to myself. This was going to be a long night, but it might be kinda fun!

I danced myself to a frenzy to a couple or twelve inch records (music on vinyl, remember them?), managed to encourage a few nice lassies up to dance with me, and showed them a few dance moves which they seemed to enjoy. Diane would be keeping a close eye on me, in case she thought I was flirting too much! Sigh - having a partner can be such a ball ache sometimes, and she would insist on coming along for 'moral support'... yeah, right! Anyway, I am showing at least four nice ladies how to dance and more were getting up. As expected, no guys would dare get up and were still too 'NED'-like to have the balls to ask someone for a dance. Twenty minutes later, I go to shake the snake and about six of the 'NEDS' follow me into the Gents. So, there I am, standing, having a pee, and these Neanderthals have chair legs, and one even had a chair (minus a leg) - they were obviously going to smash my brains in and I was a little bit worried at that point. Tomorrow's 'News Headlines' flashed before my eyes... 'Murder in Stonehaven - extremely handsome disco dancer beaten to death'.

These socially inept, hairless apes were shouting and screaming at me, saying I was stealing all the birds from them! I mean, fuck's sake! All of them? (Well, I probably could have if I had wanted to, hehe!) They were blaming me for them not having a chance with any of the local talent. So, thinking very quickly, I said, "Guys, guys, you've no chance if you can't dance, girls like guys who can dance!" Ergo, there I was, in the gents toilets, teaching a bunch of thugs how to do dance moves so they could hopefully engage with the ladies - where, in actual fact, I was only making sure they did not beat the shit out of me. Time for a major rethink on the dancing career… Taxi!!!

Disco was, sort of, losing its appeal in the '80s, and punk was slowly but surely becoming more mainstream (which was paradoxically what they did not want - fucked that up, huh? It's strange how easily you will prostitute your beliefs for money). 'The Clash', 'The Damned', 'The Sex Pistols', and 'The Stranglers' were all now in the charts and played in what was now being called 'Nightclubs', so all the 'poseur' stuff was going out the window and, so, I found myself becoming unemployable as a dancer... which was one of the reasons I thought about being in a band, and why I had been saving up for a 'Mini Moog' Synthesiser to make the next leap forward in my life. I think this was the very first time I had delusions of wanting to be a pop star.

I was a fan of 'Steve Harley and Cockney Rebel' and loved some the synth stuff done by Duncan Mackay, especially on 'The Best Years Of Our Lives', 'Timeless Flight', and 'Prima Donna' - the sounds always fascinated me. We have all done it, stood in front of the mirror with a hairbrush or something to pretend we are the singer or guitarist of our favourite band. I was also listening to 'Jean Michel Jarre's brilliant 'Oxygen' album, which was all synth and beautifully crafted. 'Tangerine Dream', too, were a firm favourite to listen to, and they were using a 'Moog Modular' - huge, wall to ceiling, racks of synth modules. They sounded fucking monstrous! I was gagging to have a synthesizer.

I had just heard the music in the cinema advert for 'Gordon's Gin', by the original 'Human League', and it's a brilliant piece of music, which I would eventually play along to with my 'Moog'. I really wanted to be famous, or on TV, or 'Top of the Pops' at least... or any of the current pop shows that were kicking around at the time. One of the most under rated bands of the '80s was 'Japan' - utterly brilliant songs and great synths by Richard Barbieri.

I have to thank Jim McKenna for letting me mess round with some classic little synths when I had no chance of owning one at that point in time. He showed me some gritty little 'Roland' that was a not a million miles away from the sound of a 'Moog', a 'Prodigy' and a 'Liberation'! All this stuff was great gear, and it made me want one all the more!!!

My experience of dealing with 'NEDS' was not restricted to discos, unfortunately. Back in the late '70s there was a prolific explosion of 'NEDS' all over Glasgow, and in the area I lived, 'Springburn', there was a gang in every district. 'Young Springburn Peg', 'View Toi', 'Milton Peg', 'Possil Fleet' to name but a few of these. We had moved from '18,

Keppochill Road', essentially old Springburn, to a different world from those tenements - to sprightly 'new builds' called 'maisonettes'. They looked a bit pretentious and dystopian, and I would find out the darker side of living in these faceless, communal blocks of grief not long after.

Knock, knock, and knock - Someone is at the door of our new house on Viewpoint Road. The knocking came again; I am the only one home as everyone else is out in town helping my Mum pick out new bedding and curtains for the new house. I open the door and three fucking 'NEDS' are standing there, right, fucking, ugly, obnoxious looking, low life, cunts - immediately one blurts out, "Fucking new guy... right, here's the rules! We run the fucking street, you do what we say or your life is not worth living!" Feeling a bit taken aback, I sort of mumble, "Err, well, umm...", at which point one of these low life, cunts spits right deep into my mouth, a big, dirty, fucking green bastard! I gag and close the door, hearing them laughing as I run to the bathroom, gargle with hot water, and brush my teeth for about ten minutes.

I felt better, but so fucking angry - and this is not the usual me - but something in me wanted to teach them not to fuck with the 'Scott's', and I knew if I did not do something, my life would be made miserable and I would be the dick who let someone spit into my mouth. I could still hear them outside the front door, still laughing and still sounding very pleased with the way things had went. I opened the door and coldly pointed my older brother's airgun at the spitter's groin, I pulled the trigger and he went down with a whining scream, as the other two 'hard men' were offski - running like greyhounds chasing a hare. I calmly closed the door, went downstairs, and waited... knowing there would be consequences.

An hour later, there was a loud knock at the front door and there was this woman with the spitter and a cop.

"Fuck's sake," I said, under my breath, "no one's home yet and I have to deal with this all by myself!"

I blurted out, "That fuck spat in my mouth," and "No, he was fucking mistaken - I did not have an airgun. Come in and look, if you want!"

His mum had his trousers pulled right down to show a beautifully painful lump on the inside of his thigh with a nice, big, red, impact spot.

I said, "Looks like a bee sting, to me."

He was crying like a little girl.

The cop says abruptly, "Any witnesses?".

And, to his credit, the spitter said, "No!" I think he was scared to get his cronies involved. "Okay, nothing I can do. Behave yourselves!" and the cop was on his way, leaving the spitter and his Mum to walk away and take the shame.

Am I glad I did it? I don't know, I did not even think about it, but at least they never bothered me again and my older brother, younger brother and sister were a bit safer on our own street after that day.

(I later found out, years later, this guy had died in a motorbike accident while travelling across India... which made me kinda reflect on it all.) As for 'being safer', I was about to find out how fleeting that feeling really was.

It was a Friday night (1973), and my older brother, Harry, his friend, Ricky, and me went to see 'The Exorcist' which had just come out that week. I really wanted to see it, but it was 'X' rated, so my brother took me and somehow I managed to get into the cinema without anyone asking any questions. The film was great, scared me shitless, laughable and tame these days, of course, but back then it was one of the scariest horrors I had ever seen. We had no money for hotdogs, popcorn, or for the bus home that night, so we did what all teens did back then - we walked the seven miles home, through some of the craziest, gang infested, areas of Glasgow. It was a bit like the cult movie, 'Warriors', where we were trespassing through other peoples 'hoods' to get home to ours. We were sneaking around streets, making sure we were not walking into trouble and checking our backs the whole time we were walking. I think this was even scarier than 'The Exorcist' movie we had just came from. We finally made it back to Springburn and started to walk up Balgary Hill, and we were just passing the corner of Galloway Street when five or six older guys shouted their gang war-cry at us - 'Peg, ya bass', and they started running at us! We shot off like whippets, but one guy caught up to me and, as he was right behind me, I stumbled out of fear and he just missed the back of my head with a thick bottomed beer glass - I felt it whoosh by my head and I scrambled up and ran like 'The Six Million Dollar Man'.

Harry and Ricky were down on the ground and they were getting a horrific beating by these sick, fucking animals. I came back minutes later with my brother's fake 'Samurai Sword', expecting to start swinging it at these evil bastards, but they were long gone and all I could see was my brother and friend lying in heaps with blood from their heads all over the pavement. I really thought they were fucking dead as they were not responding to my shouting and screaming - there was blood everywhere and a small crowd of people had gathered to stand and stare at the horror in front of them. I could already hear the wail of sirens getting closer, so I dumped the fake sword into a bush just as the cops got there... moments before the Ambulance did.

Harry and Ricky were in 'Stobhill General Hospital' for many months and, personally, I think they were never the same again. My brother seemed less vibrant and energetic, and, as the years passed, he certainly seemed less cognitive. We later found out that these guys were known to the police for being trouble makers and causing all sorts of mayhem at the weekends. They were a family of morons called 'The Colquhoun's' and they did not deserve any kind of freedom let alone existence. They were the lowest order of life, being two steps below an amoeba strain - these oxygen stealers were all jailed at various points later on for violent crimes and murder, or so I had heard many years later. This fact was little consolation for my brother who had lost something that night, never for it to return. I hope these bastards die a slow, lingering, cancerous death one day! Bitter and angry? Yes, I am - but only towards these creatures masquerading as humans. My older brother has survived two bad strokes and he has brain aneurysms just waiting to explode in his head and steal his life from him - he is fifty six, has been in poor health since his forties... and I love him dearly.

The paradoxes of life sometimes makes me wonder 'what the fuck is going on?' I ended up getting work experience in the very same hospital Harry and Ricky had been, perhaps because it's only a few hundred yards from Colston Secondary School, where I was stumbling through my education the same as everybody else at that time. Maths - boring. English? Oh, please. Science? Well, maybe, Music? Kinda interesting, but all Mozart and Chopin. Home Economics and Cooking? What the fuck? French - ooh, la la... not! Then there was P.E. Now here's a funny thing - from an early age I was never ever interested in the nonsensical thing that every Glasgow brat was into at that time... fucking football! To me it was a complete waste of time and fucking energy, running to kick a ball into one of two big fucking holes at the end of a field. I've never been to a football match in my entire life! This being Glasgow, of course, people thought you were mentally ill if you did not like either Celtic or Rangers. No, no, no, fuck that fucking pile of crap which sustained and justified itself on perpetuating religious bigotry and hate for differing perspectives of the same worship of the same so called 'God'! And this is why I still hate football and religion to this day. Secular society? - Yeah, right! Biggest load of bullshit ever to leave anyone's lips - especially the retarded government at that time.

Okay, let me see - same God, but different religious practices... and if you have no idea about Catholicism or Protestantism, then you need to do some serious reading. This is why there is so much religious hate in Scotland and Northern Ireland - it's a virus of the mind and you get indoctrinated at an early age by football. You see, Rangers football club is Protestant (as are the players) and Celtic (yes, you guessed it) are Catholic. So what? I hear you say - these teams use this as a religious war on a football field, the supporters are the same religions as well, and they hate each other with opposing, equally evil doctrines and are quite happy to beat the shit out of each other over football and religious differences. I mean, what fucking chance has anyone got who is born into a family with a parent or parents programmed with this form of shite burned into their twisted brains?

I felt this maniacal mind-set first hand one morning after leaving work. I had just finished night shift at

I Wonder Why? (he's The Greatest Dancer)

the Bakery and the sky was chucking down loads of snow, it was so thick it was already a foot deep and I had five miles to walk home with no bus fare and no way was I not going to attempt a 'niggy'. Let me explain - this is not a racial slur, it's a Glasgow term for piggy-backing on a moving vehicle. Okay, lots of people who started early or finished early in the morning at their jobs usually walked to work as the pay was so shit. No-one wanted to spend any money on bus fares, so what we would do (and if you are from '70s Glasgow, you will remember this) is hang around at a bus terminus, where the drivers would change over. This gave at least three people the chance to hang onto the back of the bus where the engine was, grip a slim ledge on the back window and stand on a narrow ledge at the bottom of the bus frame with your feet, (a niggy), and hopefully the bus driver did not notice you as he pulled away. The only problem you had was trying to get off where you wanted to alight, and sometimes the bus took you past your intended destination by a few hundred yards, but still beats the fuck out of walking in the rain and snow, haha. Sometimes, if you were unlucky, there would be a police car behind the bus at some point and you would just have to jump and run.

It was snowing very heavily when I finished work that morning, and my mate, who was just starting, said, "Here, have my scarf." I said, "Thanks," and wrapped it round my neck and head like a hood. I walked about half a mile on the road home with this thick blanket of snow falling onto me. I was completely covered in the white stuff and remember walking by a parked coach and looking up as I heard people banging on the coach windows. I had no idea what was going on, so I just kept walking. Something made me look back and, fuck me, the people were getting off the coach, shouting at me, picking up bricks and bottles, and throwing them at me. Then they started to run at me like tribal Zulus with murderous eyes, intent on killing me. I ran like I had Usain Bolt's legs for about half a mile - by then, they had given up the chase.

I felt sick to my stomach after assimilating what had just fucking happened to me... the coach was full of Celtic supporters on their way to an away game and, yes, you guessed it again, my friend had given me a Rangers football team scarf! These fucking loonies who had never met me or knew anything about me were so brainwashed with religious fervour and football hatred that they were willing to seriously hurt, if not kill, me for nothing more than a piece of woven material in a different colour from their own scarves... and this is what religion promotes - it divides sections of the community and turns people into sheep and slaves to something that alters their mind state to a point where nothing they see or hear is intelligible to them anymore. If you are looking for a fucked up reason why the planet is such a shit hole, just look at religion objectively and there you will have your answer. Even my mum was twisted with this shit - she would ask my girlfriends names, and if any of them were Frances or Ann Marie, then she would tell me to not bring them into her house!!! Religion is a plague on society and turns seemingly nice people into utterly evil entities, who will fuck you up with their version of shit if you let them.

I chose not to and I am a secular, humanist, atheist, if anyone wants to know, because if there is a God, any God, and if any of the religions on this planet are right, then that God and their Gods are fucked up, jealous, megalomaniacal, child abusers who do not give a fuck about anything or anyone... and this thing called life is a sick fucking joke!

Myself, Rab and a little guy called Alan, were on a three months' work experience from school, working two days a week at 'Stobhill Hospital Kitchens', where we would be training to be Commis Chefs. There was talk of one of us being kept on for an apprenticeship if we showed enough initiative. Fucking easy! - The job was mine as the other two chumps were brainless and only cared about smoking. So, there we were, all dressed up like chefs and making an arse of everything we touched. I got shown how to make 'Windsor Soup' in a huge, fifty gallon vat, stirring it with a plastic oar, of all things. I remember thinking "This is so fucking cool!" One of the chefs told me to decant the soup and make sure it was sent out to the trolleys waiting in the corridor. I did not want to let the chef down, so emptied one of the vats and its gallons of soup into the containers and got it to the trolleys where the porters wheeled it out to the starving patients in the wards. Now, I was thinking I had done a pretty good job getting all this out and was feeling pretty pleased with myself when I had the realisation that what I thought was Brown Windsor Soup was, in fact, gallons of gravy... and I had just sent it off to the wards! What the fuck was I going to say to the chef? He would surely kill me and put me through the mincer, so I decided not to say anything. When he got back, I waited for all hell to break lose in the wards - but to this day I have no answer for what happened... there were no complaints of any kind and it was definitely gravy that was served as soup! Answers on a postcard, please, and well done to me for staying super calm, hehe.

The kitchen manager was a small, moany, cunt of a man who was obviously married to a female Nazi and had five kids. He was a miserable shit and always in a foul mood. I think he hated us, as he often told us we were there 'under sufferance' and not to get 'too cocky' or 'cause any trouble' (just as well he never knew about the soup, then, eh?). Rab and I were in the changing room and he was smoking, but before we left to get to the kitchen, he threw the cigarette into the waste bin, which was full of the paper towels you use when drying your hands. A few minutes later we hear a commotion and the tiny, moany cunt is running about with a fire extinguisher, shouting "Fire! Fire!" The waste paper bin was fully ablaze but quickly put out, and the other chefs were all having a good chuckle at the little man's panic. He knew who had been in there last, unfortunately, and he had myself and Rab in the office, ranting on about how we were a 'fucking liability'.

I am saying, "Hey, wait a fucking minute - I don't even smoke!" and then Rab pipes up and says, "Aye, it must have been my fag, I threw it in the waste bin."

The Manager went ballistic and says, "Is that right? No! No way was that fire set off by a fag - it was deliberate!"

"I said, "Oh, you're fucking dreaming, pal, it's just how Rab says it is."

Then the little dick says, "Okay, if you can tell me the flashpoint of paper and a cigarette, you get to keep your jobs - but, if you don't, you are both, out the door, for sure!"

"For fuck's sake, Rab!" I said, "What are we gonna do now?"

There was no internet in 1976 (well, not that I was aware of), so no way of easily getting the answer. In about sixty minutes we would both be walking home and have no chance of an apprenticeship (or free meals), but then I had a brainwave. I ran to the other side of the Hospital and found the laboratories where I ask one of the technicians in there, "Would you know the flashpoint of paper and a cigarette that would cause the paper to ignite?" and the guys says,

"That's funny, the Kitchen Manager just asked that same question about twenty minutes ago."

So, I said, "Aye, that's right. He forgot the answer. Can you write it down for him?" (He he)

At mid-day, the little man calls us back into the office and says, "So, you think a cigarette can ignite paper, do you? If you do, what's the flashpoint?"

I replied, "Well, err, hmm... let me think, is it... (Insert answer from the hospital lab) ...Fahrenheit 451?" ha-ha

"Bastards!!!" he screams!!! Ha-fucking-ha!!!

I fucking loved the look on the little fuck's face, knowing he had been shafted by my superior intellect, but I honestly thought we were fucked that day. So, I would like to retrospectively say "thanks" to the technicians who worked in the labs of Stobhill Hospital that day... respect! See, this is what Scottish people do - they have no airs and graces and will help anyone as they would a brother in trouble.

How not to get mugged in Glasgow 1980,

I was going home from Town and wanted to take a shortcut through Glasgow Central Station. There was an escalator on the Hope Street - Argyll Street entrance, a bit off the main street, a typically, poorly lit place with beggars and homeless dudes, but it was a quick way through to the main entrance. I had just walked towards the escalator and some NED shouts, "Hey, mate, give me some spare money!" My first reaction was to say "Fuck off, you cunt, and go get a job!", but tonight I found myself going through my pockets to dig out a Pound note (yes, we still had them in Scotland. Stick your pound coins up your arse, you Sassenach bastards :-)

He took the pound and went on his way, probably to buy a bottle of 'Buckie' (Buckfast - very cheap wine).

A few weeks later, I took that shortcut again, around 10pm, I think, and I walked into a crowd of 'NEDS' - about twelve of them, looking like they were just back from a rampage somewhere. They stopped me and said, "Give us your fucking wallet, cunt!"

I thought my evening was going to finish with a drip in my arm and a nurse calling my Mum to say I was in Intensive Care at 'The Royal', when two seconds later, this lone NED says, "Leave him alone, he's alright."

I looked up and it was the guy I had given the pound to a few weeks before! Lesson learned - if you have spare, then share... or it might come back to bite you on the arse! And, yes, they let me alone.

CHAPTER FOUR

LIFE IN A NORTHERN TOWN

We used to live in Swindon, which is South-West England, I believe (hold on, I'll Google it). Okay, it's in Wiltshire, and midway between Reading and Bristol. We lived here from 1966 till 1968 (moving from Scotland, with my Dad's Army career)

I remember hearing my mum and dad fighting again, and she was laying right into him as he was packing his bags and stuffing them into his car. He drove off, and for the next few weeks we never saw or heard from him. My mum was in a constant bad mood and had no time for any of us... and I later realised it was because she obviously had no means to pay for the house or any of the bills, which were soon mounting up.

The reason for the split (one of the many) was due to the fact that my dad had been fucking the next door neighbour's wife while her husband was away. When my mum was out shopping, he would go out to the garden and into the garden shed (a big brick thing that may have been a garage but never saw a car in it). He would disappear for ages before coming back the same way. It transpired that he was using the side window to go to the neighbour's garden, and she was leaving the back door open for him (from stories told to us, many years later, by my mum).

Shit hits the fan when the neighbour's husband finds out what has been going on and a massive row and fight is on-going for days before my dad's 'chicken genes' kick in and he runs out on us all - leaving us high and dry, with no means of support. My mum took all four of us to the local social welfare / parish office (you know, the place you go to beg for money from the state), and she leaves us there, saying she can't look after us anymore, and runs out... leaving us all behind. I remember we were sitting there for about five hours before some official took us to another room to await our fate.

What seemed like an eternity to us all passed, when, suddenly, the door burst open and my mum comes back in and orders us out, then walks us home! Apparently the 'Welfare' had went to her address and talked her into coming back with the threat that 'if you leave them here you will most likely never see them again as they would be adopted out... or worse!' Fuck, we could have been sent to a Children's Care Home, only to be gang raped by seedy Government Officials - who the fuck knows what could have happened to all of us when you see all the shit that's coming out these days about that sort of thing! But, of course, there is the other side - perhaps we could all have been adopted out to a much better life.

We were too young to know what the fuck was going on, but the fear and the hunger were all too real. I am one hundred percent certain we were all affected mentally by this experience, and that, as we grew older, it would manifest as a profoundly negative emotion in all of us and may even be there within us all to this day. I know my older brother cannot forgive my parents for all the strife we went through and all the unloved birthdays and Christmases that we never had.

My younger sister was plagued by nightmares and she was visited on many occasions by a local doctor who would administer her a sedative to calm her down and help her sleep. My sister, Wendy, vividly remembers the nightmares and the doctors' visits, and is still visibly shaken when she recounts them to me. Sometimes I forget that it was not only just me who was the victim of parental abuse, and perhaps I have been away from it all for so many years it has settled in my mind as my own nightmare. I was so wrong.

So, a few months later, my dad has come back

and has moved up to Catterick Army Garrison, but had gotten us accommodation in Glasgow less than a hundred miles from where he is based. Now, if you have no idea of 'Tenement Life' in Glasgow, this will probably shock you to the core, as it was like living on the same levels as Third World countries, but in mainland United Kingdom. Fucking unbelievable!

Tenements were built in the 18th century to accommodate local workers in certain areas around Glasgow, this one being Springburn where the 'Caley Rail Works' were just a few hundred yards down the road and also home to the 'Whiskey Brewery' in Flemington Street. So, these houses were all in a state of disrepair and the amenities were all pre-war, having wash houses out in the court yards for communal clothes washing, where many a neighbour would spend all day scrubbing the family's clothing collection of rags and bedding. It was a tough life and a humbling experience that has never left me.

We lived at number '18, Keppochill Road', diagonally across from Springburn Fire Station Our flat was on the top floor with just two rooms - one front room was the bedroom where five of us shared a bed, and the other back room was the living area and kitchenette with a small sink near the window. This kitchen sink would also second as a bath, where we would have to stand upright while my mum washed us, much to the entertainment of the neighbours, whose windows backed onto ours.

We had no inside toilet and shared the communal

one, outside on the landing, with other 'tenants'. I remember one night I had to go to the 'kludgie' (toilet) and it was well after midnight and the landing lights were all out (gas lights that hardly ever worked). So, I open our front door and can see the toilet door, just down a flight of stairs, with the flickering of my candle - fucking scary, as you were never too sure if there was anyone out there or already using the toilet. I was just about to step out the door when my eye caught a slight movement in front of me, and, as I peered into the darkness, I saw a dirty, great, fucking rat, climbing the stairs towards me. It was as big as a fucking cat, really fat, and looked evil with its grey fur and piercing black eyes - it was not scared in the slightest, and kept climbing towards me as I froze with fear. It touched my left foot, which was outside the door, and to this day I still have no idea how the sound I made came out of my mouth - it was a high pitched, girly, elongated scream, much like the little girl (Newt?) who was in the second Alien movie, 'Aliens', when she first saw a face hugger (go and on look on 'YouTube' - you will hear the exact noise I made).

The rat shot forward to get through our front door and I instinctively pulled it towards myself to prevent it gaining access - it was now trapped between the door space and stone front step. I pulled the door harder to close it and the rat exploded... and blood went spattering onto the bottom of the door and all over my exposed leg. By this time my older brother and mum were stomping the shit out of the intruder until it lay there, totally lifeless and no longer a threat.

To my shame, I remember getting a plastic carrier bag (Galbraiths or Hoeys, I think?), and squatted over it, with my mum shouting "You better get rid of that in the morning!" as she went back to sleep. After this incident, we invested in a red plastic bucket and kept it in the hall for 'emergencies' - taking turns to empty it, as and when required. This was 'Tenement Life'.

The building we were in had big red signs on it stating 'Unsafe Buildings' and 'Unfit for Human Habitation', but all of the Tenements around the area had the same warnings on them - Glasgow City Council let us all stay, as there was nowhere else to go. It made me sick, years later, to discover that the GCC still sent rent collectors to take money from the people who lived in these crumbling, officially condemned buildings... I mean, what the fuck?

Tenement life was cruel and many hardships were endured on a daily basis. Most people did not work and many were just too ill or too old to do so, but paradoxically there was a community spirit whereby neighbours would look after each other, share food, and give pieces (bread and jam) to the kids playing in the communal back yards. We could be out for the whole day in the back yard, which was nothing more than a bit of spare ground with wash-houses and surrounded by the Tenement blocks themselves. There would be all the women out washing and gabbing, but at the same time looking after the whole crowd of streets kids, and some of them would make us sandwiches and feed us, even though we did not even know them. This was typical of life in a Northern town.

The ones who were lucky enough to have a job got home about 6 or 7 pm, then had to prepare dinner for their families and going to bed at 9 or 10pm, for the cycle to start all over again the next day. I know my mum had about three part time jobs to keep us all going and pay the bills - she worked in Collins Publishers as a packer, in a Cinema (I forget the name) in Renfrew Street as a cleaner, and a third job as a cleaner in the doctor's office in our street. Sporadic jobs and sporadic wages, but we still survived. I used to think this was 'normal' life and that everyone lived like this. We did not have a TV, so we had no other source of information apart from school - but even there, I had no idea we were on this pale blue dot and that life could be better... we had only needed the knowledge that the world was bigger, and have the will to climb out of the mire. All people need in life is a chance!

Our Tenement was opposite the local Fire Station, and next to this was Springburn Cemetery. Now, seeing as there were no parks near to us and the 'Gravy' being the only bit of greenery around for miles, it was used as a playground for the local kids playing football between gravestones and 'Kick the Can' (a famous Glasgow game whereby we all went and hid while someone stayed behind to protect the can, because if it was kicked, the game was a 'bogey' and it was all over One side would hunt down the other, and if caught, you were held until the game was over or one of the 'hiders' had sneaked back to 'Kick the Can'. Another variation of this game was 'One Man Hunt' or 'Two Man Hunt' - who needs computer games? We all played outside, together, as kids... not like today's misanthropic teens who prefer texting to talking, or 'Facebook' messaging to actually meeting up with their friends.

After we were living in Glasgow for a few years, it just became normal. Although the place had a bad reputation with such stories as the tales of Jimmy Boyle, the infamous small time crook who was famously dragged out of a bar and had his hands pummelled to a pulp by a hammer, and some other guy in our street who was 'knee capped' by the IRA or UDA, or one of those other, nutter, religious, home grown, terrorist groups masquerading as 'righteous'. These were only stories - urban myths that were whispered after dark and held our imaginations captive in fear and loathing... and still we thought it was 'normal'. There was even talk of 'Bible John' being chased up Springburn Road after being spotted near Springburn Train station - another urban myth? But this was the kind of place we lived in and where we all grew up.

"Get dressed, we're going out," my Mum was shouting at us all. We were all dressed, washed and cleaned, looking respectable for Sunday afternoon, (fuck, hope it's not church). We were herded down the stairs and along Keppochill Road to the Cemetery where my Mum had sorted us out a picnic - that's right, we were having a picnic in the Gravy (graveyard), fucking cool! It was like going on holiday, although technically we had never had a holiday and had no concept of one... still, it was a summer's day. The grass had just been cut and it was full of families, all doing the same thing. My Mum would say to me, "If you step on a grave, say 'sorry' or 'excuse me'." I guess it was out of respect for trespassing on their bit of land. I was never scared in the cemetery and it never even registered that it was full of dead people, it was just a nice place to walk through and find peace and quiet. It had a little collection of trees at the top of a hill that was perfect for that jungle or pirate adventure. My own adventure was 'Star Trek', and I would play up there for hours with John McIver - he was Mr. Spock and I was Captain James T. Kirk of the 'USS Enterprise', but Gene Roddenberry's utopian world was still light years away, at least for us.

'Midgie raking' was a past-time that most kids did. You see, there were communal dustbins housed in a brick building in the communal back yard, 'midges' or 'middens', and I did this as well. We would be raking through all the stuff that had been thrown away from all the neighbouring houses, and it stank of old food and dirty water - I ended up with Scarlet Fever one time, and I am convinced it was through my raking days that I contracted it. Occasionally there was a gem of a find, an old toy or something shiny like an old ornament. I found a Venetian styled, plastic boat of gold and black that I took home to my mum and she proudly put it on her mantel piece. The grand prize found by raking the midges was empty 'ginger' bottles (Sassenachs call them pop bottles) as these had a recycled value of two pence. Competition was fierce as others kids and often adults went looking for these glass hunger-saviours, with which, if enough were found, we could trade for food instead of cash. Most times traded for sweets, adults would trade them for cash or cigarettes. I remember I had found around nine bottles and, feeling pleased with myself, had them all in a wet box I had dragged out of a puddle - this was about five hours' work hunting them down, when a gang of four 'NEDS' jumped me, gave me a good kicking and took them all off me, then said to me, "Right, fuck off or you'll get some more!" I turned and swore at them, then threw a stone - feeling brave, being twelve feet away from them gives you the balls of an Elephant! My stone missed all of them but the bottle they threw back, an empty half bottle of whiskey, hit me square in the face - striking my nose and top lip... bastards! So, now I was bleeding, had no bottles, and had wasted five hours of my life raking though bins.

Undefeated, I went to a different tenement block

and started looking through the bins for more glass gold, then I had a brainwave - if some people just threw them away, then why not knock on their doors and save them the trouble of taking them to the middens? Thirty minutes later I had five bottles in my possession, and from that day on it was my preferred method instead of raking. One day I had collected fifteen bottles and had enough to buy some cut ham and bread from 'Christies Store', just at the bottom of our close - so, thanks to Mrs Christie for being such a kind hearted person and taking them all off me for food... I will never forget that. Although she passed away many years later, I can still feel her kindness when I think of that moment. Next time I am back in Glasgow, I will visit the cemetery and put some flowers on her grave. I know she helped lots of poor families in the area and gave them 'tick' (pay later, when you have it). All this community spirit seems to have just about gone from our daily lives with a more and more mercenary approach to life. Social Darwinism is not pretty, but it seems to be the way of the world at this present time. I am not too sure if we are all being manipulated to think this way by the Government or the current austerity measures that will turn neighbour and friends against each other when it comes to the 'haves' and 'have nots' - only time will tell, and I have a feeling we won't have to wait too long to find out.

I sometimes miss those halcyon days from '70s Glasgow and wonder what the hell happened, and why we seem too obsessed with no one but ourselves. Is this the result of capitalism? Live, Buy, Consume, Die? I remember reading this somewhere many years later 'You can take a person out of the Tenements, but you can't take the Tenements out of the person'. I like to think this is not a slur on a person's character - for all the hardships and lack of money, we all had a sense of belonging and we lived in a skewed version of our own harmony, looking after each other and bonding on very personal levels. This is what hardship does, it strengthens your resolve and gives you a sense of perspective that a lot of people have never been exposed to in the UK, and I like to think it grounded me and prepared me for the life that was to come.

Marriage number one, sometime in the early '80s

What the fuck have I done?

Three months prior, I am going out with Diane, my long time, suffering, beautiful girl friend, and next thing I know, I am with this 'other' woman, who I have just asked to marry me! For fuck's sake, when did I hit my head on concrete, and why did no one fucking stop me from making an arse of myself?

So, here I am, making my Mum's worst nightmare come true - me, marrying a Catholic, Anna Maria something or other from 'Govan' of all places. It was funny, the Pineapple (Chapel) had all her lot on one side and mine on the other. My lot did not sing one

Hymn or do the double shuffle (cross yourself), and no knees to the floor malarkey. When we came out married, the sky was full of thunder and lightning... and pissing it down with rain. It was mid-November, but I remember thinking, what the fuck did I get myself into? Have I just married 'Satan's' daughter?

CHAPTER FIVE

SAVE A PRAYER

Our band 'DanceVision' are playing a gig in a little venue called Maestro's on Scott Street. It was just off on the left hand side of Sauchiehall Street and it was a steep hill, an impossibly steep hill, and a nightmare to get the gear into. Luckily it had its own P.A. system, mixing desk, and lights, so all we had to do was plug in our synthesisers. Myself, the other keyboard player (whose name escapes me, but I am reliably informed by Jim McKenna that his name is 'Robert', so I will call him that from now on - thanks for the email, Jim), and Michelle are keen to play.

We are on stage at 10pm with all our own songs. The place is a disco venue, quite small, but the people who attend are select and seem open to new music as Disco is slowly but surely dying out. The only annoying, fucking thing is these prick DJs do not know it's dying out or do not have the skills to move onto another scene. We had a mere five minute sound check and Michelle's gone through her vocal range - sounding more in tune than our synth's oscillators that would drift in and out of concert pitch every twenty minutes or so. It's already 9pm and the place is jumping with pussy, a mixture of disco-dancer guys, some punks, and new romantics (I guess we called them).

The venue itself had a sort of 'Blitz Club' feel about it. I recently learned that, sadly, the legendary Steve Strange had died on February 2015 - he was one of the founders of the original Blitz Club in London, a place I managed to visit once in the '80s whilst on a visit to Mick Karn's art exhibition at the same time. At the exhibition, I got to speak to Mick for all of four minutes and chat about the most recent 'Japan' album, 'Gentlemen Take Polaroid's and I was sure he noticed how much I sort of looked like him - I even had on the same coloured shirt and I was hoping I did not come across as some sort of delusional stalker... fuck, what was I thinking? Sorry, Mick, I hope I didn't sound too stupid that day - and for those that do not know, Mick Karn died in January of 2011 aged 52. Rest in peace, dude, I will miss your earthly presence and unearthly bass lines.

The DJ stops playing disco tunes and announces

our impending stage appearance, and it all goes quiet as we get into position. It's not our first gig, but my hands are shaking, like it's my first feel of some girl's tits, as we are about to be judged by our peers in the court of public musical opinion - how the fuck would we go down, would they boo and hiss or throw chairs at us? You never know how it's going to go at gigs. At least Michelle is looking hot and so fuckable - man, did she know how to sex herself up. I should have made a move on her instead of that nameless fucker (oh, right, we are calling him Robert - whatever!). Well, dude, if you are reading this, I hope you got what you wanted out of life and p.s. thanks for fucking the band up, you cunt, as well as fucking Michelle - we could have been famous and you could have had your pick of women... small minds often have small dicks and pathetic egos.

I start the drum machine up and it's pounding out a steady 4/4 beat as Robert starts playing a chopped up bass line that sounds so fucking cool through this 3K rig. Michelle starts singing and swaying her hips - I can see right through her short dress and she looks like she is pantie less. I start playing my riff and backing her up on vocals as the crowd looks on, dribbling at the mouth to our electronic vibe that is pulsating with sex and teen spirit. The song is called 'Sex Park' that originally started out as 'The Park', which was really about my time working near the 'Botanic Gardens'. Every lunch hour, when it was Summer, I would lay on the grass in the park and watch all the gorgeous woman sunbathing - I usually had to lie on my stomach to hide the tent pole, ha-ha, but managed to give the park a sort of golf course kinda look with all the mini holes poked into the grass by Mr Cock.

My mate from work was there too, and the sheer number of beautiful women made us smile and enjoy our lives a little more. This was the day I met Rose McDowall (so sexy) and Jill Bryson (not so sexy) aka Strawberry Switchblade. I knew instantly who they were due to their striking looks - a sort of Bohemian, punk look. I had actually seen Rose play in a punk band in Paisley a few times before, 'The Poems ' or something like that. I went and spoke to them and we had a conversation about music and where it was all going - they thought that electro was shit and disco was cancer... and these are the girls who hung about with Edwyn Collins from 'Orange Juice' of 'Rip It Up and Start Again' fame! WTF? Incidentally, Edwyn stole a Mars bar for me, once, just round the corner in a shop called Presto/Safeway's? (Thanks, mate, but I never asked you to... but it was sort of cool that you did it anyway!)

I would meet lots of people who would end up on TV at some point and always wondered when it would be my turn. The BBC Scotland studios were just opposite the Botanical Gardens in Glasgow, and I used to sit and dream about my tomorrows as I watched stars drive in and out of the gates on the right hand side. I met Tracey Ullman once, as I was walking home from work. I would always deliberately pass in front of the impressive BBC building and saw her just walking back from the park across the road, and I said "Hello, Tracey!" To which she replied, "Oh, fuck off!" She's a bit rude, I thought, but she said "Sorry," right after it and added she was "...having a bad day."

I asked her what she was doing in BBC Scotland and I think it was some sort of Comedy show she was doing, but to be honest I have no fucking idea what it was called as I never watched her on TV except for 'Top of the Pops' - hehe - Sorry, Tracey. She said goodbye and wished my band luck for the future. Fuck, here's me trying to get a back way into TV, but my charm skills were not as honed as they are today ;-) ...maybe I should hang about near the STV studios on the other side of town... on second thoughts, perhaps not as all they were generally interested in was kilts and accordion music for TV. It would be at least fifteen years before STV caught up with the rest of the world and had already 'missed the boat', in my opinion, as most of the great talent had migrated south for recognition a long time ago.

We are halfway through our set and the place is jumping - it was the right decision to go electro pop after all. There wasn't one person not dancing, even the usually disinterested 'punks' were doing something rather than ignoring us... they were part of it! "Fuck me," I said to myself, "we're going to be huge!" I saw Midge Ure at the back of the room and

I am sure he stole my pointed side burns (which were my nod to 'Captain Kirk') - I never saw him before the gig or after, but I am certain he went to gigs back in those days, borrowed people's styles, and reinvented them into his own... it's the only reason I can come up with to explain his frequent change of styles in such a short spaces of time.

Midge's name, as a matter of fact, was given to him from some other guy in a band called 'Salvation' (which eventually became Slik) as his real name was James, and there was already another 'James' (McGinlay, on bass) in the band - so, they reversed his name to 'Mij' (with the'd', 'g' and 'e' getting inserted later on to complete the phonetic reversal). I'm not even sure how the fuck I know that, I think I read it in Midge's Autobiography, 'If I Was' - Hey! Maybe he will read mine?

I do like Midge Ure, only partly for his 'Ultravox' stuff which I thought was great. I'm not too sure what would've happened to 'Ultravox' without him after replacing John Foxx (who was a fucking mastermind, in my opinion) in 1979 - I mean, who else was up for the job after Foxx? I used to sit and think what if Gary Numan was lead singer in Ultravox, or David Sylvian, or even Bowie! Might have been very interesting, but, again, hats off to Midge for making them more mainstream at least. With some cracking songs and good use of Billy Currie's skills on synths, Ultravox reached a level of success the Foxx-led version had failed to achieve. Billy and Midge were also responsible for the rise of 'Visage', with Steve Strange on vocals and make-up duty.

Back at the gig, it is now the last song of the night and it was something slow and moody with a little perky string bit in it that was used by another band I would be in shortly. Jonn Harton heard me play this riff once and I said could we use it? I think he was a bit reticent because of the simplicity of it, but, to date, I owe him a great debt, as he had written one of my favourite tracks of that time, called 'I Don't Believe in Love' with this riff incorporated into it... and to this day it is still eminently listenable.

We had people asking for our autographs and shouting 'Brilliant - Great stuff' at us - adulation is one of the most emotive and rewarding things, especially when it's directed at you for your own material and imagination. Little did I know that there were people in the crowd that night who wanted to sign us up on the strength of that little gig? Fucking, yes! There were 'A&R' (Artiste & Repertoire) people in the venue that night and we had no idea - essentially talent scouts for record labels... and these ones were from London, maybe that's why Midge was there? Who knows, but a few days later, there I was, meeting an 'A&R' guy in a restaurant in Renfield Street, with Michelle and 'Robert' - the record company guy was saying all the right things and was fanatical about our sound and Japan-eseque look from me, the 'New Order' look of Robert, and stunning sexiness of Michelle and her vocal range.

The man was talking singles, albums and tours, but wanted us to do a few support slots for a tour starting in Birmingham (way down south) - he could not tell us who for, as it was all hush-hush and all that… I was guessing he did not know ha-ha! These 'A&R' guys are famous for bullshit amongst other things.

As it transpired the 'secret' act he wanted us to support was none other than 'Hazel O'Connor' (and what happened in between makes me choke back tears even to this very day). She was a sort of a handpicked, movie star in a film called 'Breaking Glass' - all about the depiction of the music industry, the sleaze and manipulation for profit at the artist's expense …a great movie, if you have not seen it, go rent it today. Personally, I thought she was an ugly, fucking hag with a drug addiction - but, years later, I have sort of mellowed to her in a way I can connect with now (not that I am ugly or a hag or have a drug addiction, I might add). It's actually a very gritty movie, and hats off to the lady - she did a grand job of portraying it 'as it was'... sleazy, underhanded, and downright mercenary, and anyone who has been in a band will tell you the same thing.

Remember, a few chapters back, I said 'Robert' would fuck the band up? Well, he did this big time and I still hate part of him and Michelle to this day as things could have been so different under different circumstances, and perhaps if I had made better choices and decisions earlier on, isn't hind sight a wonderfully useless piece of shit.

We had a band meeting and discussed the events of the week with the 'A&R' guy and his offer of getting us the support for the upcoming Hazel O'Connor tour starting in Birmingham. Man, I was so excited I could not sleep - I mean, we had ten great tracks, a small following of fans, and I lived next door to a Scottish 'Radio Clyde' DJ... none other than Billy Sloan. I was going to get him involved with it all and see what he could do for us, as we were doing something for Glasgow hehe. It was all decided and another meeting was due in a few days, so we had to have our shit together - money, how were we getting there, did we need to hire a van or a mini bus, who's driving, where will we stay? I got my big brother on board as a driver/roadie with my next door neighbour Alan West as acting roadie and possibly Michelle's dad, as he would want to come just to keep an eye on his daughter - and here is the tragedy... three days before the meeting with the record company guy (Frank?), the phone auspiciously rings about 6pm.

My Mum's shouting, "Tam! Roberts on the phone for you!"

I grab the phone and he starts saying that he can't do the gig in Birmingham and he is sorry! I said "Fuck's sake! What's wrong?"

He says he will come and explain at my house and bring Michelle. Three hours later they turn up and I am trying to keep calm by playing Kraftwerk 'Hall of Mirrors' on my Mini Moog. They sit down and he says, "Michelle's pregnant and we need to get married... and her Dad doesn't want her being in the band and travelling to England, and will kill me if I don't marry her soon." She is already three months gone, apparently, and I feel the cold hand of fate slap me hard in the face, and then kick me even harder in the balls.

I feel sick and stutter out, "But this could be it! I have a feeling this will make us! Think of the exposure, it's only for two weeks and we will be back in Glasgow again!"

They disagree and think it will just be small time as Hazel O'Connor is shit.

I said, "So, fucking, what? We can use this! We can get something from it. It's a test from the 'A&R' guy - it's our initiation…" But, no! They are both more interested in saving up to get married - they are in love and having a baby! Oh, for fuck's sake, please! I interject, "What about the band and our futures?" They explain their future is already starting and that's what they want, so I scream, "Oh, get fucked! No, sorry - you already have! Get the fuck out, just get the fuck out!"

As I watch them drive away I am still swearing, "Fucking idiotic, selfish, cunts!" ...and yet a small part of me is perhaps happy for them. I call Frank the very next day and say "Sorry!" I explain that we can't do it and he says, "No problem, thanks anyway," and he wishes me well for the future and hangs up.

To this day I still get weird over this when I think

Save A Prayer

about it - to realise just how close we came to being so fucking huge! And to this very day, I have never met or heard from the 'happy couple', but they know, as I surely know, that the band that eventually got the support went on to be quite big... and I hope this chokes Michelle and Robert as much as it chokes me! The band who eventually did the support? None other than a new, 'up and coming', band from Birmingham itself who were called 'Duran Duran'.

Don't save a prayer for me now, you two selfish bastards!

So, if either of you two are reading this - do you see what you actually did? Hindsight is a wonderfully useless thing, but do you know what would be even more useful now? A 'Tardis' and a packet of condoms for those two numbskulls! Hope you're both happy with the life that you chose for yourselves.

It's like one of my friends used to say, "Don't jump without a parachute - as it will kill you!" (Meaning don't have sex without a rubber or the consequences will fuck you up.) And you two certainly killed a part of me when you jumped.

Will you just politely say 'Goodnight'?

Still reeling from this, and now looking for a project of my own, I have never been so motivated in all my fucking life. I had an idea to recruit new people into the band and breathe 'New Life' into it, so I started looking for a new singer and a new keyboard player and... Oh, fuck me, I knew it was going to be bad interviewing people for the band, but come on! The dicks and wannabes that came through my door were just so abysmal - no talent, no style, delusional, or just downright ugly. One guy that came eventually went on to play in a band with a minor hit... what were they called? Oh, yes, 'Friends Again' - but, so what? I thought he was crap, sounded too funky and definitely not good enough for someone who had nearly went on tour with Hazel ha-ha! Oh, I had it bad and was fuming with malcontent.

For the next few months I ended up playing with a few bands and doing synths for them - I am sure the only reason they had me play with them was because I had the Moog! I used to go to this Music shop on Bath Street, called 'McCormack's Music' and I sort of knew Jim, the synth engineer that worked there. I'm still not too sure how I ended up in this band called 'Zoneheim', but I liked them from the start. The front man, Jonn Harton, played guitar (Ziggy?)... Which nearly put me off, but he was actually skilfully minimalistic with his playing, so the songs still sounded synth based with a floating guitar interspersed with it all - which gave it a sort of Japanesque sound to everything.

So here I am, rehearsing with the new band and enjoying it. Everything still sounded raw, but in a good way, a bit like 'John Foxx' and 'The Maths', lots of raw synth energy and punch, with catchy lyrics (some with a political intent) and some with skewed versions of what 'love' is.

The drummer, John Healey, was a sort of cross between a Japan band member and a typical Glasgow 'NED', but was funny in a direct kind of way. Back in those days I was wearing makeup and dyeing my hair and some people had a real hard time trying to ascertain my gender (which was kinda fun at times ha-ha). One night myself and the drummer had went to a get a drink on Sauchiehall Street in a trendy bar called 'Nicos', and the girl behind the bar came up to me and asked me what I wanted to drink - when she came back with the order, and clearly unable to work it out for herself, she asked me in a quite 'matter of fact' manner if I was a guy or a woman? John Healey swiftly retorted, "Why don't you suck his dick and find out?" I nearly spat my drink out and almost fell backwards off the chair, but it was a brilliantly delivered response to a slightly cheeky, Glasgow Waitress who was now completely lost for words ...and looking down at my groin

Hurricanes Bar Glasgow 1980-81

There used to be a bar on West Regent Street near Blythwoods Square (yeah, that square ;-), a bar for the semi-famous, pretentious or famous to hang about - Hurricane's. I remember seeing Boy George here one night and he was surrounded by lots of wannabe gays - he seemed to have their attention for a very long time.

I was in here with my girlfriend, enjoying the

talks, spotting the wannabes and mixing with up and coming bands - it was a great place to hang out ...no 'NEDS' here! Zara was in here a few times and I managed to talk to her one night. We were just generally chatting about music, her latest chart single, and her past movie debut. My girlfriend, who was not standing beside me at the time, was giving me a very strange look from across the lounge - a look which I have seen before and perhaps should have paid more attention to. Next thing I know she has followed Zara to the 'Ladies' and they are having a fight. Apparently my girlfriend had thrown water over her, out of jealousy, for talking to me! A few people broke the fight up and I called Diane a taxi to take her home. I stayed and apologised to Zara who was okay with it as she said it happened a lot, bought her a drink, and to this day I have no idea how it actually happened... but we saw each other for about nine days and we used to hang out at her place just off Great Western Road. We were passionately kissing and heavy petting when she said to me, she was 'sort of' seeing someone else - I said "and?" in my head and thought no more of it. Nine days of a whirlwind romance and it was all over - then I was back with my old squeeze, Diane, who was none the wiser... phew!

Karma came to visit me a few weeks ago in 2015. I had never told the aforementioned story to a particular someone in a band I was in, as they were sweet on Zara and I did not want to be kicked out of the band because I was rolling in the hay with his dream girl - but I finally told him a few weeks ago, after some 29 years and he just said, "It's okay, I was with her too!" Then I thought to myself, "Fuck, this is the guy she was 'sort of' seeing," but to my relief, it was a whole year before me. Then I told Jim (the other keyboard player in Zoneheim) of my dirty deed, and Jonn's, and he laughed aloud, saying he had the chance with her in some pub he was in a few years ago (they used to go the same school) and he passed on her... so my little dream of the sweet little Zara has been thoroughly tarred and sullied, ha-ha - thanks, guys!

Thanks for making it seem like some sort of twisted, love bomb across time and space (its cold outside, some kinda atmosphere...?)

CHAPTER SIX

SPACE ODDITY

"Tommy, if you play that fucking annoying tune again, I am going to rip your fucking hands off!" Jim McKenna would scream in an irritated voice. Thoughtfully I just kept playing the short riff again and again until it blew a fuse in Jim's head and he jumped up from his seat in front of the bank of synths he was in charge of - the problem was that Jim was around six feet two and the height of the basement was about five feet ten with the result being that Jim's anger at the riff was mammothly exacerbated by jumping up in rage at listening to the annoying riff playing again and again, only to be enhanced by smacking his head forcefully into the wooden roof with an ugly, thumping echo before slumping back down into the chair like a wet dish-rag... and that just sent everyone else in the room into uncontrolled hysterics! It's a hard life being in a band ha-ha.

He was one half of the Synth combo from 'the new band' I was in, 'Zoneheim' - myself being the other half. He is a gifted musician, has a genuine talent, and came up with some great riffs and bass lines that are still very listenable near thirty years on. He was actually a guy I had met a long time ago in 'McCormack's Music Shop' in Glasgow, and he was in fact the Synth engineer - what a cool job to have at that time! Although I do remember finding a pair of red pliers bouncing about inside my very expensive PolyMoog after it had been in to the shop for repair and returned them to Jim shortly after (devoid of any sense of guilt, Jim simply smiled and stated "I wondered where they had got to!") - we were all very relieved he was not a heart surgeon, imagining the horror of Jim mislaying his watch or something else that should not reside inside a human body!

As a teenager I used to hang about that music store, waiting for a chance to play some of the cool synths that they sold. There was a downstairs bit where they had stacks of synths stashed, and I would have to blag my way downstairs as, to be honest, they were a bunch of snobbish cunts on the shop floor, and if they didn't think you had money or talent, they were not letting you touch anything! There was a cheeky fucker with longish black hair and a moustache who used to annoy me immensely and he always refused me entry downstairs, so I wanted to twat this fucker most Saturdays - I guess he just looked at me and thought, "NED with no money," and that was enough for him.

At the time I think this was the only shop in Glasgow that sold this kind of gear, there used to be another one near the Toll Cross, but that was a few years in the future. All the, up and coming, Glasgow bands would buy their gear from McCormack's and finance (buy now, pay forever) was a new concept that made things seem affordable with weekly payments and interest.

I also used to hang around the record shop just along from 'McCormack's Music' shop, I think it was called 'Precinct 29', and it had a bright yellow facade, shop front and steps leading downstairs to the rows and rows of vinyl. This is where I would go and listen to tracks from albums with synthesisers on them - 'YES', 'E.L.O.', 'Steve Harley and Cockney Rebel', 'Jean Michele Jarre', 'Paul Brookes', 'Kraftwerk', 'Bowie', 'Be Bop Deluxe', and loads more. I was captivated by these sounds and so desperately wanted to get my hands on a synthesiser as they utterly fascinated me! My mate next door had loaned me a 'Bontempi Organ' and I had learned a few tunes on it from Kraftwerk's 'Autobahn', but became increasingly frustrated by the lack of sounds and control of this thing, which vaguely sounded like a really bad imitation of a piano or an organ, and that was it.

The irritating riff was something I came up with just to annoy people, but Jim took it too seriously hehe (sorry, dude). He was a very likeable guy with strange tales of bohemia and sinister doings, I used to liken him to 'Freewheeling Franklin' from the 'Fabulous Furry Freak Brothers' comics my older sibling would collect - he was just so funny, a bit loopy and a lot like Stephen Hawking, but on acid. We also eventually likened him to 'The Doc' from 'Back to the Future', he would go off in little tangents and I would revel in them as they were highly entertaining and perhaps I was too 'innocent' to understand most of them, but, in retrospect, I now know these sort of experiences would come to my life later on and I could relate to them and dispense them out at dinner parties like a witty raconteur. (Dinner parties? Fucking behave, Tam.)

Thinking about it, I think Jim looked more like the lead singer from '10cc', with his long hair and pilot sun glasses… looked okay and kinda cool.

I remember one time we were rehearsing and he came limping in (he was always doing something or something was always happening to him).

"What's up?" we would ask, knowing there would be a good story in it.

"I jumped out of bed (was it the top bunk?) And my bare foot landed on a stupid, bloody electrical plug lying on the floor and the three prongs nearly sank all the way into my foot!"

We were all howling at this, and thinking if we needed a spare power socket we could always use Jim's foot as an adapter or plug-in socket for an extension cable ha-ha!

I remember him driving me home one night with two girls from the band in the back, I forget their names, but one was kinda sexy with shiny lips! Anyway, Jim was driving across the 'Erskine Bridge' and had his right arm out the window banging the side of his souped up 'Mini' like a drum and whistling some obscure song in time with the banging as passing drivers gaped, open mouthed at the sight - fucking insane! And to this day I still smile when I think about it.

Jonn Harton was the 'Zoneheim' frontman, writer of all songs, and the guitar player - he seemed cool, focussed and I thought we had a good chance to get somewhere with the current line up. I was still reeling from the last band break-up and what might have been a turning point in my life that was blighted by the fucker Robert's cock and his desire to procreate with the band's singer, Michelle - I never told anyone in the new band this as I wanted to keep a low profile and see what would happen when we started knocking some songs out... and I was also a bit worried in case they saw me as some sort of jinx to have gotten an offer to tour with a named artist and have it all fall apart in the space of a week! Anyway, onwards and upwards, we rehearsed at least once a week in Dumbarton in this soundproofed, basement in Jonn's parents' house. We knocked out some good tunes and, although our synths were basic, it still sounded good - a bit raw and a bit jagged, but still good tunes for Glasgow at that time. We had our first gig as Zoneheim in 'Night Moves', a sort of disco, come club, come band arena thing.

I said to my younger brother, "Do you want some cash to come and roadie for me?"

"Oh, aye - no problem," he says.

Anyway, on the night, he turns up late and pissed. I said, "For fuck's sake! Okay, just help at the end, you dick."

So, I get up to go on stage and kick something hard with my foot. I was wearing 'Chinese Slippers' and whatever I kicked nearly made me pass out with searing pain - For fuck's sakes! I thought I was gonna keel over in agony during the set, and to this day I have no idea how I got through it.

So here we are, on stage at 'Night Moves' in the Centre of Glasgow, our first gig as a new band and I must admit I am enjoying it. The place is full of punks, who seem to think it's cool to sit right next to the speakers of a 4k rig - bet you today they are walking round saying, "Eh, what? Can't hear ya!" What a bunch of fucktards punks were, they were so anti-establishment that they were up their own arses and were in fact anti-everything - they did not like anything unless it was punk and you were jumping up and down like Zebedee on fucking crack and spitting into each other's faces.

I remember I took my younger sister Wendy to 'Shuffles Disco', just when punk was coming in, and it was her first time in a dance-club-like place - she was only fifteen, if memory serves me. So, I palm her off onto one of my friends who has just turned punk, and off she goes to dance... only to come back five minutes later nearly crying.

"What the fuck? What's up?" I'm screaming at her.

Then she blurts out, "Your friend spat on me!"

So I said, "Oh! It means he likes you... in punk."

So she sort of smiled, but did not come out with me again. Sorry, Sis.

At 'Night Moves', we're on stage and we are cruising along quite nicely until our next track, 'Boys for Sale', whereby the drummer, (John Healey) has somehow forgotten to tell us he has changed the tempo of the song to something akin to a runaway fucking freight train, bombing down a hill with no brakes! For fuck's sake - nightmare. My hands were having serious trouble trying to keep up with him and Jim was in manic mode too, I could see the sweat on his brow from ten feet across the stage - but, interestingly enough, it was one of the tracks that the 'Punks' sort of danced to. Fuck me, we must have touched something in them.

I am convinced to this day that Jonn Harton was a fucking Vampire, I swear I never saw this guy in daylight, and he always had a sallow, pale look about him... sort of a David Bowie, 'Man Who Fell to Earth' look. I remember, as a joke, I was in his flat and he was banging out Bowie on his acoustic while sitting on the floor and I chucked ten pence to him, like he was a busker in an underpass, hehe. The guy was a musical genius and was in loads of bands that all went on to be on TV or something else, so I thought he was well connected or at least fucking someone (male or female) who could make us all famous! Sometimes when we were rehearsing, we would talk about the state of the world and how life was akin to a sexually transmitted disease, a virus with no known cure - but a drug that could circumnavigate the pain of existence was money, and the path money could take you... to places you only dreamed about, and to people who you only ever heard about.

"Fucking slow down, you fucking, mental bastard!"

I am saying this in my head as the drummer has kicked it up another notch. I was seriously thinking of sticking those drum sticks in his ugly, fat head after the 'gig' and I am sure the other guys felt the same way. Thinking back, I'm not too sure what we did afterwards, but I think we all just headed off to our abodes and I went home and stuck my poor hands in the freezer compartment to reduce the swelling. My brother later told me he stopped some guy above me from hitting me with something as he went up to the balcony and punched him a few times - I offered my thanks as it would have been disastrous to have been hit by something tossed down from that height and while I was playing. After reviewing the video of the gig on 'VHS', I looked carefully at the balcony and could see nothing... I did, however, see what they guy had thrown at me - a single piece of silver, chewing gum wrapper. My brother was off roadie duty for ever, what a loon!

Rehearsals were always the same - "Come to the flat at 2pm," Jonn would say to us all, "and we will get to Dumbarton to rehearse." 2pm meant 5pm to the Vampire, even though I was always there at 2pm... And then we had to eat, and then rehearse - so I was getting back home around 11pm. I was prepared to put up with this sort of 'nightwalker' style of rehearsing as it was a good band and I liked all the guys and thought it would all come together at some point and things would kinda seem 'normal'.

The flat where we met was in Sauchiehall Street, so there was always somewhere to go to pass the time until the 'Prince of Darkness' awoke from his slumber (hehe). I think we had another gig at 'Night Moves' supporting 'Roman Holiday' - 'Don't Try To Stop It' was their single in the charts at that time, I think, but something or other went wrong and we could not do the gig - to this day I have no idea what happened to that gig... Van? Cars? Not too sure.

We had done some tracks in a popular Glasgow '16 Track Studio' called Park Lane (where Altered Images recorded their early 80s hits) and they were quite experimental and had a resonance of 'Magazine' meets 'Japan' and David Bowie without any mimicry. These 'Zoneheim' tracks had their own style and stamp, sounding sophisticated, polished and professional - but we were already heading for another style and had decided on a name change for the band, now hailing as 'VIVA'...

Now the frontman had a sweet looking girlfriend who also sang (and was also a Vampire, as they both kept time to the same clock). Her name was Lynnette - she had a great voice, looked in good shape with saucer like eyes and velvety lips, and hips shaped like a sexy violin. She hooked up with us and we got down to recording 'New Love'... I am reliably informed the song was about lesbian sex? (Citation needed here, Jonn. ha-ha). We rehearsed this for weeks before deciding to enlist two backing singers to lift the song's chorus and a variety of other parts. Fuck me, I'd never heard Glasgow accents in a song till I had heard these ones... I mean, to be fair, they were not bad singers, but the accent was there in some nuances of their singing and only to the trained ear can you hear it. On another significant point - they were dog fucking ugly and looked like they had been burped with a mallet as kids! One was a bit rotund and had to put her belt on with a boomerang, and the other one was kinda cute, but had a woeful (dumb) look about her. I remember Jonn H saying to them that their services were no longer required and I am sure they tried to sue us for ruining their singing careers - fucking delusional or what? Damn, those bitches be crazy... and should have been suing themselves for ruining their own singing careers with voices like that!

Sadly, when they left, the drummer left too as he was loved up with one of them and we had to force his hand - the band or her! He chose her, so it must have been love, after all - he was regularly cancelling rehearsals and studio time to be with her, so I think we did the right thing and there were no hard feelings about it.

So, now rehearsals were being done with a drum machine until we could find a replacement drummer that was good looking, had his own kit, own car, and a desperate drive to succeed (not suck seed, Monica Lewinsky style). Derek, or 'Dek' as we named him, came to audition and he was the most retro looking guy that had come through the door - he looked like a member of 'The Sweet', in fact, he may well have been! I have nothing against The Sweet, but I did not seriously think one of them would fit into an electro pop, pseudo-Intellectual, pretentious band such as ours... he looked so wrong with the white jump suit on and his twelve foot long hair - it looked like he had quantum leaped into the '80s from 1974 at least. But he could play and his timing was rock solid, so we gave him a go and it started to feel like a band again - nothing against drum machines what so ever, but programming them back in the '80s was a mare.

Now, in my experience in bands so far, the drummers are the ones with the ego problems - they want to hear their parts over everyone else and, fuck me, he was loud and hit those skins like he was beating the shit out of something with a sledge hammer! This, of course, forces everyone else to up their volume and, before you know it, the fucking house is moving off its foundations and we are all going to die of drummer's syndrome. He would get aerated if we told him to be quiet and then, luckily for us and our hearing, he brought a set of 'Simmons Drums'. Fucking, yes! Now we can turn the volume down on his electronic kit and get an electro compatible, synthetic sound... but, bizarrely, he was the only guy on the planet that could make electronic drums sound exactly like skinned ones - what the fuck, Dek?

I think Jonn was none too fond of Dek, but he needed a drummer to get on with the projects... and fame waits for no one. I remember vividly, we were shooting a video for one of our new singles, 'Let The Rain Come Down' and Dek turned up with two full sets of drums - crazy bastard drummers... plus, we had to cart it all up a flight of stairs so high you needed oxygen on the way up. Diane was there with me to give moral support and she also wanted to see a 'music video' shoot, first hand. It was a long, hard day - I think we 'mimed' the song about thirty times to get various angles and as many head shots of us all into the final video. The entire thing turned out well, all in all, and I can still listen and watch the video to this day without puking or laughing my head off!

Great days, but in retrospect, I wish I had taught them all to dance as none of them really could and the video would have been a bit more lively - JH would look at me with one eye as I boogied and I would say "John, I'm only dancing!";-p

I'd never had a finger up my arse up till this point in my life - one day, during a pickup to get to a late rehearsal, Jimbo, the driver of the car, stopped to pick up one of his 'mates' for some reason that would become clear a few minutes later. This guy (no idea of his name, but let's call him 'Fat Freddie') is in the car with us - so here we are, driving along Byres Road when these two cars pull up in front of us, forcing us to a stop, and 'Starsky and Hutch' bail out, order us out of Jimbo's car and into theirs. I am, of course, carrying my synthesiser with me and 'Starsky' asks '"What's that?" I reply, matter of factly, "A synthesiser," bemused that he did not know what it was... but I should have realised that he was only able to function on a basic level of awareness and intelligence - hence his job title of 'Policeman'. These are agents of tyranny that infect every city and every street, a lot of them these days are nothing more than policy officers or revenue officers as they are more interested in collecting fees and issuing tickets to the 'Sheople' for daring to walk down the street, drive a car or, even worse, park one.

Being Boiled

I never met one who could string a sentence together coherently or quote a law or bylaw to explain why they have stopped me for any reason that they had the right to. Wrong! So wrong - no probable cause and no section number is legally applicable without a specific cause. Why don't they actually learn something or study the law before they give these morons a badge to walk on the streets - it makes me so fucking angry to see people oppressed by 'Peace Officers'. Stopping people in the street and asking for your I.D. is akin to Nazis stopping you in the street during World War Two and demanding to "Zee your paperz," or be arrested! I mean, what the fuck, if you want people to respect you, then learn to do your fucking job!

It seems to me, at least, that our freedoms are being eroded just like the USA's constitution is being eroded - 'The war on Terror' now gives them all the rights to stop, search or detain without cause! Back in the early 70s, the 'IRA' did more damage to the UK mainland and threatened us on a daily basis, bombing major cities and selective targets, killing dozens and dozens on trains, the underground, shopping precincts and murdering people under the banner of sectarianism, all they did was murder and kill regardless. They even had a go at sending homemade missiles to bomb the Conservatives at the Grand Hotel in Brighton during their Party Conference. Not that anyone would have been too bothered if they had managed to get rid of Thatcher as she was a fucking crazy bitch taking the

Unions out and flushing the country down the toilet. I absolutely get that one man's freedom fighter is another man's terrorist, but my point being that the fucking Government of the UK did NOT take away or erode everyone's freedoms back then, so why now? The so called 'Islamic State' have done far less in the UK to merit this erosion - but don't take my word for it, it's all on record for anyone to investigate if they can be bothered... but, perhaps watching the next episode of 'X Factor' is what you really live for? Which, if it is, you deserve everything that's coming your way soon.

Someone said a long time ago, maybe it was David Icke, that the best way to enslave people is not let them know they are slaves... and I know that is indeed what we are - enslaved. We are free, but only to a certain point, even the police are slaves to this system and they will eventually have to answer for all the wrongs they have protected higher up the 'chain of command'. Just take a look at the Paedophile scandals of the last half century (and longer) that has all been hidden and with only a few celebrities thrown to the wolves to pander to the public outcry! Stop protecting the scum and filth that are our Government and those sick Catholic priests from around the stinking mess of a Planet we are trying to live on - we need a Revolution of some kind, but we are sadly a nation of sheep now! We are good at policing ourselves, for tediously inane things like litter, swearing, cannabis ...for fuck's sake, grow some balls, UK, and wake the fuck up before we find ourselves living in a Fascist, Totalitarian state where we have no rights and have no balls to stand up to anyone, anymore... and they can do whatever the fuck they want with us! This makes my fucking blood boil! And, for fucks sake, don't get me started on Israel and Zionism! Apartheid gone insane! I smell the Rothschilds' kiss of death all over this.

Babylon, Osiris, Isis, and Horus - people, wake up! This is where religion was founded and bastardised to become a perversion of Christianity and all sorts of other religions - do some research and educate yourself, Rome did not fall! It simply became 'The Vatican' with a man who could make no mistake as far as the 'word of God' was concerned and rule millions around the world. It does not matter if you do not believe in God, or any other Gods, the ruling elite do, and they are in control. We are nothing more than the profane, beasts of burden, like meat on the table to the Initiates of the 'Mystery Schools of Babylon' - don't take my word for it, look at history... and this is why they win all the time, because they study history and learn from it. History can be used to predict events and fashion them to do your bidding - have you ever asked yourself why there are so many 'Obelisks' in major cities around the world? They represent the phallus of Osiris - yes, a penis, reflected in the pool that represents Isis... for fuck's sake, do you think they are there for another reason? If so, what? And while we are at it, where is the largest

'Obelisk' situated? Yes, that's right, America's capital city - the penis of Osiris is standing firmly erect in Washington DC!

The Freemasons of the Masonic order love their symbolism and love to have it all around them - its right in our faces in every city and everywhere we look there are Masonic images... all too glaringly obvious if you care to open your eyes and look for them. Even the Muslims despise Osiris and stone an Obelisk as part of their traditions. I think it's too late for us, but maybe we can save the planet from these penis worshippers for the next generation! They are not in awe of prophesy, they are making sure that prophecies happen and we remain as cattle and slaves to do their bidding. If you really want to educate yourself on this, just Google - Bill Cooper, 'The Hour of the Time' and the 'Mystery Schools of Babylon', a fascinating series from a very knowledgeable man.

So, here I am in Maryhill police station, with a copper fingering my arse for drugs (or so he said), it was not unduly unpleasant, but I made a mental note to look at policemen fingers from now on to see if there was any discolouration to indicate that they practiced on themselves to get it right.

"I don't do 'drugs'," I said to him, and he said, "I know," and let me go. They were after 'Fat Freddie', who turns out to be a New Yorker with a habit, and they had been watching him for a few days - wrong place, wrong time, with the wrong person in the car! Anyway, we carry on with our journey to get to rehearsals (minus 'Fat Freddie', who is now in a grey bar hotel for the foreseeable future). My arse is twitching and indignant to some faggy, twat copper's fingering techniques.

Backyard Tenements; Keppochill Road 1974

We were all playing in the backs (backyards) of the place where we lived and we were raking the midges for some bottles to claim the recycling fee of 2p each, and I stupidly put my arm into this broken part of the outbuilding, then screamed in agony and pulled my arm out... and there was a dirty fucking rat hanging off the flesh of my left arm, its' jaw locked in a bite right through my flesh. I was screaming like a constipated donkey trying to shit a bag of nails!

A few neighbours had heard the commotion and had come out, they were trying to get this rat off my arm, but it was not budging and only bit harder into me. I was now bleeding badly and someone, I don't know who dragged me across to Springburn fire station where a fireman drowned the rat in a deep basin of water that was in the yard. With the rat now dead all they had to do was get it off my arm somehow as, even in death, its jaws were locked firmly shut. An ambulance was on its way, but would still be another fifteen minutes before getting here and I was near passing out with the sight of this evil thing attached to my arm. The fireman came back and cracked its' jaw open with a pair of pliers, and it dropped to the concrete with a spongy thud. They washed my arm, put me in the ambulance, and sped me off to the infirmary. I spent a few hours getting sorted and, a few days later, all the tests came back negative for anything that could kill me, but I was sick for a week or so and my mum had some weird old lady, who stank of fags, to look after me as I was not going to school - I think I preferred the rat! This old lady was rank and I had smelt better drains

I'm made of stronger stuff and all the things that happened to me in my youth have only made me tougher in myself and perhaps, despite all the hardships and poverty, it has made me the person I am today - not too sure if I am grateful for that, but it's done and it's a part of me now.

CHAPTER SEVEN

ONE NIGHT IN BANGKOK

'...And the world's your oyster,

"Sawadee ka," the air hostess said to me as I stepped off the plane, and I replied "Sawadee krab, sabai dee mai," to which she smiled back with a sincerity which I found very refreshing. I needed to get away from Glasgow, away from my feuding, fucked up family, and the emptiness that was now making its self at 'home' in my shattered head. The band I eventually joined had scored some chart success and TV appearances, we had also went on a US city tour with another, annoying, teen-pop band that had achieved a lucky number one single in the charts - but all this was fast becoming a memory and I was at a loose end with my music career now. So, here I am, on a night flight to Bangkok or 'Sin City' as it's known to a lot of 'Farang' (Foreigners).

I wanted to expand my mind and my musical influences, to find inner peace on the banks of the 'Chao Phraya' river, to visit 'The Grand Palace' and 'The Wats' (Buddhist temples) which have always fascinated me. I book myself into a modest backpacker hotel just off 'Sukhumvit Road', I think it was three pounds a night (five pounds a night with air conditioning). I remember standing, looking out my hotel window, and seeing all this energy encapsulated in vibrant neon colours and swirling traffic. Even in the daytime it had a certain 'appeal' and I have never regretted my decision to go there. Sure, I could have chosen Spain or anywhere in Europe, but I was sick of seeing white people - it sounds strange, but I wanted to find somewhere different enough to shake me up, somewhere I could rise up from the dust of a crumbled band and past, and exorcise it from my synapses

Fucking, yes! This is just what I needed - to get out of the abyss of malcontent and reinvent myself... no girlfriends, no bands, no family, totally on my own - I am a 'Stranger in a Strange land'. Some of the local language I had read and memorised in a guide book (no Internet for years to come), so I had to do everything the hard way for now. Up to this point in my life, I had never been a drinker as I feared I would become just like my afflicted 'Dad' and be a full time arsehole with a wife and kids to beat on a daily basis, but I found myself going into bars in Nana Plaza and Soi Cowboy at night - being ushered in by sweet, beautiful, Thai girls who would 'love you long time' (or short time if the price was right). I am essentially a sensualist and I was also in search of 'The Pleasure Principle'. Thai girls are very, very friendly and it is so hard not to fall in love with them, but I am no fool and I know that the 'bar girls' are, in reality, eye candy and distractions, sometimes obvious and vulgar, but relentless at pursuing money from 'Farang'... and they are very good at getting you to part with it. I later changed my name by rearranging the letters from 'TAM' to 'ATM', as that's what the bar girls saw me as, as did all the others that frequent Pat Pong (Bangkok's notorious area where anything and everything happened), internationally known as the 'red light district' at the heart of the sex industry.

I'm up and out in the Thai streets, walking towards 'Wat Po', one of the more famous Temples in Bangkok, where they teach Thai massage, and I am reliably informed that most diplomas are attained from this temple. I am walking down the street, but my spider sense is tingling and I look behind me and see a Thai guy (poo chai) is keeping up with me, so I stop a few times and look to see what he is doing and it seems apparent that the fucker is shadowing me. I think I am in for a mugging and perhaps look like a first timer in 'Bangkok', so I make a few turns, cut through some alleys and, lo and behold, this cunt is now three feet in front of me - so, I go up to him and say, "What the fuck are you doing following me?" He blurts out in broken English, "I like shoes - can I buy?" What the fuck? He likes my trainers? He wants to buy them! I say "Pai kai kai!" (Which is a very rude way of saying 'go away'!). The guy looks shocked and the fucker moves away - I did not see him behind me again for the next hour it took me to get to the Temple.

Now, I am not saying Thai people are racist, but the price to get into the Temple is graded by 'Thai price' and 'Farang price' - Thai price being 90% cheaper than the price for the foreigner... what the fuck? I nearly start to make a scene when this Thai girl stops me and says sweetly, "Not to make the noise - very bad for you, many people will kick." So, I park my tongue and smile at her. She calls herself 'Ao' (pronounced ow) and she is a shop worker of some description. This girl is a 'stunner' to my eyes and senses, I chat her up for a good twenty minutes and ask if she would like to go out one evening... and she eventually gives me a number to call her on, but stipulates, "Thai lady always go out with chaperone on first date!" What the fuck? I start to think to myself, 'is she's bringing her Mum?'

I pay the five pounds entrance fee to the temple and I'm ordered to take off my trainers as no shoes are allowed into the temple at this point. For fuck's sake! The Thais are obsessed with feet and the top of their heads - but more on that later. The temple was very calming and very beautiful, intricate carvings on the roofs, walls, and doors - all very alien to western culture, like nothing I had ever seen before in my entire life. I am awe struck with the beauty of it all and spend the next two hours in intellectual and spiritual ecstasy - absorbing all of this is very intoxicating to my mind and I am not 'missing' Glasgow at all.

Fucking, little, smiley, Thai bastard! I shout when I leave 'Wat Po' - my trainers are missing and I do not need to be Sherlock fucking Holmes to know who had lifted them while I was inside. Unfortunately, a lot of Thai people are now looking over and frowning at me, whilst some were saying something I had not read in the guide book - 'Farang kee ngok!' ...I later learned this meant 'bird shit, foreigner' and was an insult meaning that foreigners are like bird shit and leave a stain - meaning we are a western stain to Thailand. This is, sort of, weird, when they call it the 'Land of Smiles' - 'fucking two faced bastards!' I say to myself, but in years to come I will learn that Thailand is a very organised and respectful society, and that I am the one at fault, feeling a little bit ashamed of my outbursts of anger in a land where they would not say 'boo' to a goose.

Thinking of 'two faced bastards'! Fuck me, no, the memory of the band is filling up in my head once more and I find myself drunk on Chang beer in my hotel room, thinking about it all again. The Thailand heat has driven me slightly wacky as well, not helping my state of mind. Eighteen months previously the band I got to join currently had a recording deal and had already recorded the 'single'. I start to hear a song in my head - 'The Worst Band in the World'.

'....It irrigates my heart with greed,

The '10cc' track is full on in my head now and I have just fully grasped the real meaning of it! The word 'greed' hangs in my head as I recall the last days of the band, despite fondly remembering my joining of the band on a happier note (although I still thought the singer was a delusional cunt - but what the hey?). I will not mention the actual name of this band as they may well read this and disagree on some points I make... and maybe arrange to sort me out at a later date, be it by hook or by crook - but anyone who knows me personally will know exactly who I am talking about and will have to be content with that.

1983, the year that I get a chance to be on TV with a freshly signed band. I had a phone call two weeks before asking me if I still had my 'Mini Moog', and would I be interested in standing in for their keyboard guy who was in hospital for the duration of a booked European tour. I am clearly saying 'yes' and now wishing this keyboard guy is in some sort of five year coma - yeah, fuck him... looks like the wrong time to get sick, dude! Will I stand in for him? You bet your fucking life I will! So, I go to rehearse with them in some Glasgow Studio, which was a bit posh and with decent equipment stashed in it. The tracks themselves were basic and guitar based (how the fuck they got a deal was beyond me), and my synth was the only source of electronics in the band - it was not really my kind of thing, but I wanted to see what transpired at the end of it all... for me! Easy peasy japaneasy! Ten songs, all learned in the space of a week. The job was mine for two simple reasons - Firstly, I looked good with black dyed hair and a slither of guy liner, and secondly... I had a Mini Moog!

The band got their single into the British charts 'Top Twenty', I think it was, and although I was not officially one of the original members, it looked like I was going to be on TV for the second time in my life (first time being the ill-fated dance competition on STV). I told my family, who were far more interested in fighting over cigarettes and beer... although my Dad did ask if he would get some money off of me for being on TV - yeah, right, you dysfunctional twat! I was not at all surprised by the lack of interest in me and my band antics, my Dad thought my music was crap and would not get me anywhere, suggesting that I should play stuff such as 'The Shadows', 'The Beatles', etc. ('now that's real music', he would say).

My Dad was a guitar player, and for all his married life he blamed my Mum for his lack of recognition in the music world. He claimed he left us to make his fortune as a guitar player when we were young, but all he did was play seedy working men's clubs for beer money and have sex with ugly, loose women. I had never bought the line that he was held back by a wife and four kids - he was just a plain, old fashioned, bastard with a sadistic streak that came out when he had no money or was getting 'bored', being back with his wife and kids.

Karma would come to visit my Dad one day. It happened like this - he was out driving a van (probably up to something dodgy), he stopped the van on a blind bend on the road to pick something up that someone had dropped or had fallen out of a car (he was only thinking of making money from whatever it, was, undoubtedly), when his greed was cut short by a Transit Van coming the other way... it hit him at forty MPH and sent his overweight body violently across to the other side of the road with a sickening thud on the concrete. He was left for dead as the Transit simply took off!

I remember the police coming to the house and giving us the grim news. My Mum looked sombre and we all looked... well, nothing really. The outcome was that he was in hospital for at least six months and had lost the use of his right arm and his left leg was shattered to pieces, needing to be pinned together. He'd be on pain-killers for the rest of his life and never play the guitar ever again - nor would he ever lift a finger to my Mum or any of us again... what goes around comes around, and everyone who knew him said he deserved it. I remember when he came out of hospital and my younger brother said he was going to pour Whisky on his grave, if and when he died. Well, my Dad thought that was kinda cool and said "thanks, son" then my brother, David, added, "But, I'll be passing it through my kidneys first, you cunt!" Nice one, bro!

No fucking way! Just no fucking way did I just see what I saw? I am sitting in a club in 'Nana Plaza' and this Thai girl is on stage, dancing and writhing around, looking very hot indeed. I am sitting right in the front row when she shot a ping pong ball right out of her pussy and, as it zoomed towards me, I toyed with the idea of stopping it with my teeth... then thought better of it! Fucking hell, serious internal muscle control or what? She did a few more as I sat there in total amazement and wondered where she learned something like that? I was thinking that this city was going to be very interesting indeed, and the only worry I had in my mind was... would I be able to survive it? I think I did fairly well - I stayed for eleven months, doing visa runs to Cambodia and Vietnam to stay sort of 'legal' in the kingdom.

I called Ao a few days later and we arranged to meet in 'Siam Square' - a few checks on the map and the next thing, I was in a taxi whizzing my way to meet a Thai beauty. I got there and she was standing, waiting for me - and she looked utterly stunning! Dressed in tight trousers with a camel toe you could park your bike in! These perky little nipples were protruding through her top and I found myself very aroused indeed, although I felt a bit guilty (but only a bit).

I asked her, "Where's your chaperone?"

And she answered "We meet in restaurant, later - okay? But, for now, we can walking and the talking... chai? (Yes)"

I am drunk on her beauty, her smile, her sweet perfume and her sexy little giggles to my attempts at talking to her in Thai.

"You very good to speaking the Thai," she said.

To which, I replied, "Khob khun mak mak krab."

She took my hand as we wandered about all the shops and she was constantly stopping, looking at lots of shops. Most of them, I noticed, sold gold items of one kind or another, and, at that point, my spider sense was tingling once more - "Fuck's sake, don't ask me to buy you anything," I said to myself. She just looked at the glittering objects behind the window and said, "So sad, mai mee tang (no money)."

I answered, "Well, there's more to life than money!" and she laughed, then said how silly I was.

I really did not care what she said, I would let her stick chop sticks up my arse if she asked to. She was breath-taking and I had never been with anyone so alluring and sensual.

About an hour later she said, "We go to eat now, chai?"

I said, "Yes, of course."

She added, "Okay, I take you to meet my Aunt now - she is waiting in restaurant, not far."

Actually, I was a bit miffed about her chaperone, but I guess they look after each other there... but, oh boy, I had a lot to learn and was about to be taught a big time lesson on how not to get involved with some Thai girls - especially tricky ones. I had been warned well in advance, by many people... don't fall in love, don't go to meet her family, don't loan anyone money! Yeah, yeah, I get it. My mate, in UK, who was a Thailand expert and went on in later life to write his own blog or website called 'Stickman' (where he would post up stories on Thailand every other week to help out guys who were thinking of going there on holiday or to live) knew everything there was to know, and I just didn't listen to him when he told me what to be careful of.

The restaurant was quite small and had had about 20 people in it laughing, eating and generally having a great time. I was introduced to her Aunt and a few of her Aunts friends, who just happened to be there as well. It was no big deal, just smile and say nice things. Their English was limited, but they seemed nice, friendly and seemed to approve of me immensely... which made me relax and just enjoy the evening. We sat and talked for hours - about her job, her life, her childhood, and every now and then a Thai would walk by and say "Khob khun," (thank you), and I simply assumed they knew her. This happened about thirteen times and I thought, "Fuck, I'm lucky if thirteen people talk to me all year, back in the UK."

The whole place is quite empty by now, and her

Aunt's friends have now gone too. Ao then just pipes up, "Okay, pay bill now - chai?"

"Yes, of course - no problem," I reply.

Thai food is cheap and I do not mind paying for her food and her Aunt's, so the waitress hands me the bill and it equates to nearly two hundred and seventy pounds - that's £270! I check it again and do some addition on a napkin and suggest - "Sorry, this can't be right, I only buy little food!"

But the waitress says "It's for all restaurant."

I stand up and say, "Fucking what? What the hell do you mean, the whole restaurant?" I turn to Ao and ask, "What the fuck is the waitress talking about?"

She just looks up at me and says, "You have to pay all!"

I shout back, "Why?"

Ao says "You pay for my family to meet you!"

Now I am trying to keep cool, knowing Thais despise confrontation or making a scene - So then I calmly inquire, "So, you are saying I have to pay for all the people who were in here tonight?"

The stunner says, "Yes, it's Thai tradition for to take out Thai relatives on first date."

"Fuck, no! I did not know or agree to this - I'm not paying for these others!"

Helpfully she tells me, "But if you not pay, they will arrest you for sure and put you in 'Bang Kwang'. (Bangkok's famous grey bar hotel for mugs!)

I now know, with absolutely no doubt, that I have been stitched up and it was all a scam to feed a few families on the pretence of a date.

Finally, I say, "Okay, fine - I pay... but you can fuck off! ...and take your ugly Aunt with you!" At which point I felt a sharp blow to the back of my head which made me spit some blood and I turn round to see an angry young dude ready to Muay Thai me into unconsciousness.

Tip #1 - When in Thailand, do not offend anyone's Aunt!

I stare him down and think about going 'Vin Diesel' on this Ong Bak look alike, but self-preservation gets the better of me - I say, "Sorry," to the old lady and 'Wai' (bow to her with my hands pressed together in front of me). I pay the ridiculous bill and then leave, step outside and jump into a TukTuk to take me back to my hotel... a few hundred quid lighter and a whole lot wiser.

"Fucking, fuck me!" I am swearing to myself.

The TukTuk driver is staring at me in his mirror, he shouts back to me, "You want to buy the real diamonds?"

Feeling sick, I just say, "For fuck's sake - please stop!" I don't need another Thai bastard scamming me today!

I pay him and walk the rest of the way back to my hotel - I had already heard about the gem scams that TukTuk drivers try to get unwary travellers involved in... And I was currently in no mood to be fucked around with.

Feeling wracked off, I go out to the bars across the street and console myself with a few cheap beers - all the while having sweet, Thai girls dance seductively all around me. All of them are in bikinis and look very sexy indeed... eye candy and food to a starving man. They are making my senses reel with the overload of flesh all around me. I am starting to weaken and now have 'localised, high blood pressure'! With only one obviously effective cure in males, I start to wonder what I can do to cheer myself up to forget the day's events.

Still pissed about being ripped off earlier in the day, I start to feel myself slipping more and more into 'la-la land' with the beers and the loud music. I can remember a lap dance and kiss on my lips, here and there, and someone rubbing my cock under the table in the bar. I am too drunk to care or object and it all feels very nice, but a part of me is wary that I may end up in trouble, so I get up and wander across the road, back to my hotel to sleep it off!

The next morning I awaken and look up at the ceiling. My head feels like it's been ripped off and screwed back on, but I feel weirdly serene and calm. I suddenly realise I am not alone and there is a beautiful, naked Thai lady on either side of me in bed! 'What the fuck did I do last night?' I slip out of bed, go and check my wallet to find my money and stuff is all still there - to my immense relief, nothing is missing. I look at all the clothes strewn across the floor - panties, bras and ping pong balls, and two condom packs (you know, the 'three in a box' ones). Hehe - I laugh aloud and wish I could remember what I did... although it was pretty obvious - but two of them?

I have a naughty thought and slip back into bed between them. One of them starts to wake up, kisses me full on the lips, and keeps on kissing me for about ten minutes The next thing I know, the other one is awake and she is slipping down beneath the sheets, puts my soft cock into her mouth and starts sucking on it like a lollipop. A tongue goes down my throat and there's a hot mouth around my pork sword - what a way to wake up! They put a condom on me and one is on 'top riding' me like a Grand National jockey who desperately wanted to win the race. They then swap over and I am very close to losing control. I gush into the safety of the rubber (I never jump without a parachute) and shudder with pure delight as I float up to a fluffy white cloud. They both giggle and laugh, then run off to the shower together whilst I lie there and wonder what their names are... and are they really prostitutes? Fuck's sake, Mr Scott, what are you doing? The pair come out of the shower twenty minutes or so later, get dressed, and then say "Bye, Mr. Tam!" I watch them leave and I am still worried that I have just fucked two whores, so I check my money once more - no, it's all there... so obviously I did not pay for anything untoward. The matter is a subjective one now and I leave my head to deal with it on a lower level as I think about breakfast and perhaps catching a Taxi to 'Pattaya City' in the south west of 'Chonburi'. I had a feeling it was going to be a great day!

The drive to 'Pattaya City' takes a few hours, more or less covering the same distance from Nottingham to London. The Thai taxi driver is chatty and stops a few times to pay toll fees over a couple of bridges before he stops and buys me some food and a can of much needed 'Coca Cola'. He drives like Steve McQueen in 'Bullitt' and gets me there almost like James Bond's Martini - shaken, but not stirred. The man then asks me for the equivalent of eight pounds - I am fucking embarrassed and give him twelve pounds, whereupon he starts bowing to me and I say, "No, it's okay - you deserve it, man, that journey would have been about two hundred pounds, back in the UK for the same distance!"

Why is it so cheap over here? Thais eat four or five times a day - how the fuck can they afford so much food? But, in all honestly, it costs pennies to feed yourself here - just three pounds would get you four meals and a drink in Thailand... what the fuck is wrong with the West?

'Pattaya' looks very different from 'Bangkok', it has a beach and it looks like a holiday resort - I am already liking it. I find a reasonably priced hotel and stow my gear into the room, then head out for the sunshine and the beach.

"This is fucking great!" I shout aloud, "No worries and no one to nag or harass me."

I start down the Beach Road and immediately see bar after bar after bar - it's like running in a 'Scooby Doo' cartoon... lamp, window, door, lamp, window, door, and on and on.

It's just gone lunch time and the bars are full of beautiful Thai girls dancing outside or on little stages raised up from the floor so they could be seen from the road. I felt a slight panic, wondering if I should keep myself in check here and not let my mind or cock wander too far this time! I come across this girl and she is fucking crazy or deranged or something - she has a black scorpion on her head, her shoulders, her cleavage, and on each bare foot... it's a 'street theatre' thing to make money from tourists, but, fuck me, I could think of better ways to make money. I continue to walk down the road and this gorgeous lady stops me and asks if I want a 'Thai Massage' for only a hundred and fifty Baht. I always wanted a massage like that, so I said, "Yes". Now, Thai Massage is like Yoga for lazy people - they will bend your body into the shapes for you and exert the pressure needed to release tension and muscle spasm. The massage girl was called 'Apple' and she said, "Please follow me to my apartment," ...which I did. It was only a couple of minutes walk and I soon found myself lying on the bed with a soft white towel covering my arse and the back of my legs.

Apple begins to rub my legs and feet, she is expertly pressing down with enough force making me sigh with appreciative, 'ummms' and 'ahhhs' every now and then. She is wearing a short skirt and seems to be able to bend herself at will to reach all parts of my tired body when I feel something warm on my leg. I think nothing of it until I feel it again and realise it's not her hands - it's something under her pants that must be touching the back of my leg with such persistence that... Oh, my, fucking hell! It suddenly hits me like a ton of bricks - it's a 'Katoey' (Lady-Boy) and she is rubbing her cock on my leg with the intent of getting me aroused for what I guess must be paid sex. I try not to instantly leap off the bed as I want to get out of the situation in one piece.

I feel this thing getting harder and pressing into my leg even more and I say, "Sorry, but are you a guy?", and she says demurely, "No, I'm girl!" I ask, "Are you sure?", and she replies, "Yes, I'm sure!" I ask, "What's that sticking into my leg?" and she/he giggles and responds with, "It's my lollipop - do you want to see it?" Very firmly I state, "Mai chai" (no), and she/he finally stops the rubbing and continues with just the massage. Beating the crap out of him seemingly now averted, I go for a shower and get dressed in thirty seconds flat, and then I am out the door at the speed of light. Bloody fuck, my brothers will never believe me, and to this day I have never mentioned it to them. Now I can spot a 'Katoey' a mile off - too pretty, too much make up, and too revealing clothes with no subtlety about them... oh, and too flirty and forward as well - real Thai ladies would never be like this.

I love 'Pattaya City', its wild, it's funny, it's kinda seedy, and is a bit like 'Pat Pong' but with a beach, a beautiful ocean and spectacular sunset. I am walking along Beach road (again) and there are scores of Thai ladies and Lady-boys, they are all obviously prostitutes and called 'freelancers' as they do not work in the official, 'unofficial' sex industry. All of them are beautiful and all of them a little desperate, all of them with a story of woe and hurt, pain and heartache, all of them in need of love - but for now, all they need is your company for a short while and some much needed money. All of them have families to feed from whatever village they come from, usually from the poor North such as 'Laos' or from 'Vietnam' and 'Cambodia', searching for a way out of the poverty trap and to send money back home so no one goes hungry.

I start to look around and see how widespread it all is, before I wonder how bad things would have to be in the UK for more people to do this kind of 'work'. I remember how poor we were in the late 60's and 70's, living in a life of shadows and eating food from litter bins like a feast - old chips from the night before and scraps of leftovers from the neighbours. I vividly remember looking for food in the house and there was nothing there, but perhaps there was something left in the Cornflake box. I shook it and it sounded very empty, we had no milk but I did not care and poured the last of them out, only to see a mouse fall into the bowl - it was dead and had probably been there for a week or so. I still ate what was left of the Cornflakes, and I cringe now every time I think of it, hunger knows no shame.

My mind comes back to me as I continue to walk down the Beach Road in 'Pattaya City', looking past the eyes of all those beautiful ladies who have no choice and probably hate themselves for what they are doing to survive, possibly realising that looks are transitory and wondering what will happen to them and their families when they are no longer beautiful or wanted by the 'Farang'. I realise there is no real work in 'Pattaya', it's a 'Las Vegas' world of lost souls on the 'Chonburi' shoreline - a place to gamble with your life and live the illusion of happiness for as long as you are able to... or can afford it. I find it vile that we are the only species on the planet that has to pay to live on it.

I now know that we are all slaves to something or other, and do things we have to do in order to survive. Most of us are chained to a desk or a job that will not let you go and will suck the very life out of you until you are no longer of any use to it... when you then waste away into a life that is supposed to set you free to enjoy what time you have left. But the truth of the matter is that unless we are very privileged indeed, that freedom still seems a long way off... and what a sad way to expire - getting older and weaker in the UK, with occasional trips to hypothermia, worry, and the illusion that you actually have a life.

I leave 'Pattaya City' and head back to 'Bangkok', feeling a sense of freedom I have never felt before - fuck me, is this place getting to me? I feel an affinity with Thailand - The Thais seem well adjusted, happy, appearing to be having fun and enjoying what they have, even though for some it's very little. I am sitting at the 'Chao Phraya' river looking across at 'The Temple of Dawn' (Wat Arun), and the serenity of it all is opening my mind and my heart. Glancing around, I see a lovely, sweet, Thai lady walking near the river... and I say to myself, 'how beautiful you are'. The woman looks at me as if she had just read my mind - did she somehow hear what I was thinking on some level? She smiles at me, and I say, "Hello, how are you?" The beauty introduces herself, and says "Sabai Dee". I don't know it at that moment, but this Thai Lady will be in my life for the next nine years.

She takes me to a place called 'Tiger Temple' in the 'Saiyok District', 'Kanchanburi Province' - here, we are allowed to hold and feed baby Tigers and help out around the 'Wat' with some menial tasks that she assures me with be good for 'merit'. I say "uh!", and she says "Jai dee mak mak" which translates to 'having a good heart', and I understand now what she means - I am being selfless and it will make me feel better. The Monks give us some food and water, and after a few hours more work, we leave and I feel an intense satisfaction. It makes me remember when I used to feel like this, when we lived in the tenement slums of Springburn in Glasgow. There is something humbling about living basically, and it seems to bring out more of the community spirit from individuals, making people seem nicer and more caring. Perhaps being in Thailand is making me understand that money is not the sole purpose in life.

She spends the whole day with me, taking me to the 'Grand Palace' and the 'MBK Shopping Mall' where we have some food, laugh and talk about life, and how much freer everything seems to be in 'Bangkok' than the city I live in. It's obvious to me that Thai people seem very relaxed and happy with what they have, something I think we in the 'West' have lost in ourselves - we seem more wound up and angry with everything around us. Surely this is not healthy and we will undoubtedly suffer for it at some point in our lives unless we can find a way to cope with the stresses of everyday, modern living in the UK... and it's getting worse - people are just being turned into 'Automatons'. We will all burn out like an old light bulb, and the sad thing is... no one will care. We have lost the thing that makes us, 'us'.

She take me to 'Chainat' to meet her family and they are really nice. They own a farm and some local shops - they are sweet and very friendly, conversing with minimal English... but that does not stop us laughing and having a great time. Her Mum is a great cook and this has to have been, by far, the best Thai meal I have had since I got here. She has a sister called 'Tuk' and a brother whose name I forget - but he was a really funny guy, and I liked him a lot. In a way I felt more at home with them than I did with my own family... and I felt a real twinge of sadness at how dysfunctional we all were.

I suppose she is one of the lucky ones from a lucky family, and my mind wanders off and I start to picture all the girls standing along the 'Beach Road' in 'Pattaya' and 'Nana Plaza' in 'Bangkok', who dream of being a lawyer or a shop keeper instead of a vessel of iniquity. I feel really sad inside, deep within myself, and I want to help all of those lonely ladies I saw, promising myself that if I ever became rich, I would spend my days helping people out of misery.

Boston Massachusetts - 1980s

I have just woken up in my hotel room and I'm getting dressed for breakfast. The gig last night was fucking brilliant and I loved all the adoration from the crowds swarming around the 'Boston Garden'. The American crowds could not have known who we really were, as we were the support act for the 'Pop Band' that we had managed to get on tour with, but they gave us a rapturous welcome and I am feeling hyped up and a bit like a 'rock star' - should I trash my room and call up some hookers later? Lick a line of cocaine off their pussies? Perhaps throw the TV set out the window into the pool below? Oh, no, I do something much, much worse.

I am walking down the hotel corridor and I see the lead singer's room door is open.

I'm just about to walk by when I hear his girlfriend shout, "Hey! Who's there?"

So, I knock on the door, ask if he is there and coming down to breakfast. She says, "Come in."

I go in and she is fucking starkers on the bed, with the sheet wrapped around her leg and inner thigh. She says he went for breakfast and then going for a run in the park, a mile or so away.

I start to walk away when she throws back the sheets and says "I need a fuck!"

Right up to this very day, I still think about it - the reason why I jumped into bed with her and fucked her brains out, I will never know... but she was a dirty, little slut - the kind I adore (just like me), and, after all, I am only a guy.

The singer was always a bit of a cunt anyway, and although he never knew what happened, I could not look at him or her in the eye ever again - but my cock's eye seemed to wink at her whenever she brushed by me with that lovely arse of hers! Sorry, dude, I don't know if you married her or had kids, but she was naughty and I can personally verify that she had more suction than a top of the range, Dyson vacuum. Hey, it's all rock and roll to me! ...Shit, just checked online - it took me ten minutes to find him on Google and, yeah, he married her and has two kids.

Maybe I should have just thrown the TV set out of the window after all?

CHAPTER EIGHT

COMPLEX

In Freudian psychology, 'The Pleasure Principle' is the instinctual seeking of 'pleasure and avoidance of pain in order to satisfy biological and psychological needs'. Specifically, 'The Pleasure Principle' is the driving force guiding 'The ID'.

Here I am again, in bed with another lady. I have been in 'Hanoi', 'Vietnam', for only three days and already I am in need of some 'intimacy'. I think back... is this something to do with the lack of parental attention from my beleaguered past? I think Freud would blame it on that, at least, or blame it on some sort of sexual fantasy involving a carrot and a bag of dead chickens - in any case, isn't that what your cock's for? Surely not just for some animalistic coupling to beget more life like some dumb, retarded followers of Christ who live in Rome, giving out 'Papal Decrees' on what you can, and can't, do with your own body or enjoy with another consenting adult. Well, it's a good thing I am not Catholic or I would be going to hell on a one way ticket. To quote 'John Milton', 'It's better to reign in Hell than to serve in Heaven' and I am clear where I would rather be if there is such an entity called 'God' to send me there.

I am shafting this rather pretty Vietnamese lady called 'Dung' (which translates to 'Beauty' in English) ...fucking hell! It's a rather unfortunate name and one I find hard to call her, so I call her 'sexy', which she seems to like and accept. Man, did she know what to do with her tongue! I had met her in a 'Go-Go' bar and somehow ended up in her 'room' just above the bar. The room stank of stale sex, and I was more or less sure it was a short time room for 'other bar girls'. Dung insisted, "She only work as waitress and not the other," and I believed her, as she was not dressed in the same way - no cheap perfume and no tits spilling over a bra that was two sizes too small. She had a son who lived with her mother in another part of 'Hanoi' and I guess she had to live where she worked for now. It reminded me of 'Bangkok' on some levels, with the exception of a different language and slightly less appealing food, which was still very edible and savoury.

I said 'bye' to her and decided to go for a walk

before returning to my hotel and, fuck me, I was scared a little. This motor cycle gang just roared up from behind me and all stopped at the swinging set of traffic lights that a gust of wind had caught and was making them jump and jingle like outdoor Christmas decorations. The thing that scared me was not the loud roar or the menacing looks but the helmets they were wearing.

On each and every gang member's head was an old 'US Army Helmet', complete with bullet holes and dents - a keepsake of the Vietnam conflict with the US of A. I was later told that the Vietnamese people have a long memory and still despise the 'Americans' to this day - a bit like the 'Scottish and English' sentiments of 1746, during the last battle fought on Scottish soil with the Jacobite uprising and the 'Young Pretender', Charles Stuart, better known as Bonnie Prince fucking Charlie! (Who, for all intents and purposes, looked like a fucking `Hobbit' on a white horse that could have been tailor made for 'Barbie!)

I am in 'Vietnam' for a visa run so I can get back into Thailand 'legally', something a lot of Westerners do to avoid getting kicked out by the Royal Thai Police and put on a black list of people over-staying their welcome in the 'Kingdom'. It's all about fucking money and nothing else - what a fucking bunch of hypocritical wankers! But the visa run works as the 'Thai Border Check-points' get to keep some of the money for stamping your passport for another sixty days. I have been here nearly eight months and I have no intention of going back to 'Blighty' - why the fuck would I want to? What the fuck is back there for me? Who the fuck is there for me? I cringe at the very thought of going back to 'Scotland' and starting all over again - fucking well fuck that - big time! I need a plan and I need one fast! My funds are dwindling and I want to make sure I don't delve into my last twenty thousand pounds, which is for a rainy day, or my return to the UK at some point... I called it my 'Disaster escape Fund'.

I have met a few ex-pats and they have been fucking great at helping me sort out visa runs and the language barrier. They usually hang out in an Irish bar called 'Finnegan's Irish Pub' (honestly). I met a guy there called 'Big Andy', who was from 'Dundee', and he says, "Fuck, man, you've gotta have a fucking plan!" (Yeah, thanks for pointing out the blindingly obvious, Andy.) I'm thinking 'how the fuck can you afford to stay here permanently'? Just as soon as I actually ask the question aloud, I don't want to know the fucking answer... he says, "Just take a suitcase back with you on your next visa run and you'll earn enough to stay another six months easy!" I hear exactly what he is saying and I break into a cold sweat as the honest guy inside of me, who I have always trusted, says, "Sorry - no! That's a line I will not cross, so I guess I'm going home." He looks at me with slitted eyes and says, "Are you sure you're from Glasgow?" I replied, "I am!" ...but not the Glasgow he thinks I am from.

Complex

Helpful Andy punches me in the gut and I double up, instantly feeling a bit sick. He shouts at me, "Fuck off then, ya wee cunt... and don't come back here or I'll rip your fucking throat out!

I'm back in Bangkok, living in a flea pit hotel to save some money, when I call 'Noi' - the lady I met near the river. I asked her if she wanted to join me for a meal later - she says, "Umm, yes sure. I thought you go back to UK last week?" I answered, "No, I had a few things to do and stayed in Cambodia and Vietnam for a few weeks." Noi inquires, "Ahhh, you visit all Temple chai?" I confirmed it, "Yup, I did, and loved it all... but would be going home to Scotland soon and wanted to see her before I went." (Translation - not had sex with her yet!) Oh, dear, my 'id' is clearly in control ...and always gets me into something more troubling than just sex.

According to the model of the psyche, the 'id' is the primitive and instinctive component of personality, made up of unconscious energy that focuses on fulfilling urges and sexual desires (well, having studied some Freud, I know what my weaknesses are... but, fucking hey, it's something we can't control - so stop thinking that I'm a cunt. He-he)

I meet Noi near the 'Amphawa Floating Market' about eight miles from where I am staying - there are lots of nice places to eat there and, if you ever get to Bangkok, I can recommend it. I have been going there every time I return to Thailand Anyway, Noi turns up, smiling and very pleased to see me - she has a very 'shagadelic' arse and my 'id' is biting at the bit to be let loose and savour her fruits and inner sanctum. I wine and dine her near the river, and she is so sweet and caring - such a delight to be around... how the fuck am I going to be able to leave here?

So I ask her, "Noi, can I stay here with you, in Bangkok?"

She looks at me and replies, "Mai chai u la ngu hua mak mak."

"Errr... what?" I enquire.

Noi says, "If you stay Thailand, you will be sexy pest with all Thai ladies - all Farang who stay always leave girlfriend and have many other, Pakwhann mak mak." (Which means Sweet-talker or, more to the point, 'Jack the Lad')

I said, "No, no, no - I would never do that!"

But Noi is adamant that it is inevitable that I could not resist what was on offer in Bangkok on a daily basis. She said, "Sanuk nid noi," but soon 'ngu hua."

"Oh," I said, "so you think I am like that now, with you?"

Shaking her head, she says, "No, I am nice now and she not want me to change!"

Damn it, she was right - and I knew it! I had already succumbed to the fatal charms of Thailand and slept with at least eight ladies in the first six months of being here - nothing paid for (I had not sunk that low) but I guess if you stay here long enough the temptation will get to you.

I decided to that now was not the time to try and charm the knickers off her to 'bump uglies' as she would probably hate me forever... and something told me she was worth holding onto - fucking hell, am I actually falling for her? I walk her to the taxi and she gives me a hug and a lovely thing Thai ladies do when they rub their noses on your cheek and make a little exhalation - so sweet and so very charming. This country is full of wonderful things and I am drunk on its passionate life style and free thinking.

John Lennon's great song 'Imagine' is echoing in my head.

I admit being in a Buddhist country with no religion dictating your daily life gives you a sense of freedom. I feel very at home here, but realise I have not accomplished anything on my personal path - to get back to my music, to reinvent myself, and to move on from the 'Pop Band' thing. I feel elevated, much like The Beatles must have felt, after years of teeny bop song fodder, to come out with 'Sergeant Pepper's Lonely Hearts Club Band'.

The UK's dismal grey skies loom a few miles ahead and already I feel alien and nauseous at the thought of landing in Glasgow. I am not even interested or excited about seeing my family, but I have nowhere else to go for now. I get a taxi to my Mum and Dad's house, and they seem sort of pleased to see me - but I know they are thinking about money... and if I am going to ask them for help. My Mum cooks a great beef stew and dumplings, and I am very grateful for it. I fill them in about my time in Thailand, and I know they are not interested in hearing any of it. I decide to sleep on the sofa when they go to bed, my trusting friend 'Damien' sleeps with me - the family dog who has shown me more love than both my parents put together. He snuggles up close to me, but his breath smells of dog's balls, and I turn my back on him... but he never leaves my side.

I dream of Thailand and wish I was back there or able to go back soon. I miss Bangkok and I miss Noi's company, I miss the food and the weather - What the fuck have I done? Why did I come back? To write a fucking album or join a new band? Self-doubt is creeping up on me fast, and if I don't act now, I am going to become another casualty of Glasgow and sucked into a life of utter misery. I have a brainwave and think to call my Aunt in England - she lives in a city called 'Leicester' and I wonder if she has a spare room. I tell my Mum my plan and she says, "What the fuck do you want to go there for? It's full of 'Pakis' and 'Blacks'!" My Mum has never been shy about her racism and it pains me to hear her speak like that - another by product of the UK's ever-present 'xenophobia' ...and she has it as bad as they come.

"Hi, Tommy!" This is an annoying name that my Aunt has given me and is short for Thomas, an

English pronunciation and translation of my Scottish name 'Tam' - for fuck's sake, am I doing the right thing here? Two weeks later, I and all my worldly possessions are in Leicester. I had money when I was in the band. I think, all in all, I had about one hundred, thousand pounds (£100,000!) at some point - not all at once, but over eighteen months ...it was coming back to me in 'dribs and drabs' as 'P.R.S.' cheques (Performing Rights Society), and Record Company 'Royalties' for my parts in the Single and 'Live' shows. I felt so fucking rich a year ago, but now all I had left was twenty grand - a tidy sum to have in 1986, but where did the rest go, I hear you ask? Did I have a drug habit? Was I an alcoholic? Did I gamble? - No, on all counts... I had 'my family' - and what a bunch of leeching fuckers they turned out to be.

My brothers and Dad - "Hey, can you set us up in business?"

"Yes... I can," I foolishly said.

I bought them a burger van, on a good pitch outside one of the big Football Stadiums in Glasgow - guaranteed money every Saturday... easily enough to sustain the van and three skanking fuckers who did not want to do an honest day's work. I bought the van, some stock and paid for six month's rent for the pitch in a prime location right outside the football grounds. It was a no-brainer to make money and that was only for working a single day per week. On the one day, the takings should have been about three thousand pounds for the whole shift on a match day ...and five hundred pounds on any other day they wanted to work by moving the van around to various points in the city. I felt good - I had managed to set these sad fucks up in business and did not need to concern myself with them anymore. My part was done! But, I also bought them a six berth, static caravan home - you know the ones, you see near the beach... big spacious and about twenty thousand pounds worth. I bought them this with the view that they always had somewhere to go for their holidays, but could also rent it out at times to make some money too. It was near Arbroath/Dundee and was a great location - my Mum was very pleased with this as it was her most favourite place on Earth.

Fucking complete idiots and wankers! I had come back from Leicester for a few days, just to see how they were doing, and had only been gone for six months.

I asked my siblings, "How's the burger van going?" expecting great tales of how rich they were now... but these fucking 'Muppets' said, "Oh, errr... we had to sell up!"

"For fuck's sake, why? What the fuck did you do? It was a no-brainer, a monkey could practically run it blindfolded - all you had to do was make burgers, put them in fucking buns and take money off people!" I responded, angrily.

"Aye, but we weren't getting any pocket money to keep ourselves, bro!"

So I did the maths and worked out they had fucked it up on month three. They had taken all the money they had made up to then, about three and a half thousand pounds, and split it between the three of them - and then they each gave a hundred pounds back to buy stock... which is grossly fucking obviously not enough. The fucking greedy cunts - I try to help you and you fuck it all up because of your own selfishness.

I asked, "Where's the fucking van?"

"Oh, aye... Dad had to sell it!"

At that point I realised they have screwed me over and were only thinking of beer, fags and drugs.

"What a bunch of retarded twats," I called them all.

They had no intention of running the business, they just wanted access to quick money so they could debauch themselves once more. The 'id' knows no bounds.

"Hoist by your own petard' I said to myself, paraphrasing Shakespeare... but Shakespeare's 'Hamlet' would be wasted on such low-vibrational 'Muppets'

I stormed out, disgusted with them, and go to see my Mum.

"Hey Mum, how are you?"

"I'm alright," she says.

I told her about the fucking Marx brothers and she nods.

"Aye, I know... they fucked it up big time, from their own greed, as always!"

I asked her about the Caravan and if she had used it a few times for holidays and to think about renting it out for some income, every now and then. Her face fell and there was silence.

I said, "What? Don't fucking tell me the cunts sold it as well?"

"No," she says, "it was an accident."

I felt a bit weak and asked, "What fucking accident? What's going on?"

"Oh, Tam, it was one of their pals!

My Mum explained she had given my brother the keys to the Mobile Home so he and his mates could spend a few days 'up North' for a birthday do.

"...And?" I enquired.

"Oh, well, they had a wee party and they got a bit drunk."

"For fucks sake, Mum, what where you thinking?" says me.

"I know," she replied, "I wish I hadn't given him the keys now."

"So, Mum, what the fuck did he do?"

"Oh, they put the chip pan on to do some chips and they all fell asleep. The chip pan caught fire, set the kitchen up, and they couldn't put it out ...and the whole thing went up in flames."

"Fucking hell - did anyone get hurt?" I asked and saw her shake her head in denial.

Twenty thousand plus pounds gone - up in smoke! But I know I also left them money to buy insurance... so, I asked what did the insurance company say?

She went all white again and said, "I didn't get it. Your Dad took it and drank it!"

"That's it," I shouted, "I've had enough of you bastards! I try to do the right thing and give you the means to support yourselves and all of you fuck it up in the space of six months - I am fucking done with you lot as a family ...all that money gone, out of greed and stupidity - gone for good!"

I am so pissed off I drive back to Leicester the same night and tell my Aunt the story. She tells me they are a waste of space and especially my Dad, who is a loser of epic proportions. My Aunt's husband is called Danny, and is from Leeds City - they met and lived in a caravan until they could afford to buy a house in 'Gypsy Road', 'Leicester City' (a place that has now been swallowed up into the 'Golden Mile'). My Aunt lives in 'Leicester Forest East', and I am happy to be there for the time being.

So, after all that, my current situation at that point is... I'm back in Britain, I have a job, some money left from being in the band, a place to stay on 'London Road', I have a car and nice furniture - but I've not done much with the music so far and I'm at a loss as to what style to write in. Then I meet a lady called 'Ashley', (name changed at your request, hehe), and she is wild, crazy, sexy and very naughty indeed - she reminds me of some Thai ladies I met a year or so ago and she makes me feel very alive. Ashley is always doing something crazy and is involved in some very, very weird shit - she heals people with 'laying of hands', she reads 'Tarot Cards', and is the most interesting person I have met since being in England. One day, right out of the blue, she seduces me. I am in her 'Healing Room' and she is using 'Crystal Therapy' to help me heal my 'Aura', when she suddenly says, "I'm going to give you a treat." I'm slightly baffled and I'm thinking, cream scones and tea or something, when she says "I want to suck you off!" I sort of say "Hhmm, huh?", and she leaves the room. I thought to myself, 'Fucking hell, up until that point we had not kissed or done anything - hell, I never even asked her out... we just hung out together!' Ashley comes back into the room and I am still sitting on her bed-sofa, she smiles and says, "Come on, get it out!" Who am I to refuse such a cheeky and naughty lady? I pull my zip down and there he is, standing proud, erect, and ready for action. She gets down on her knees and gives him a little lick, then looks up at me, and with a cheeky grin puts my cock all the way in and 'Deep Throat's me! Oh yes! 'This is nice,' I'm thinking when she starts to speed things up, moving her mouth up and down with expert rhythm.

Occasionally she looks me in the eye, pausing only long enough to ask, "You wanna cum in my mouth, huh? Do you? Huh? Hmm, Come on, give it to me!" Now she starts to go faster and faster, then moves her head from side to side, grabs my balls and gently tugs them till I feel a sudden rush. I feel like my head is going to burst off my neck, I am in total ecstasy and I explode in her eager and willing mouth - but she just keeps on sucking and licking for another five minutes at least. Fucking hell, does that qualify for the best blow job ever?

She looks up at me and smiles - I think how sweet she is, how demure she appears... she then proceeds to spit my ejaculate out, all over my stomach. 'Hmm', I think to myself, 'a bit slutty, but I'm not going to argue.' Ashley says proudly, "I don't swallow, just love to feel it squirt out of a cock and into my mouth!" "Well," I say, "Wow that was fucking great!" To which she replied, "Yeah, I know! I really know how to suck!"

I went round to her place most days and she drained me even more - she was insatiable and her sexual repertoire was nothing short of incredible. I was starting to think she was an ex-porn star as I could barely keep up with her sexual cravings. We were never officially a couple and I knew it could end anytime when she got bored of me or found someone else. I went over to her house after work one day and knocked on her door, she shouted on someone and I went to where I heard her shout. Ashley was in the dining room, which she had converted into a 'massage/healing' room, and when I went in. She was on the sofa kissing a girl, a pretty lady called Cathy, and, man, were they kissing! They were both naked from the waist up and obviously enjoying themselves. I stood dumbfounded and wondered, 'What the fuck do I do?' when Cathy just gets up, pulls me to her nipples and shoves one in my mouth. I start to suck on her as Ashley pulls my eager stiffness out of hiding and starts sucking on it... then Cathy does too, and soon they both are doing it - taking turns, and I am starting to think 'I am in a dream and this is not real!'

Cathy starts to kiss me passionately and Ashley leaves the room - she comes back five minutes later with a naked guy... I am too far gone to care who the hell he is, but Ashley start to suck him off in front of me and I feel a little ashamed, hoping we can still be friends tomorrow. I needn't have worried as we were friends for a long time to come and she regularly took me on hedonistic journeys, but telling me that as soon as I get serious with her, "It's over". I managed not to fall in love with her for a long time... she did, however, have a darker side, and I experienced it one night laying in bed beside her.

I was sleeping soundly when I felt a sharp pain to my head and woke with a start. "Oowwwww," I screamed and looked at Ashley -- she had a glass ornament that she has just smashed into my head while I was sleeping. I got scared and jumped out of bed, shouting, "What the fuck are you doing, you crazy bitch?" She throws the object at me and claims I've been cheating on her. I said "You are fucking nuts, I am not seeing anyone and you were the one who said 'let's not get serious', etc. etc. So what's your fucking point?" Still acting bizarrely, she screamed, "I know you are, I know you are!" The truth was that I really wasn't, but she was off her head with something, so I decided to get dressed and leave sharpish. I called her the next day and she did not remember doing anything at all, then asked me to come round that night. I really had to give that notion some serious thought, wondering if perhaps she was drunk or something, maybe she had been having a bad dream, or...? Finally I decided to go over and that evening went round to see her. After a marathon bout of sex, we lay in each other's arms and fell asleep... only to feel her punch me in the face, hard, a short time later - making my nose and top lip bleed. I demanded to know what she was doing, but she never answered - just kept raining punches to my face and scratching the back of my neck. "Fuck this, I've got to get out of here," I said to myself. I grabbed my clothes and ran to the car, dressed only in my boxers, hoping the neighbours were not awake to see such a spectacle. Ashley then ran out and started throwing crystals at my car - big, heavy, amethysts and quartz gems. One of the tossed crystals cracked my windscreen as I pulled out the drive, but I was too scared to get out and complain. I put my foot down, drove off, and got back to my place, where I lay, shattered, on the bed.

I had to go to work later on and was looking at my cut lip and all the scratches. The fucking bitch! What the fuck was wrong with her? I called her on the phone again for an explanation and she said she was sorry, but sometimes she just became a bit crazy and violent. I said, "Sorry, but I've had enough - I just can't cope with it, Ashley." She said she would give me some healing if I came around later. I made the situation clear, "No fucking way - you need some serious fucking therapy, and fast! You are dangerous to be around and I don't want to be in any kind of situation with you... ever!" On the other end of the phone, she cried and cried... and I hung up. It was right then that I realised that I wanted to board a plane to Bangkok that very night - I missed the gentility and calm of Noi, the sweetness of her face and the kindness of her eyes. The very next week I had bought a return ticket to Thailand.

Leicester 1986 - Wigston

Have you ever been lonely? And a bit, well, desperate? I had been in Leicester for a few months and had not really went out much. Finally I had decided I needed some, 'intimacy' with someone soon or else I was in fear of it falling off with lack of use - 'use it or lose it', as the saying goes. So, like some sad bastard, I somehow sign up for a 'lonely hearts club' - how sad is that... what the fuck is wrong with me?

I get there, park up, and wander in - fuck me, I'm too early and I am the first one there. So I'm sitting in an empty bar with an empty dance floor and empty tables all around me... oh, this is great! I wince, when about twenty minutes later, about twenty odd guys come waltzing in and take up position at the bar. Now I'm a creature who likes to study and watch from outside the circle, so I move to one of the tables at the back, with just enough shadow to be covertly obscured from the bar and the entrance into the lounge.

Some ladies wander in and the guys at the bar, who are all on their own and not talking to anyone, stand up like Meerkats as the women stroll over to a table. I laughed so loud that the Meerkats glanced at me with a look of derision and I scowled back at them with contempt. 'This is going to be fun', I say to myself. I know I have no intention of 'meeting' or 'hooking up' with anyone as I now know it is as sad as it looks... but perhaps I can get some twisted pleasure out of other people's predicaments, hehe.

I watch as ladies in their late 40's and 50's walk on by and the Meerkats do their thing while I sit watching. I am thinking back to the times when I was a 'warm-up' dancer, many years ago, in the same situation when no one would make a move to dance let alone talk to the other members of the opposite sex. I could feel the tension in the air and this circus of cruelty was about to start its performance. Now, we all masquerade our true selves to a certain degree and live vicariously as someone we admire or aspire to be like, even if it's on a subconscious level - we all do it! Fuck, I've been Captain Kirk, Gary Numan, Ed Straker (from Gerry Anderson's 'UFO'), Mr Spock, and even Gene Kelly - and I'm sure I had business cards for all my personalities at some point ha-ha. Fucking hell, I even know a guy who lives as Bowie ;-)

I sat back as guy after guy made complete twats of themselves. I was laughing under my breath and toying with the notion of leaving, when I noticed two ladies on the next two tables away, looking at me and smiling. I smiled back (I'm polite), and they smiled back once more. I said to myself 'I will go in about fifteen minutes, but just want to see if they are interested'. Both women were in their 30's and looked like they had seen bit of grass on their ass in their time, but I noticed they were also laughing at the Meerkats and whenever they got asked to dance they refused and laughed to themselves afterwards. I realised they were there for the same reason as me, to deride the situation and tease as many of these sad fuckers as they could - it was a game to them and they were enjoying it immensely. I mused, 'what cruel bitches', we all deserve something in life, even just a dance with a pretty lady- it wouldn't kill them to say 'yes' to someone.

Fucking hell! One of them gets up, looks over,

smiles at me, and starts to walk over to my table. I see her friend laughing behind her hand and I sense this is a piss take... and being Scottish, I am more than ready for the rebuttal that will surely come.

"Hello," she says, "how are you?"

"I'm great," I reply and stand up to shake her hand.

Then she says, "Oh, I'm sorry, I thought you were taller," looking back at her friend with a secretive glance.

She was not expecting the answer I gave to her.

"That's ok, I thought you were prettier!"

I sat back down and looked at her friend, who was by now open mouthed and did not know whether to laugh or be quiet. The woman standing in front of me was lost for words, looked a bit upset and walked away from my table - leaving me feeling very chuffed with myself. After giving the Meerkats a slight nod, I walked to the door and went home, laughing all the way to the car. Ha-fucking-ha, serves her right!

And from that night on, I have never been to another 'Zombie' meeting since - I'd rather have a wank, to be honest.

Now, where's that magazine?

CHAPTER NINE

ARE FRIENDS ELECTRIC?

Jonn Harton comes in from the freezing night air and has a plan - "Fuck those bastards, it's time for another musical adventure... and this time it's going to work!"

A few weeks before meeting up with Jonn, I am playing what I did not know to be my final gig as the synth player in my own creation - 'DanceVision', the band that should have toured with 'Hazel O'Connor' but didn't... the tour that 'Duran Duran' went on to do and the rest is history.

I'm sitting in my room, playing on my synth, feeling fucked up, and in a dark place, and thinking of ways to get back into the limelight and make some money... and get some fame. I had nearly accomplished that, but for the cock antics of my band colleagues who had just stolen it away from me. I was playing some Gary Numan tracks from his album 'Replicas', actually I was playing the track called 'Replicas' itself, on my synth and pissing off the whole street as the volume was cranked up to a head blasting two hundred watts. The track is very atmospheric and builds up after a few minutes using more and more keys to fill the sound out. The room was shaking and the windows were on the verge of exploding into a hail of shards onto the street below when my amp fizzed and died. "What the fuck now?" I screamed, "Oh, fucking hell, now I've got no amp!" I plug a set of headphones into the back of the synth and they sounded shit, but it had to do.

Jonn placed an advert for a synth player to compliment his other two choices so far - Jim McKenna on synth duties, and John Healey on skins and sticks. I do not recollect where or when I saw the advert, it may well have been on a poster in a music shop somewhere, but I made contact and had an audition with 'Zoneheim'. What the fuck was that name all about? Sounded sort of Germanic or political to me. I met up with them in Glasgow somewhere, I think it was 'Centre Court', a sort of cocktail bar for pretentious twats just like me! I think I turned up with jet black hair, makeup, eyeliner and black nail varnish - I looked the part at least. They were a bit more 'relaxed' in their dress sense and I was a bit disappointed that no-one had made the effort, in my own band I always thought that image was half the battle to success! 'If you have it flaunt it - If you don't have it, fake it'.

Jim was dressed like a poorly paid office worker and Healey was only slightly better, at least he had a passable haircut, but had a face like a cheap pizza... man, wash your fucking face now and then! Jonn Harton was more interestingly dressed and I could tell there was more to him than met the eye. So I ride along with the conversation of - we have a street buzz, it's all going to happen, blah, blah, blah ...and record companies are sniffing in our direction. I felt they were honest and seemed to rate themselves as above average in the Glasgow music scene, which was going through the jangly guitar phase - something which I thought was the wrong way to go.

My love of music was all things electronic and I had been studying such synth keyboard wizards as Duncan Mackay (Cockney Rebel), Tomita, The Motors, Kraftwerk, Jean Michelle Jarre (whose album Oxygene was just fucking brilliant - all those keyboards and synths he used to complete that project made me want to do the same sort of thing). Another really good album I loved was by Paul Brookes (the UK's answer to Jarre) - his album was called 'Steps From Beyond' and was every bit as good as anything else that was going around at that time.

Okay, so now I am in a rehearsal room with 'Zoneheim' (still none the wiser as to what it means), and again no-one's made an effort, looking like they have just fallen out of bed and I starting to think, "Oh, fuck!" Then I see a guitar and say to myself "Oh, no!!!" I was primarily interested in electronics only and thought about leaving when I saw the guitar. "This is going to be fucking rock drivel," I thought, "A fucking hippy on keyboards, a fresh faced pizza guy on drums, and a Bowie clone on vocals... and probably a Mick Ronson trip on guitars!" Then I remembered some great Bowie stuff with synths and a fucking great song by Ronson, 'Billy Porter', so I thought I would give it a go.

The songs were gritty and painted some sort of dystopian landscape to my eyes and ears. I was surprised... this was fucking okay. I had been given free reign on what sounds to use and left to improvise, so I felt better about it all. As the months went on, it was more and more enjoyable, filled with dirty and gritty sounds. The guitar was cleverly interspersed, sounded rhythmically minimal and sort of Rob Dean, early 'Japan', in some respects - all of which I enjoyed immensely. The drums were flat and harsh, more style than shit drums, and the synth guy, 'Jim', was obviously classically trained to some degree as his fingers were all over the scales... and I was thinking, "Fucking hell, Richard Clayderman lives in Glasgow!" I still thought he was a bit of a hippy, and thought it would only be a matter of time before he was playing fucking organ sounds on everything, like 'The Doors' or the 'Velvet Underground'. It took me a year or so to realise that Jim was a tremendously talented keyboard player, could transcend over to synths quite easily, and was by far one of the best blokes I have ever played with. I, on the other hand, thought of myself as more of an 'experimental' sound designer, creating soundscapes rather than lead lines and bass. I later managed to combine all three and had my own 'style', much like anyone who used synths - Wakeman, Rhodes, Sakamoto (eventually) ...and, no, I'm not delusional, you fuckers!

Rehearsals are, by definition, a nightmare - usually undertaken at the weekend and somewhere dingy and dark. Realistically, it's something that just has to be done and I enjoy that part of it as long as it's all going to plan. The only annoying fucking problem was most of them did not stir or wake till mid-afternoon. I used to think, "That's fucking shit, let's get it done ASAP, and then we can still have a life or most of the day to do something else," ...like fuck my girlfriend before the end of the night! It was always the same, get to Sauchiehall Street at 2pm, Healey and I always got there on time and he was as eager as me to get started! Jim would get there about 3pm-ish and looked mellowed out, whereas Harton and his 'Squeeze' would wake about 4pm - luckily it was a shared flat and the nice 'Teaching Student' was always awake to let us in.

I used to hate the waiting about. When they woke up, we would be in their room and they were still in bed, or on the bed, then we would sit and talk for hours and they would smoke hippy shit - "Oh, fuck's sake, can we fucking get going?" I'm a bit impatient, I guess, but like to get things done in an orderly fashion... and preferably when there's still some daylight remaining. I think we were the first, real, 'Goth' band... well, we had two fucking vampires in it, anyway - ha-ha!

I was actually eager to get out of the house, before my parents woke up and the daily ritual of hate would start. They would fight constantly over nothing, or money, or some other crap, or just have a go at their kids because they had no money and shitty lives. Why the fuck do people stay together when they obviously hate each other so much? It's something I would never understand, and still don't.

A few years before, my Dad was 'missing' and my Mum somehow found out he was living in 'Nottingham' - she went down there to get him and bring him back to Glasgow (why the fuck she did this, none of us will ever know). I remember he was back about a week when he started fighting with her over money for beer and she said, "No! Its rent money, you are not going to fuck up the rent!" He grabbed the chair she was sitting on and flipped it against the wall, breaking her nose in the process, then taking the rent money. He left and did not return for at least a week... my Mum still let him back in! I can only guess there's something retarded about them both that I will never figure out, but she is still my Mum... a view and feeling I never ascribe to my

Dad - him, I just see an evil cunt who uses and abuses all of us for his own demented, twisted pleasure, and as a way of life.

We were all used to seeing violence throughout most of our days in Glasgow. It was a violent city in the '70s, and was that way long before we were ever born, but there was something nasty about the violence - it was mindless, brutal, and was meted out with regularity at any time of the day. Perhaps we just thought it was 'normal', and that's why the things my Dad did were seen as an extension to slum life. Obviously, looking back on it all, it's so very wrong on so many levels and people would now be in jail for even the smallest of things they got away with back then. I am not making excuses for my parents, or even Glasgow, but I knew so many friends at school with the same bruises and black eyes that we had.

I was always jealous of Jonn and Jim as they seemed to have had a better upbringing than me or my siblings, but only jealous in the fact that their parents seemed nice and well-adjusted - unlike the sadistic cunts my Mum and Dad were back then. To this day, my Dad has never apologised or thought he had done anything wrong to us... what the fuck?

We had already played our first gig together in 'Night Moves' night club and it went down reasonably well, I thought, with lots of energy and lots to reflect on - but we felt a little bit restricted in what we were playing and the direction we had chosen, so decided on a name change and getting some vaginas in the band. Jonn's girlfriend, Lynnette, was the obvious choice as she was a decent singer and well known around the gig circuits in the West End and surrounding city (and she had already done some back-up vocals on the first Zoneheim demo tracks - 'Dream Detectives' & 'This Island, This City'). Jonn and Lynnette did a joint, lead-vocal role and we added two other female backing singers to allow some sophistication to the vocal arrangements of the material.

'New Love' was the first offering in our evolved format to radio land, and Billy Sloan (one of Radio Clyde's foremost DJ's) had played it regularly and was excited about it - I wonder if he knew it was actually about lesbian love? He He! Anyway, we were now called 'Viva' (long live, I guess), but this line-up was to be short-lived and perhaps a few tactical errors played some part in our downfall. Lynnette was a bit of a lazy singer and I know Mr. Harton would have a go at her for wasting time in the recording studio on occasion. Healey, the drummer, could not keep his cock in his trousers and was soon merrily bonking one of the backing singers to the point he became more interested in her than the band - so we got rid of him... and the two girl, backing vocalists, and things seemed to sort of chill after that.

Our new drummer, Derek, was at least reliable, if not a bit predictable - but at least we had a new drummer and we could get started once more on the important job in hand... to get a recording deal!

Reincarnated as 'Viva', we had some very good songs, all strong hooks, catchy synths, danceable bass lines, and good vocally, and as commercial as anything out there - it was only a matter of time before the big signing. I had always thought Jonn was bit of a control freak and obsessed about how everything needed to be done, but I just wanted to get signed.

Jonn had managed a few well-known Glasgow bands, worked with a stack of people who became internationally famous... and was prepared to walk away from anything he didn't feel was being done 'properly' - irrespective of success peeking over the horizon. He plugged the band and got interest from companies who had never heard of any of us, simply by being smart, astute, and having some idea of how the industry worked. There was a level of charisma and confidence around him that could be quite surprising at times... but there was also a problem which came with that - managing a band and being its front-man did not sit well with record companies. This was why we decided to look for a good manager.

There were a variety of candidates who were, not to be cruel, utter toss-pots and fucking clueless about the world around them, never mind the music industry - and some of these people were well-known figures in the business... DJs, promoters, and journalists. One of the first that wanted to plug the band to death and make 'Viva' into a household name was a significant figure from the '70s and early '80s... 'Mr. Superbad', of radio and television fame. He and his daughter had a promotion and management company, together they looked after some successful Glasgow acts and came courting the band. There was a general consensus about the man - he was great at doing his own thing, but seemed unable to count to twenty one without getting naked. Finally Mr. Superbad got down to the nitty-gritty of his proposed deal... and we all ended up in agony - laughing so hard, it hurt! The deal, essentially, meant he would own 50% of everything - recordings, publishing, concerts, merchandising, and absolutely anything else that came into the communal 'Viva' account. It was hard to believe he was upset when we politely declined, suggesting we'd get richer selling our spare kidneys!

The next candidate was less experienced, but more realistic... he was very impressed by the band and knew we could sell shiploads of units by signing the 'right' deal. This Manager (we'll call him 'Kenny' - although his real name was Kenny!) seemed fairly clued up, was prepared to capitalise on the interest we had generated on our own (and there were some significant, Record Company figures who were now watching what the band were doing, including the manager of 'The Police, and a variety of A&R headmen... not just desperates looking for the act that would make them figures of influence in their own, cut-throat, Gladiator arenas). Kenny was a journalist and wanted to make a real career in the 'Music Biz'! We voted and decided to take a chance on him - we never imagined for a moment what was going to happen with 'Kenny, the Manager' representing us. The first hint that he was less astute than he sounded was his idea for the next set of promo photos... suggesting it would be great to feature the band as 'already successful' and 'dodging all the Paparazzi photographers' - a brilliant and astute concept... if it was 1973 and not 1983! We went in another direction, something in tandem with the kind of acts we had a commonality with, such as Japan, Duran Duran, Gary Numan, Magazine, Visage, Ultravox, Heaven 17, Bowie, and our own sense of what made an impression.

We had just recorded a new demo in Edinburgh - three new tracks that secured some decent airplay on Scottish radio stations... and Kenny was sent to London to sew up a decent deal for the band - or so we expected! Were we going to be fucking disappointed? While Kenny was in London, hustling the new material around the companies who had been exhibiting interest in the band, a senior Record Company A&R man phoned Jonn and asked if he had been in an accident, or was abusing medication, or had just lost his fucking mind in the past week. "What the hell is this shit meant to mean," Jonn asked... never suspecting what was coming - "Your manager is down here trying to sell 'Viva' and some shitty rock band at the same time!" I remember hearing the volcano blast right across Glasgow. When we were told what had been going on, there were a number of 'Viva' members ready to go and fuck this twat manager into the next world. We settled for a meeting, bringing our 'Manager' into town and inconveniencing his own work routine as a matter of urgency that we needed to speak to him about. Kenny was confronted with his crime and wriggled about like a snake on a hot-plate, whining and justifying what he had done with a lot of shit that no-one except him cared about. He got the bullet in a professional, sensitive and concise manner... Jonn looked round everyone, turned to Kenny and smiled. "Everyone with anything to do with 'Viva' - sit back and relax," he said - someone looked at Kenny and asked, "What the fuck are you still doing here - ex-manager?" The prick left with his tail between his legs and his rock band never even dragged their arse from unknown hopefuls into total obscurity. Lesson learned, for us... but the damage was done - we had to start again to repair it all.

After firing a dickhead manager who was a parasitic cunt and had all his fingers in our pie, we still had had some small time interest... but it was always the same story - not enough, no way, shit contract, it's a rip-off! It seemed Jonnny boy was turning things down left, right, and centre... and I was getting pissed off, as was everyone else. He would always say, "The only thing worse than no deal, is a bad deal!" I later learned that being the control freak he evidently seemed to be was actually the best thing for us, as signing your rights away is the best way to get fucked for years in this business - look at Wham and George Michael, Frankie Goes To Hollywood, even the Beatles signing for a farthing per record in '62... So many bands were signed, famous, selling millions of records, had no money, and were locked in legal battles for years! So, I guess, he was right in the end.

We had done dozens of live performances with Record Company, A&R guys flying up from London to see us - but nothing worthwhile ever came of it... the offerings were just not good enough, our Illustrious leader would say!

Our next song was 'Let The Rain Come Down', and it was a funky, upbeat, synth-dance, classic and I can still happily listen to it to this very day. We had shot a 'promo video' for the track, something which would be laughable by today's standards, and anyone with a 'Smartphone' could make something better in about twenty minutes. Technology has come on in leaps and bounds over the last twenty to thirty years and we all have sophisticated, multi-function phones, computers, Ipads and tablets, 'Smart TV's, etc. I often question if we would have 'made it' quicker with such technology if it had been available back in the 80's, and I can honestly say, 'No, it would not'! Back then, it was down to raw talent, dedication in mastering your own instruments, and writing our own songs - the turgid, fucking manufactured crap that is about today is abysmal and I am confounded as to how easy it is to dupe the public with such contrived, crass, shit, impotent music (the kind of material that the 'Punk and 'New-Wave' revolution hoped to destroy). To some extent, I blame technology for letting loose the drivel that pervades the airwaves, television and Internet channels - there are a few fine examples that have not been manufactured into existence, and I would certainly listen to them and not any of the others.

When we were working in 'Viva', I was sick of these bastards that would claim, "Oh, you only need to press a button and it plays itself!" My tight, round arse, it does. If there was a magic button that I could press to make a hit song, I would have been pressing it every time - but there isn't, it's always down to hard work, good song-writing skills, and bucket loads of talent... ask any real musician and they will tell you the same thing. Rest assured, if there had ever been a magic button to press that made a hit record, I would have been pressing it until the fucking thing was worn out!

Records Companies are now as bad as Industrial Corporations, and look at profits before talent - in fact ninety per cent of the these multinational, music businesses do not care one iota about talent... signing a deal these days is akin to selling your soul to a devil who will own you, crush you, and unceremoniously dump you when they see fit (or the money stops rolling in from some manufactured act that has slithered out from another tedious, reality TV, 'talent' show).

Are Friends Electric?

It felt like going back to square one, even though it wasn't, but we were slogging away and going through material at a rate of knots - new songs, shifting style, and trying to get ahead all the time. Jonn was back to running things and becoming obsessed with writing things the Record Company would like, instead of following the natural direction we were all moving toward.

There was also one last attempt to secure good management - this guy had a strong track record, had secured contracts for bands that hardly sold any records, but scored incredible deals. Bit by bit, Jonn generated interest in the band and the notorious Glasgow manager came along to see us in action - with all of us hoping his contacts, facilities, cash and contacts would pull us out the nose-dive we suspected we were heading towards. The band performed well, tossed out the best material and watched the Manager and his sidekick look professionally distant. The pair said little to the band after the performance and asked Jonn to come and see them the next day at 'The Venue', on Sauchiehall Street, where his offices were. It wasn't what any of us expected. Jonn went to meet them and hear their opinion, reasonably confident they were interested... he was mistaken. The Manager said he didn't like the band, told him to get rid of Lynnette, dump the drummer who looked like he should be in some '70s pub-band... and might be as well sacking everyone - the only way he would become involved with 'Viva' was if it was a Jonn

Harton solo act and supported by a backing band. It was not the news any of us wanted to hear. Jonn was definitely a control freak, Bowie-clone, but unlike Bowie [who dumped the 'Spiders From Mars' when he had become famous enough not to need the people who had worked for years to build him into a massive figure], Jonn was a control freak, Bowie-clone who was loyal to the band he believed in... No matter how bad things were becoming for 'Viva'. Jonn told them both thanks for their interest, but if there was no band, there was no him - the end. From here on out he was back to performing, running and managing the band.

I was in the bowels of Jonn's parents' house, where there was a small rehearsal room in the basement - not much room and a very low ceiling, claustrophobic and noisy... I'm sure my hearing suffered as a result (deaf as a post now and wear digital aids now and then). The light would flash on and off, to indicate that there was a phone call, which was great as Jonn would leave and I could get to play my annoying riff for Jim and fuck about with other stuff, hehe.

I felt a bit weird one day, I was there by myself when Lynnette came down and was a bit teary eyed and I said, "Are you okay?", and she said "Yes, just having a bit of a falling out with him, (Jonn)". I said, "Take it easy, relationships are like prison sentences, sometimes!" to which she laughed and smiled, then walked over, kissed me on the lips and replied "You're a nice guy, thanks!" then went back upstairs.

Jonn and Jim would argue about anything they were both philosophically opposed to, on many things, and I enjoyed watching them tear strips out of each other - and the silence that followed. We would normally be eating a curry at this point, after rehearsing and trying to solve the world's problems... as well as our own. "Fuck you!" - "No, fuck you!" was the mantra of the evenings. Oh, joy!

Another six months on and the cracks were beginning to show - badly. I had no idea what was going on - we had lost direction and purpose, and I had a sneaking feeling that Lynnette was just not interested in any of it at all now, becoming more and more aloof as the weeks went by. For the second time in my life, I could see fame slipping away from me, I was never sure what was going on between Jonn and Lynnette, but they seemed like 'Burton and Taylor' - in love, but desperately trying to hide it, or use it like a weapon against each other to hurt and control, to disparage and rage against their lives. They were another couple who would ruin what I needed to succeed and bury it along with any chance of escape from my misery. I believe it was this mix of toxicity that was part of the reason we failed on some levels. I knew then that the end was coming soon and I needed a plan, I could not go back to living at home, I needed to break free even if it meant sleeping in the streets or skipping the country.

"I know the heat is so crazy, hotter than Marrakech" - we had just finished this song, 'Please, Be Strong', and had now drafted in a saxophonist! "For fuck's sake," I was thinking, "we're gonna be like 'Showaddywaddy' now! What the fuck's going on? Electro/synth and brass? Not going to work in my opinion, and at the very least we will sound like 'The Teardrop Explodes' - it's already been done!" He was a nice guy, actually, but I thought Jonn had lost the plot at this point. I think 'Burton and Taylor' were on sabbatical in a foreign land, leaving the rest of us to do the overdubs and mix the track together... and it turned into a right mess with bickering and fights in the studio, and me saying, "No, that's too fast, why are you changing the tempo? Oh, fuck this, stop it, look... I'm going home!" I know Jonn was livid when he heard the finished track - I still cringe when I hear it, that saxophone does not belong in the song! For the first time I wanted to walk away and felt even more isolated than I had ever felt in a long time.

I think Jonn was seeing it too, nothing could save what was left of the 'Viva' cadaver - Derek was becoming a cunt, I was bored with all the fights and Jim was being, well, Jim. I don't remember the night we all fell apart, but I was kinda glad as I now needed to connect with myself and the reasons I was trying to do this... which was to better my shit existence, so far. After all the hard work, good times and music we had created... the coffin was finally nailed shut!

There was one last indignity to be added to the sad

end of this project, after 'Viva' had broken up... Derek had organised some kind of deal with Andy Scott of 'The Sweet' - a cover of his track 'Invisible', to be released as a single and featuring him on lead vocals. Derek asked Jonn and myself to do the guitars and keyboards for this single and we both agreed to help him out. The recording took place at CaVa Studios in Glasgow and, ironically, was recorded on the same '24 Track' tape we had recorded 'Let The Rain Come Down' on. When the recording was complete, Derek oversaw the mix and we had nothing more to do with it, simply waiting for a copy of the single to arrive. It never happened - Derek explained something had happened to Andy Scott or his label and the entire thing was shelved.

Derek did not like Jonn and had a personal grudge against him and I am sure it was mutual (although Jonn claims he simply had no time for Derek as he was, in his words, 'like wallpaper - devoid of any personality'. When CaVa closed down, Derek bought the '24 Track' master and thus gained control of the last 'Viva' tracks - something Jonn was furious about... especially as he had finally secured a solo deal with a small, French label who were willing to put out and promote a Jonn Harton single, so long as the master was simply provided to them and no recording costs were involved to the company. Jonn had no choice but to ask Derek for the use of the tape, fully expecting there to be no problem (especially as he had recorded the 'Invisible' track for Derek, simply as a favour)... he was going to be disappointed. According to Jonn, when he phoned Derek, explained the situation, and pointed out that, legally, the '24 Track' tape should have been wiped of the 'Viva' recording before Derek was allowed to buy it from CaVa... but since it was still in existence, he wanted to borrow it to do some re-recording and see the track he had written, released as a single in Europe. Derek's answer? "What's in it for me?" Jonn indicated that "...being able to walk for the rest of your life would be one thing!" Derek refused to assist him in any way and finally got to demonstrate who he was and why no-one ever found any common, social ground with him. There was some legal action started by Jonn against both CaVa and Derek, but the moral of the story was 'possession is nine tenths of the law'. After demonstrating loyalty to the band, recording on Derek's own projected single and a couple of years working together, Jonn feels he was screwed over by the drummer's petty jealousy - no tape, no single, no European career.

Derek told me a story, years later, that he had bought the master tapes from the studio and burned them in his garden when he was threatened with legal action - thus, validating exactly what Jonn had claimed. If all this was true, then it was a nasty thing for Derek to carry out - a bit fascist and mercenary... so shame on you, Dek! What were you thinking, dude?

'Stayin alive.'

The song echoes in my brain and I wish for a return to the '70s where everything was a bit simpler - not less shit, just simpler... now, everything has gotten complicated. I wanted out of my parents clutches and needed a way out fast. I met Anna Maria somewhere, somehow, and ended up losing Diane in-between all the 'Viva' debacle. I wanted out and took the most dire direction I could take... and made the worst mistake in my life up to that point - I asked Anna Maria to marry me, only for the reason to get out of 'Dodge City' and buy a place of my (our) own.

She was sort of attractive and she thought she had a brain, but in fact she was as dull as Politics and had an even duller family to boot. What the fuck have I done? But, I'm free, have a job, and my own house at twenty one! I remember some cunt coming to the door once, selling something, and the guy at the door asked, "Is your Mum or Dad in?" I said, "It's my house!" He looked a bit shaken, ha-ha! Twat!

Anna Maria had a bit of a problem with alcohol and would come in drunk every time she went out, and she usually brought her alcoholic Mum and two sisters back with her - oh, fucking great! They would all fight and argue while I was trying to sleep upstairs - I think it was quieter in my Mum's house. I know now I have made a terrible mistake and I tell her, "Look, sorry, I'm about to leave. I don't want to be with you - I could not, would not, be with you at any price. You are the opposite of everything I need right now!" So, all in all, we lasted nine months and I had my first divorce before my twenty second birthday. If only I had married Diane, perhaps we would still be together and maybe everything would've worked out right - but that's a question I would never get to know the answer to, although I did get to meet Diane many years later and say exactly that to her and felt better for it. I had learned that regret is as poisonous as guilt, and I was not going to let it eat away at what was left of me.

Am I going crazy?

I am now in a very dark place and I fear for my sanity and my very life. I have never had these thoughts in my head before now - no 'God' to help me, no one to count on; no one to care or even talk to... this is 'absolution'. I did not know it, but I would spiral down into an abyss of hate and self-loathing.

The darkness is tangible and very very real, no voices in my head except my own

Telling me it's all over, what's the point, why live? why bother? Why? Why? Why?

My head is spinning, I am going down hard and fast - is this what insanity feels like?

I was sure I had crossed over into depression my fragile mind was spinning out of control and I was losing my grip on reality nothing is real I just can't feel anything

I feel like a living ghost and nothing I do helps.

I know this is affecting me deeply, I don't want a

mental illness not now not at this time in my life , please go away ! please let me be!

I eventually go to the doctors and he manages to get me to talk about my stresses and nearly prescribes me Valium .. what the fuck! happy pills? No thank you I'm not that crazy …yet!

Weirdly they work as I discovered years later after a bitching bad marriage I was in depressed mode once again and spiralling down that abyss ,and this time I took the damn pills , fuck me they do strange things to you,

Did they make me happy? , well no not really but what they did do was sort of stop me thinking about anything I was able to function at least on a certain level , they take the edge of intellect that's for sure and they suppress things in your brain , sort of turning you into a cabbage that can walk and work like a robot.

The pain goes away and the fear and the dread are numbed into submission , you don't care about what was hurting you and you really don't know why anymore , it just fades away,I find these drugs very scary , how the hell can they do what they do?

It took me months to get off them and get my sharpness back and for a time I felt alone and wanted to have them again to drift into that place where nothing mattered and nothing ever upset you,

I think if they gave all the world leaders and

maniacs in the world these pills , the world would be a very different place.

It reminded me of a song by Thomas Dolby, called 'May The Cube Be With You' it was about this happy pill in which you could lose yourself in a fantasy world, after all what is 'real'?

More and more people took 'The Cube" and less and less people went to work or fought any wars ……maybe …one day …eh?

I remember something from a film I watched as a child, 'The Day the Earth Stood Still', where 'Klaatu' states that the Earth cannot be allowed to develop and move it's violence out into the Galaxy, among peaceful worlds, and would have to be destroyed. When Professor Barnhart states, 'but your own civilisation must have reached a point where you nearly destroyed yourselves and you rose above it. Only on the precipice of self-destruction do you find another way, another way to live and evolve - we all deserve that chance!'

Tam 2.0

The more complex the mind, the more the need for the simplicity of play,

I'm in Los Angeles and have no real idea why, other than it's somewhere else to be, but I feel safe and I feel sane for the time being. For a while I thought I would be 'pushing up daises', but somehow I have managed to crawl out of the abyss and into something else - whether it's the right thing, I do not know yet, but for now I am okay. I am no longer plagued by delusional thoughts or trying to hide from my past, seem stable and looking forward. I don't know who I have to thank for that. The 'City of Angels' is a place where I learn to play and let go, to be a sensualist, and learn some new things about life and how to cope

I'm in a bar in downtown LA and there is a Korean lady on stage telling some jokes. I'm not really paying attention, but the crowd seem to laugh now and then. I learn her name is 'Sung Hee Park' and that's her stage name as she is actually called Suzanne Whang and she hosts a TV show called 'House Hunters' on American TV (CBS perhaps?). After she has finished her act, she is at the bar and I offer to buy her a drink.

She says, "Oh, nice accent, where are you from?"

"Scotland," I replied.

"Oh, cool! What are you doing all the way over here?"

"Sabbatical," I state, and she uncannily knows I am here on an escape mission.

She tells me, "You can't run from your issues, Tam, no-one can! I'm on TV and I still get racist mail, calling me a 'gook' (a derogatory term for Koreans or anyone from North/South East Asia).

I said, "Well, in Glasgow you get called gay for combing your hair."

To which she laughed.

She has an American accent and I feel stupid

asking her why she is both dressed as and sounds Korean on stage.

"It's how I cope with it all," she says, "I'm a TV personality, but I am well aware of the racism towards Asians in the US."

"Yeah," I said, "the worlds a fucking mess, as always, but you have to make of it what you can, I guess."

"Very good, Tam," she retorts, "There's some hope for you, then!"

She then makes her apologies and leaves to go back on stage for part two. She is dressed in a pink, Korean dress with a fan she holds to hide her mouth when she talks. Watching her makes me laugh, and I can see the undertones to her act now - she slowly pulls the fan down, looks shy and immediately pulls the fan back up to mask her face. This makes the audience laugh, she moves the fan down again and looks around for ten seconds before she starts her joke - she says in typical Korean, broken English "Two nigger walk into bar" and the crowd erupts into laughter and she once more hides her face with the fan. After the laughing dies down, she goes to her watering can shaped handbag and pulls out a piece of paper and goes over it silently before returning to the microphone with a look of relief on her face - she then starts again and says "Sorry, sorry! One nigger walk into a bar..." Ha-ha, brilliant! Her next joke makes me spit my drink out. She says in broken English, "Last night my boyfriend, he ate me out... and half hour later, he hungry again!" She is so infectiously funny and uses comic routine and jokes to take the racism out of racist - I highly recommend her.

I have not seen her for a many years, but she has had 'bit' parts in movies such as 'Constantine' and some Hospital show. Unfortunately the last few years have been a bitch for her as she had breast cancer and had a mastectomy - she, of course, uses this in her stand-up routine to great effect. She even had a rap song out called 'Fuck you, Cancer!' I miss her laugh and naughtiness. I've asked her to do the 'Edinburgh Fringe' many times, so I may get to see her again one day.

I take Suzanne's advice and look for fun in LA. She chaperones me for a few nights, takes me to some great parties, and I meet some very sexy ladies who love my accent. I am just enjoying this, I feel part of the human race again, and my natural shyness seems to be gone. I'm standing in 'Echo Park' and I think, "Fuck, I could be a star in LA." I have four weeks to write a hit and present it to Suzanne, who knows people in the business. Oh, things are looking up for Mr Scott.

I have a new friend, and it's because of her I go to Thailand - she is the first Asian I have ever really known and I foolishly make a move on her, but she is lovely and stops me, saying, "Oh, dear... you have 'Yellow Fever!" in her 'Sung Hee Park' voice, "You should go to Thailand or South Korea, Tam, you will find someone lovely there - they are not like the 'white ladies', they are different, here and here." (She points to her heart and her head.)

She has a boyfriend, Paul, who is a musician, and says I can use his gear to write something... and he wants no money from me for using it. He stays in Suzanne's nice, big house and has a little studio with some drum machines, synths, vocal mics and a 'Tascam 38' - '8 Track', Reel to Reel, 'Half Inch' tape recorder. Fucking, yes! I messed around with the synths and eventually write a song reminiscent of 'Forbidden Colours' by 'Sylvian and Sakamoto', or 'Easter Parade' by 'The Blue Nile'. Okay, it sounded a bit morbid and mournful... but luckily for me, that was in vogue. The track was called 'Eternity' - all done and polished in the mix. Suzanne and Paul thought it was great, and she said she would get it to some people she knew. True to her word, I get a call in the UK, six months later, to ask if they could use the music for a scene in a TV show. "What the fuck?" I said, "My tune in a TV show?"

"Yes," they said, "we just need the first twenty eight seconds and the last forty five seconds for two parts."

So, I said, "Yeah, sure!"

They gave me three thousand dollars ($3,000!), and although not a fortune, it was something! To be honest, I did not really care about the money - it was the fact that the track was sort of going to be on a TV show. What fucking show? Something called 'Wise Guy', a detective/gangster series which, to this day,

I have never seen and I'm unsure of what episode it was used for, except it was in a death scene ha-ha! Unfortunately, nothing more came of it... but that was okay, I was back and I was in the mood for writing something more.

Thank you, Suzanne! Love and Blissings always. I make a mental note to visit Thailand or South Korea very soon, never fully realising that once you go there, it stays in your blood for a very long time.

Glasgow 1977: Scars Bakery

My apprenticeship seems to be going well, and at least I am making money. My Mum had threatened to kick me out when I leave school. "Get a job or you're out the door!" Thanks, Mum! Today I am in the recipe room, where you stay all day and just make up the ingredients for Sponges, Cakes, Snowballs, and Biscuits etc. I notice some of the Bakers going into a side door next to me and, as far as I know, there's nothing in there - it's essentially a cupboard about the size of a lift. One at a time they go in and close the door, coming out minutes later with a big grin on their faces - what the fuck are they doing in there? It's always the same time, every day at 8am. So, one day when it's quiet, I go into the cupboard and see nothing but bags of flour and come out again - but, sure enough, someone goes in at 8am and comes out minutes later, smiling! What is it? What?

I go in again and have another look - this time I

see a crack of light. There is a locked door inside this cupboard, but the frame has a slight, one inch gap in it, and I put my eye on it... and, lo and behold, it all becomes clear to me! It's the 'Girls Changing Room' and, right about that time, there is a part-time girl called 'Izzy', about twenty two, and a medical student of some description... and she is getting changed on the other side of the door. Ahhh, so now I know why the Bakers shout out "Wan Eye" at 8am... it means to peek with one eye.

I brave it the next day and see her getting dressed - she is in her bra and pants, and she is fucking beautiful - I mean, simply stunning! The thing is, though, I feel guilty and bit pervy - despite it probably being fairly normal for a teenager to take a peek. I come out red faced and a bit ashamed, and think all the guys here are fucking pervy... but later on they tell me, "She knows we do it and she takes her time getting dressed!" Yes, nice to now know she is the 'Bakery Bike', but I think I will pass at having a ride on it (lol). No way do I want galloping dandruff in my nether regions - only in Glasgow, eh?

I found it all a bit 'Benny Hill', and the experience made me think that it's about time I looked into having a girlfriend, instead of having a relationship with my right hand.

CHAPTER TEN

TINSEL TOWN IN THE RAIN

Glasgow 1986

The dark skies and hard rain seems endless, it's 6am on a Saturday morning and I am on my way into town for some breakfast, something I do now and then to reconnect with myself and watch the world come alive all around me.

It's always fascinated me, how a city as big as this one is seemingly all quiet and minimal - no rush, no panic, no people, no cars... nothing's going on. I imagine all these horizontal, unconscious bodies in every house, in every apartment, in every street - lying there with no cares and no worries, dreaming of something that makes them happy... dreaming they do not have to work as a debt slave. But all this exists in the mind and not outside of the mind, for if it existed outside, then we would not be aware of it.

As I walk down towards Union Street, I glance up at the everlasting icon - the neonesque 'Irn Bru' sign on top of Central Station. It's always been there, and for me, at least, it makes me smile, like an old friend I pass from time to time and just nod an acknowledgement to as I stroll on by.

I chose my seat near the window as I order breakfast. I watch closely and savour the awakenings as every ticking minute brings the city closer to its new life - buses start to slowly drift in from the outlying, 'desert', housing schemes, bringing their human cargo to the hungry streets. People are drifting in from near and far now, the daylight is just starting to illuminate and cast shadows from tall buildings, banishing the dark from every corner and filling every crevice with light - bringing the hope of a better day. A better day for me?

An hour has passed and my coffee refill keeps me from attracting too much attention from the cafe staff as I watch in wonder at the streets filling up with workers, like ants scurrying around for their Queen. Drones for banks, drones for the railway, drones for the initiates... we, the profane zombies of the elitist ruling class - we who know our place. Watching the city wake makes me feel reborn.

I see the city burst into life, there are now hundreds

of drones and clones rushing around, pushing their way past other, faceless, zombies, who neither care, nor want to care. Their mission for today is only to survive another day - is that too much to ask? Most people walk with their heads down and avert their gaze from each other's eyes. No-one wants to admit that they would rather never have to speak to anyone, and if, by chance, someone bumps into you or you them, a curt apology is all that's offered for that brief connection between strangers, a collision of thoughts reflecting a moment when both say 'sorry' to each other, never meaning it.

I will never understand my life, or anyone else's life for that matter. What determines us after birth to become who we are also is a mystery to me. I have no idea why I am alive and why I am here... or why anyone is here - someone must know and they are not telling anyone else. I don't quite see the point to life. I'm not suicidal, I just ask questions and I ask others what they think life is? No-one I ask knows either, and no-one can justify their existence. Are we an accident? A virus in a 'Petri Dish' on someone's desk? I have no fucking idea, but I certainly understand the concept of death... and want to live - but then, paradoxically, I do not know why. But for the moment, music is all I have, music is the best of me.

I get a call from a Hypnotherapist and she introduces herself and then asks me if I can score an album for her. I asked, "What kind of music?" She says, "Oh, like the other one you did a year ago - 'Nirvana Symphony part 1'!" I reply, "Ah, okay. I guess someone put you onto me?" Then she acknowledges the fact, "Yes, someone gave me the album and I must admit I have been using it with my clients... and it has been played constantly in my sessions for over a year now. It got me thinking that I would love to make a 'Hypno CD' with your music and my voice - what do you think?" "Sounds fucking great and sounds like money to me," I say to myself. I go to visit her at her 'clinic' and she seems very nice and not unappealing to the eye either - an early forties, blonde with a good figure, a nice arse and heavy on top. I'm guessing the little general is thinking something naughty right now - he knows no shame.

I listen to what she has to say and agree on a price of two thousand pounds (£2000) to write the album and record it in the studio with her. I also pitch in to design the cover for six hundred pounds (£600). She indicates she only wants four hundred copies to give away to her clients after each session, and I think this is a great way to get my new style out there! Moneys a strange beast and a means of influence - as soon as she pays upfront, she thinks she owns me and is coming round to hear me create this music for her. For fuck's sake, I can't work like that. The hypnotherapist was in my little studio room telling me, "No, no, no - that sounds too harsh... quiet here, and more uplifting there." I was starting to think that perhaps this would not be the easiest money I had ever made. Every fucking night she was round at my house for three, fucking, bitching hours. My wife of that time (No.2 - Maria) thought she was a stuck up freak and I was inclined to agree with her.

On one occasion I was playing something back for her and she was an inch from my shoulder, looking at my fingering (now, now... not that kind of fingering!). I stopped and said, "Right, fuck it! Either you let me write on my own or you can have your money back and leave right now!" She just about spat at me and finally shouted "Okay... but you'd better do it right!" I responded harshly, telling her to "Get fucked - I know how to write music, you blonde tart." I don't know how it happened or why, but she grabbed me and kissed me very deeply, shoving her tongue halfway down my throat. I pushed her off, saying, "Fucking hell, my wife's downstairs - what the fuck are you doing?" Apparently, as she told me weeks later, being chastised makes her horny... so, no more shouting at her, I guess. Man, I meet some strange people in this life.

My wife at that time was Maria, a cross breed between an English rose and an Italian bitch. Now I have no idea what I actually really saw in her, but when she was nice, she was nice - but if she did not get her own way, she would be throwing dishes at me and cussing at me in Italian, "Manna chana marina aff, fan go!" (Well, that's what it sounded like, and I still have no idea what it meant.) I am pretty sure she was not saying, "I love you, handsome man! Can you help me put the dishes away?"

Despite her moodiness, she was quite nice - fun, and sexy to be with. She was no stranger to things in the bedroom and was very forward and demanding when it came to sexual gratification, and I have some intense, sexy moments with her as she was quite the tease and nothing seemed to shock her much. I remember she wanted to be tied up, and had a fantasy about being used by 'other men' - a harmless, but evocative, piece of 'role-play' came into my mind for her birthday, one year. I tied her hands and feet together, blindfolded her, put her on the bed in the 'all fours' position (on her hands and knees - yes, arse up), I tickled her with a feather, probed her with a cucumber (just a little), and then tied her down in the same position to the bed. Then I told her, "Okay, I'm going to call someone, and he will come round and 'do things to you'!" Maria said, "No, no, no, no... Okay, yes!" Ha-ha, the kinky bitch.

What she did not know was that it was a fake telephone call and I was the 'other guy'. So, I went out the bedroom and made noises as if to let someone in, claiming loudly, "Just go upstairs and help yourself - she's ready for you!" Obviously, it was me who went up as no-one else was present in the house. In the midst of all this, I thought to myself, "This is quite a titillating game that other couples should play now and then!"

I got back upstairs where she was now trembling in an excited way and, being blindfolded, she had absolutely no idea that it was me - clearly thinking it was someone else in the room with her... someone who was as naughty as us and wanted to 'play'. I had put leather gloves on and different shoes so my footsteps sounded different - my wife had absolutely no idea that it was me with her in the bedroom. After a long pause, I touched her raised arse with my leather clad hand and she let out a soft moan of pleasure, wiggled slightly as I caressed her back, and was panting rather hard now. I cupped her firm breasts and squeezed the nipples till they became long and hard, then I went behind her and very slowly pulled her white briefs halfway down to expose her buttocks. She was still trembling and I imagined how she must have felt - helpless and blind -undoubtedly feeling very vulnerable right now. But it was apparent that part of her wanted this. Most people never live out their fantasies and most people also never realise that fantasy is closer to reality than they think... they just never know it.

I pulled her pants down a little more, caressing her smooth skin with my rough gloves until she lets out a really long moan. Her breathing is now deepening even more... so, I up the pleasure and pull her cheeks slightly apart as I let my finger glide up her, now very wet, slit to hear her having a mini orgasm. Maria was trying to suppress the noise that she was making - low, guttural sounds, very animalistic and very much, not her. She seemed to be enjoying the predicament she was in, tied up and not being able to see who was stroking her and making her feel waves of unadulterated, exquisite, shivers of delight spreading throughout her body. I noticed she was glowing with perspiration and was very flushed around her neck. I wondered if she had thought about where I was... perhaps she thought I was downstairs while the stranger was interfering with her, or perhaps she thought I was in the bedroom as well, watching my wife being cuckolded by another guy.

I then found myself feeling very randy indeed. I am not sure if it was the thought of her believing she was being pleasured by someone else, or if I had just become so sexed up with the masquerade that I had forgotten I was pretending to be someone else - perhaps that's what made me so fucking horny and hard? I went behind her and then rammed it into her, hard and deep, hearing her moaning like some sex-crazed, porn star, as my orgasm exploded into the bag (the rubber... not her).

I pulled the blindfold off her and she looked shocked, not wanting to turn round - but when she did ...bastard!!! "Ha-ha, you fucking bastard!" she screamed at me, "that was fucking brilliant!" , There was no other cock needed, but just imagination and a fantasy to fulfil is all that's required! Right then, I suddenly considered the idea of writing erotic stories - so watch this space, as they say!

Maria had a young son from a previous marriage and usually I do not get involved with women who are just recently divorced and have kids in tow - which usually means they have an ex-partner in tow as well... and, by fuck, was he a pain in the arse.

This guy was a serious, fucking twat, and probably had the very term 'twat' named after him. He was constantly on the phone to her or knocking on the fucking door. At first he did not know I was seeing her, and I was getting pissed at the cunt being at the door all the time - so, one morning when he came round and was talking to Maria at the door, I made sure I walked down the stairs in my robe (bathrobe, you thick cunts - I'm not royalty). Anyway, he must have seen me, and the next thing I know is he's thrown the maintenance money at her and sped off like a spoilt, jealous, ex-lover in his BMW. Maria was fucking livid with me, shouting and screaming, "Why did I not stay upstairs and out of sight?" Ha-ha, naughty Tam ...and serves him fucking right.

Unfortunately for him, he came round one day when Maria was out and I was there. He knocked on the door, stared at me and sneered before asking, "Is Maria in?" I told him, "No," and went to shut the door, but he put his foot in to stop it from closing. I'm now thinking he has something he wants to say to me, so I open it again and look at him. After a long pause of about six seconds, he starts ranting, "He's my son, you are not his Dad, I fucking am - so don't get any fucking ideas of taking him away from me!" I said, "Whoa, you thick, fucking cunt. I'm not interested in your kid - I'm only interested in her... is that okay?" This tool made a grab for me and that's when I gave him a hard, five knuckle introduction to my fist. The 'Ex' fell backwards, then came at me again just as Maria's car pulled up onto the drive, whereupon she jumps out and proceeds to verbally abuse him. Fucking magic, as I was not in the mood for removing all his teeth and putting them in a bag for him to take home.

He finally got the message and would phone rather than just show up - and, in the end, we became really great friends! Fuck that! I'm kidding... but I'll bet I had you fooled for a minute there hehe! Maria and I were like chalk and cheese, and never the twain shall meet. I was always upstairs, writing music or chatting on the Internet - yeah, baby, a fucking 'BT' modem with a ping rate of a thousand milliseconds... fucking dire now, but back then it was brilliant. I can remember downloading a six megabyte game, and it took from 11pm till 8am the next morning. Sometimes you would get up and the fucker had just frozen halfway through the download, forcing a reboot and trying again later that night.

Anyway, whilst I was otherwise engaged, Maria would be watching some brain dead stuff like 'Coronation Street', 'Eastenders', or some other shit aimed at GCSE level minds. I was upstairs making music and dabbling in MP3 technology back in 1996 and was writing music on my 'Atari ST 520 Computer' with some 8/16 track midi sequencer called 'Cubase' on floppy disc that was just fucking brilliant! I recorded the 'Audio Out' onto an outboard

'DAT' recorder I had bought from 'Richer Sounds' in Nottingham a few weeks earlier, and then transferred it into the sound card of my '486' PC, saving it as a 'Wav' file and then converting it to an MP3 (not quite the full quality DAT at 44.1khz). This could take up to a week to get right, but the results were definitely worth it. I would eventually get some software for the PC to do the same sequencing and retire my much loved 'Atari' to the loft (I still have them to this day, along with the original monitor and mouse - those were the days and I felt like a pioneer, learning all this stuff and making music in a totally different way).

All this was lost on Maria, and she was not even interested in my musical past or what I was trying to do now. At this point I found 'BBS' Bulletin Boards and would join many online chats on differing subjects taking place in virtual rooms, whiling my time away into the small hours while she was snoring in the next room like a fucking Gorilla with a breathing problem. What the fuck did I marry into? Occasionally sexy - yes, but nothing else was going on with her.

I am undoubtedly being a bit harsh on her, but most of the people I have been romantic with have never had much going on in their heads apart from babies, shoes, and new kitchens. I guess it's not really anyone's fault that they don't bother with anything but the simple basics in life and having no need to learn anything else. This a great example of society being programmed to think we are less than what we actually are.

Being Boiled

The Hypnotherapist would call me several times a week to see how I was progressing with 'her' album of music and when she could get into a proper studio to record her voice onto it, (impatient bitch right?). Anyhow, I spent three months writing it and finally had it completed for her to come and have a first listen to it... and, guess what? Yeah - she fucking loved it and I was very proud of it too. She brought a bottle of Champagne to celebrate and Maria went out. I showed her some album cover designs and she started cooing, "Oh, Tam, these are bloody great - you are so talented!" (Yeah, I know.)

I put all the album artwork on the floor, as there was masses of it, and she is down on her knees looking at it all. I noticed she undid a button on her blouse and, from the chair I was sitting on, I could see her braless tits swinging as she leaned over, examining the artwork. Sensing she was trying to seduce me, I said, "Errr, umm, Maria will be back soon." To which, she just snorted. Maria and she had not liked each other from the very first time she had come around. Why are women so fucked up and intimidated by another pretty woman? It fucking pisses me off - I can't even work with one without getting the, "You'd better not be fucking her!" look every five minutes - something I would not do as I am certainly no cheater. (Not like Maria, as I was to find out later. Fuck me, I can pick them.) Okay, so you can look at the menu without ordering anything from it ...and that's as far as I ever went whenever I was in a relationship.

So, I'm at work one day and Maria calls me. I ask, "What's up?" as she never calls me at work. Nervously, she says, "Are you sitting down?" I told her "No, just tell me whatever it is." Then she says, "Erm, I'm pregnant... and it's not yours!" Fuck me, that was like a bullet going through my head. I slumped down and asked "Why? And who?" She would not tell me, so that confirmed it was someone that I knew. I hung up and felt like crap - okay, I can deal with someone telling me they are bored with me or I don't love you anymore and don't want to be with you... but to have that sort of betrayal thrust onto me, in my opinion, is nothing fucking short of emotional abuse. I finish work and drive home, thinking about what sort of mess a chainsaw makes and how long it would take to dig up the patio. I get back and I'm rather calm and collected, as I knew I would be. I ask her how long she has been fucking around and she says about a year! Oh, fucking great! Fucking well done, Tam, for not seeing that anything was going on behind my back.

She told me that the guy who 'knocked her up' did not want anything to do with her. She's already had a month or so to think about it and knows she did wrong, but now wants to know if I can find it in my heart to love her and still want her? Fucking hell, she's got a fucking cheek - right? I said, "No, sorry... it's over! I can deal with you telling me you don't want me, but not this. This is the fucking wrong way to do it and you do not deserve anything from me or even any decency regarding the whole situation." My head's a bit fucked up and I tell her I'm going away for a few days to clear my head. I decide to go to Sweden - I have always liked Stockholm and have not been back there for many years. I had a great time and had my head completely sorted out when I came back... but, as I turned the corner in my car, I instinctively knew something was wrong - I just felt it. Well, the fucking bitch had emptied the entire house and left me with nothing but a broken vacuum cleaner and a fork.

There was a quiet knock on the door and I answered to find my neighbour, a nice lady next door, whose name escapes me. She said "Sorry, Maria left a few days ago - about ten people turned up with two vans and had the place emptied in about two hours." "Fucking brilliant," I responded. The neighbour told me, "I did not want to get involved, but whenever you weren't home, a guy would come round in a van and stay there for hours." "Oh, this is just getting better and better," I said to myself, "the whole fucking street knows my 'wife' has been screwing other guys," (although it turned out to be a couple). As I already stated, I have no problem with people getting bored with each other and then splitting up, but I have zero respect for calculated cheaters! I find out she has rented property somewhere, and go round to see her. Maria seems mildly surprised to see me and says, "I don't want to talk about it!" I told her, "Neither do I, but I would like some of my furniture back or compensation for it. She actually laughed and slammed the door in my face, shouting, "Fuck off, before I call my brothers to kick the shit out of you!"

Well, you might think you know someone... but it just goes to show that, no matter how long, how intimate, and how loving you have been with someone (and having it returned), there is no way of knowing if they are going to fuck you over. What are the reasons? For the sake of another cock? A guy with a better house? A better car? Or just more interesting than me? I always knew that marriage vows were a bit too ambigious and, essentially, a load of bollocks - especially in this day and age where people are more selfish than ever. I mean, what an insanely, idiotic thing to say, state, and believe... 'Till death do you part'! Especially bearing in mind this is my second marriage... and the exact same vows applied back then too, - sigh.

Nothing is forever, not even love. It may be for some people, but I have yet to meet them, and I suspect I never will. Marriage is nothing more than exactly what it realistically is - a piece of paper with contractual obligations and an expensive 'get out' clause!

I ran off four hundred copies of the Hypnotherapy CD, printed the artwork and called the blonde to say they were ready. We had already dubbed the vocal on it that she had wanted. It would be two CDs she would be selling or giving to the clients at her surgery

- one was all music, and the other was her Hypno, meditational journey, spoken softly and interspersed with my mood music. It sounded fucking great, actually, and it turned out better than I had expected.

She was actually a natural in the studio and did the voice-over in one take with no mistakes! Something of a feat in itself, I can tell you.

There was now cash in the bank and CDs of my material that would be out there, with a possibility of another one being added in the next few months. Things were looking good for me now and I was getting back on my feet - the marital home was sold, all my debts had been sorted and paid for, and I bought a brand new, 'BMW Series 3' car. At the time I was renting some place to live as I had no intentions of getting involved with anyone and having a mortgage at the same time. I could hear 'Scotty' from 'Star Trek' (The Original Series) from the episode, 'Fridays Child' echo in my brain - "Fool me once, shame on you. Fool me twice, shame on me"

I get a phone call a couple of weeks later, and it's from one of my friends in Glasgow - he says, "Errr, your CDs are for sale in some supplement magazine in the 'News of the World'!" Shocked, I asked, "What the fuck are you talking about?" And it was right enough. I went out and bought the 'NOTW', went through the supplements and, fuck me, there it was! CDs - 'Nirvana Symphony part 2' (The Music), and 'Health and Happiness' (Voice and Music)... but with her name on them, not mine. I wondered what the fuck was going on?

Promptly, I called her and demanded an explanation.

She told me, "Oh, Tam, I was going to call you! (Yeah, right) The CDs were all gone in the first week and I had some more copied."

I said, "You, fucking, what?"

She claimed, "I was going to tell you, but things have been so hectic. Let's meet up and we can discuss some money, okay?"

I asked, "How many have you sold from the new copies?"

"Oh, about five hundred, so far," she told me.

I indicated, "That's not what I had written it for... so you could make money out of me and my talent!"

Then she interjected, "Well... my talent too, Tam!"

"On one of the CDs," I said, "but not on both! You retarded, leeching bitch!"

She said, "Okay, for every one I sell at seven pounds (£7), I will give you fifty pence - seeing as I am covering all the costs of printing and copying."

Now, I know that side of things can be pricey, so I conceded to her offer, but added...

"Okay - but if you sell much more, I want to renegotiate that price and I want it in writing!"

Surprisingly enough, after a few weeks, I actually get a signed letter stating just that, and a nice little cheque for another grand. She suggested that we call it a 'business arrangement' and 'an advance for the next album'.

I went along with it, after all, she was doing all the running about and all I had to do was cash the cheques when they came. Up to that point I'd had four cheques (£700-£600-£970-£1160) arriving every quarter as promised (totalling around three thousand pounds). At the time, I was happy, but aware that it probably wouldn't last long and could dry up at any moment.

Sure enough, nine months later and there were no more cheques. I called her up and she confirmed that there were no more sales and all was quiet - she didn't have any more money to advertise etc. So, the bubble had burst, I guessed, but she informed me she would call me in six months or so to start work on another CD for her 'Meditational Journey Series'. I told her to keep in touch, and that was where we left it.

Now, I hate dishonesty in any shape or form... and it must be something instilled into me, given where I was brought up and how I lived from day to day - struggling to survive with minimal resources. I have absolutely no time for cheats, liars and sycophants.

Some time later, I was watching TV and seeing that a fairly new phenomena has started in Britain - TV shopping! I watched all sorts of shit being sold and thought to myself, "What a clever idea," when the next thing to be sold is... guess fucking what? Yes 'Nirvana Symphony part 2' and 'Health &

Happiness' as a package for eighteen pounds (£18) - not available in shops and selling like fucking proverbial hot cakes. "The fucking bitch!" I hear myself shouting, knowing I have been screwed over by a very savvy businesswoman who must know others in the business art of selling etc.

I call her up and she does not answer. I wonder why not? So, then I call the company who manage the Shopping Channel and they tell me the CD bundle has been flying off their shelves for months - selling about ten thousand (10,000) copies so far. I just about fall down at the mention of this and feel a bit sick... then try to add up all those fifty pences, but I am too mad to concentrate on my maths. Immediately, I get in my car and drive to her fucking house with a great fucking speech ready for the lying, scheming, bitch... maybe she hypnotised me - who fucking knows? Maybe I was going soft after all those years, but I knew one thing - she was not getting away with this!

I am driving there as fast as I can and my phone rings in the car (on a cheap Nokia - you remember the one?). A colleague of mine is calling me from Edinburgh and she says, "Hey, your CDs are on the shelves in 'HMV' stores!" I said, "Fucking what? How the fuck did that happen? What the fuck is going on?" It transpires that the sharp businesswoman had struck a deal with the local HMV shop manager to sell them from his shop for a fee, connecting it with the TV Shopping Channel - all of this behind my back... and I had, stupidly, not copyrighted my music as I thought it was only for a giveaway thing at her surgery. I guess greed has now gotten the better of her and the money is piling up - it's by no means a chart topper, but with her business connections, the TV Shopping Channel and now this HMV deal... she is raking it in.

I get to the witch's house and she will not answer the door or answer the phone. I am outside and shout, "What the fuck are you doing with my music? Why am I not getting any more royalties?"

Eventually she opens her window and says she has the right to sell her own work.

Then I tell her, "No, you fucking don't - the rights always remain with the artist, no matter what!"

She replies, "If that's true, then you need to take legal action against me - right?"

"Too fucking right," I shout back, "You are screwing me and making money out of my talent!"

She screams, "I paid for the albums."

"No," I tell her, "you paid me to write it, that's all - I still own them, you fascist bitch!"

I realise that this insane situation has brought out the devil in me and I am losing my usual tranquillity that I pride myself on... something I learned many years ago in Thailand - how to remain composed at all times, how to meditate and deal with these kinds of things on another level. The monks who taught me this is the city of 'Lopburi' would be so ashamed and shaking their heads at me in unified horror.

At some point, I decide that retreat is the better part of valour and I say calmly to her, "Expect a legal letter in the next few days."

And she calmly says, "That's fine."

My only option in those days was to go to the 'Citizens Advice Bureau' and hope that there was some sort of free legal action I could take against her, as she knew all too well that taking her to court to let the legal system wrangle it all out would take time and lots of money. In the end, she sent me a cheque for eighteen thousand pounds (£18,000), I guessed out of guilt, but more than likely to distract me. To this day I have no idea how many she sold or where she sold them - was it just in the UK or was it globally? Deep inside, I did not want to think of that.

Bangkok 1997

I am back in my favourite place and have just returned from meeting Noi, after enjoying a meal with her and to let her know that I had missed Thailand and her company. She seemed genuinely pleased to see me and was so affectionate that it nearly made me want to stay in Bangkok again, but I knew she would not let me stay with her, and her fear of me turning into a 'Farang', hedonistic, slut-pig, guy that all Thai women despise.

I took myself off to 'Pattaya' and then from there to the Island of 'Ko Samui', which has some of the most unspoilt beaches I have ever seen... and some of the most spoilt American women I have ever met - 'Socialites', I guessed, with too much money and probably been shot right out of a vagina, already with a silver spoon welded in their ugly mouths. Most of them were bordering on extra, extra, extra, large size and reminded me of Walruses basking in the sun, hehe. As I sat there watching this spectacle of flesh cooking in the midday heat, I saw one who was rather pretty and seemed to be only slightly obnoxious (unlike the other ones she was with). So, feeling kind of brazen, I saunter up to her at the beach bar and say, "Beautiful day, right?" and she says, "Not interested!" I come back with, "Whoa, why the attitude on such a lovely day? I'm not looking to score, I'm just interacting with you, as you seemed nice - perhaps I was wrong." I had offered my apologies and turned to leave when she said, "It's okay - I'm sorry," in that annoying, American accent that you hear too much of these days.

I give her a summary of my life so far and she stops me, making me think, "Fuck, I've bummed her out!" She says, "Wait a minute, do you have the music with you?" Nodding, to confirm it, "Yes, I do, why?" (I had brought a few copies with me for Noi and some Monks.) I assume she wants to either listen to it or buy it from me, but she says, "Can I listen to it and give it back to you tomorrow?" I made sure I gave her one with just music on it (yeah, fool me once). The next day she comes up to me at the Beach Bar and says, "Okay, this is weird, but it's actually good!" I retort,

"Why weird?" expecting her to slate something off it and then tell me how to 'fix' it. But she says, "I work for a magazine... well, I sort of work for a subsidiary of the magazine, but it's a health magazine and we are looking at alternative treatments this month and want a CD of mood music/new age stuff just like this. Is it ok if I send this to the editor?" I said to myself, "Well, fuck me!" Here is something about music that transcends most other things, and it never ceases to amaze me that something can still come out of something that you thought was gone past its appeal date.

Three months later I am in Leicester and the magazine is out - it is called 'Top Santé' (I'd never heard of it till then) and there is a CD of music fixed to the front cover. They weren't all my tracks, but a good few were there and along comes a nice little cheque that will help me put a deposit down on a nice, new, selection of music gear - Synthesisers, a 'Hard Disk' recorder, and few other bits and bobs that I've had my eye on for a while. I wonder, what are the chances of meeting someone in Thailand who was looking for exactly that?

I thought back to my band days and wondered how everyone was getting on now, and hoped that their paths had been as fruitful as mine appeared to be. What was next? What else was waiting for me, just around the corner? It was at this time that I decided to manage a band and look at making fifteen to twenty per cent from getting them a recording deal...

and me retiring to live a life of 'Sun, Sea, and Sex' in Thailand.

The dark skies and hard rain seems endless, it's 6am on a Saturday morning and I am on my way into town for some breakfast, something I do now and then to reconnect with myself and watch the world come alive all around me, live,die, repeat.

Glasgow 1982: Why it's not a good idea to beat up on your wife in Scotland.

One of my friends in Glasgow had married this guy - a right, ugly fucker with a face like a welder's work-bench. He stood about 6'3", and she was about 4'11" - they looked ridiculous, walking hand in hand together, and I always thought he looked like he was swinging a monkey around. The man was an arsehole and we all knew it, but my brothers and I never said anything as we did not want to upset her because she was, well, in love with Quasimodo - think of 'Max Wall' and 'Marty Feldman' with the skin of a pineapple and there you have it. Now, this cunt was knocking our friend around and she would have black eyes and bruises every other weekend. We bit our lips as she was not one for explaining what was going on, but we knew from someone else just exactly what was going on... and one night we decided to do something about it.

This fucking animal had kicked her in the stomach while she was pregnant and that was the last straw for us. We followed him to his favourite watering hole and marched the big fuck out and into my older brother's waiting car. This guy was shouting and throwing his arms about, but my younger brother belted him in the chops and that seemed to shut him up.

We drove through 'Lennox Town', the place of my birth where I was brought into the world at 4:15am on a Thursday morning in 'Lennox Castle' - a place where Lulu (yes, that one) had been born at some point in time too. It was always a good conversational piece when I play 'Raconteur' at parties - not quite the 'Last King of Scotland', Tam, but not bad to be born in a real Castle and not many people can say that.

We drive up to 'The Campsie Fells', a rather impressive set of hills and small mountain range just beyond the village, a place where you can get seriously lost on foot and is the back road for getting to Stirling and Edinburgh. We drive this, wife beating, cunt up to the hills and I fear the worst as my brother's deal with things in a rather ugly, old fashioned way. I am thinking, "They are going to kick the crap out of him and throw him off a cliff to his death - minus his bollocks!"

Surprisingly, my brothers had a more entertaining and novel way of dealing with this piece of shit. Once we were up in the hills and mountains, we dragged the ugly fuck out the car. At this point he was shitting himself as he knew my brothers were no softies and were well known for not taking crap from anyone, anymore - they were hard as fucking nails at this time in their lives... something I had missed altogether in my youth. I think my brain was wired differently and still is!

They dragged him to a remote part of the hill and tied him to a lamp post. "Fucking brilliant," I said. They tied his hands and waist to the post, then pulled his trousers down, and finally his underwear, ha-ha. This is so much better than just kicking his face south of his head!

My older brother then pipes up, "Hit her again, and next time you get a real kicking and left up here overnight - do you fucking understand, you sad, ugly, bastard?"

"Yeah!" he says, "I'm sorry about it!"

"We don't want to hear it, alright?" my younger brother says, "Right, you cunt - we're going to leave you here for an hour or so, you can think about what you did... alright? We'll call the cops - and you'd better tell them it's a 'prank' or we will break your fucking legs!"

So, exactly an hour later, we make a call to the police to say we have driven by a guy tied to a lamp post up in the Campsie Fells... and to this day, our friend has never needed our help again.

Of course, my brothers thought this was a great business model and seriously thought about offering it as a paid service until I pointed out that it was highly illegal... but probably very profitable in and around Glasgow!

CHAPTER ELEVEN

I DREAM TO SLEEP

Fucking great! Here I am on an iconic pop TV show standing in for the sick synth

Player and loving every minute of it - okay, the singer was a cunt (that word again), his ego was bigger than a nuclear detonation and would be his downfall one day... and everyone knew it! I've no idea why the singers (the ones who don't play instruments) think they are the band. You must know the ones I mean - the ones who think that no one else is in the band and we are all just fucking session musicians. This is the type of character that, when the band is being interviewed, the fucker steals the whole interview and we all suddenly seem to be nothing more than part of his brilliant idea and plan to bring it all together.

This is why some bands ultimately fail on many levels. Look at Japan, a fucking outstanding band, in my opinion, but internally David Sylvian's ego was bigger than the entire band and eventually destroyed them... that plus the fact he stole Mick Karn's Japanese girlfriend from him (not cool, dude, I'm thinking Yoko Ono here). Mr. Sylvian, I really respect you as an artiste, but you were kinda deluded when you were in Japan! I could name a dozen other bands who suffered a similar fate with lead singer's egos... Like, yeah, fucking Kajagoogoo (absolutely no idea what it means, and even after asking one of them, still none the fucking wiser - something about a baby's first words?). Remember Limahl, the singer they brought into Kajagoogoo to 'appeal' to the teenage girls (and boys hehe). He seemed to get too big for his (Tuka) boots and started to have delusions that he was 'The Band' - don't get me wrong, I like the guy and enjoyed chatting to him many times, but my point is they can't help themselves... no wonder they fucking sacked him. Okay, Nick Beggs was a bit of a twat too, but the momentum was lost after culling Limahl from the equation. It's a bit sad, really, you sweat blood and tears to get to that point in the business, and when you do, internal jealousy, envy or just downright fucking nastiness fucks it all up really quickly. After that, all you become is a minor search in an Internet Browser, a footnote on nostalgia

TV shows - and you say, "Ahh, I remember them..." but you can only recall two or three songs and can't clearly remember what actually happened to them.

I'm playing my synth line as the camera pans to me - I am at the back of everyone (typical) and I was sort of warned not to look at the camera as the singer says he wants 'full attention...' and if we look into the camera it will spoil the cool look of the band! Well, fuck me, the camera is coming to me and I'm thinking will I ever get on TV again? So, I turn and look into the camera, give a quick, but cheeky, Mick Ronson wink to the camera and revel in the attention for all of three seconds.

After watching the show back at some point, the singer calls me up and calls me a 'Saboteur', claiming that I 'spoiled the look' he was trying to set for the band. "Okay, Okay, calm the fuck down, Mussolini," I scream back at him down the phone - then, after a brief exchange of nice words (yeah, right), he hangs up, having made his point and seemingly putting me in my place. I'm not a big fan of people shouting at me, and if he had have been right there in front of me, he would be spitting at least two teeth out... and walking strangely for a week.

The next few rehearsals were 'tense', but I did not take it any further as I was still being paid to tour with them in Europe (and hopefully The States as well) and I did not want to blow that side of it - I just made a mental note to kick him in the nuts on my last day of service or if it all went pear shaped. It was something I regretted not doing, but do remember being balls deep in his girlfriend - so I guess we're quits now, huh? Years later, I did come across him once in the queue in front of me whilst waiting to see some 'Star Trek' thing and it made me smile to see a big, shiny, bald spot on his once glorious hair style, hehe - justice enough for me (and creaming over his GF's tits). I didn't even acknowledge him - in fact, I felt nothing and he was just another guy I had known at some time in my life. I always found it weird how you can spend years with some cunts and then forget them in the space of a week or less.

1998: Leicester

Sitting in a coffee / book shop, I am drawn to this rather sweet looking girl at the next table. I hear her talking about music and I listen intently - she is with her 'Mum', who appears to be about my age. I interrupt and ask her if she is a musician, and it turns out she is a bassist in her own band called 'CoConi' - her name is CoConi Royale and she hails from Los Angeles (a place I am not too unfamiliar with), she looks about seventeen or eighteen, and she is also a model of some description. It's at this point I introduce myself, I tell them about my past career path in the music business and suggest that perhaps I can be of some assistance in achieving her dreams. At this point I am thinking that if they are any good I will ask about managing them to get them a recording deal and get myself fifteen percent commission or more as I would like to retire early to the 'Land Of Smiles'.

They have a gig on Saturday night and I get invited along, it's in some sort of big, Chinese restaurant in Northampton and it looks quite good inside - it even has its own stage. I sit with Alison (her Mum) and wait for the show to begin, jotting down my criticisms for later. CoConi looks typically 'rock chic' American, which is okay, if not a little obvious with her accent and introduction of the songs.

The rest of the band were of no consequence, technically good players, but I could tell they were not the kind to get their hands dirty, doing what they needed to do to get on TV and further. They all looked like they had good jobs and this was a 'hobby' they enjoyed. Despite all of that, the songs were a mix of rocky, middle of the road material with a surprisingly good vocal from CoConi (or 'CoCo', as she preferred to be called). One of the songs, 'Say It Again', was quite catchy, but not mainstream pop - by that, I mean non-sellable to the musical 'sheople' customers who buy what they are told to purchase from the Music Corporations of the times.

I get into a good chat with them about their dreams and aspirations, get them all fired up, and find out Alison is their manager for now - setting up gigs and taking the money, I guess, but disastrous in the long term as there is no objectivity or strategy. I sort of take them under my wing and think to take them on professionally as Manager at some point, but want to try a few things out with them. I give them some insight into the reality of being in a band who want to 'make it'.

Firstly, if you want to be famous, you have to behave like you already are - sitting about in pubs and clubs waiting to go on stage is not how you do it... no one takes any interest in you. Now, if they had turned up in a limo with bouncers and a rented crowd, then they would have caused a stir getting on stage and perhaps they would have elevated themselves a little in the eyes of Joe Public. I did point this out to them, but all I got was, "Fuck that, what's wrong with the way we dress?" and "What's wrong with sitting in the pub and then getting up to play?" Oh, fuck, here we go - fucking ego time. I have met these types of fucking idiots so many times and they always fuck the band up with their inflated egos and short sightedness. I call this mentality, the 'SuperCunt Syndrome', and if you are unlucky, at least one band member will have it... and if you are really unlucky, most of the band has it, and they aren't going fucking anywhere.

1983: Viva concert-Charles Napier College, Edinburgh

Jim and Derek are already on stage, kicking into an instrumental of my own design. I stroll on like Bowie (No, wait, we have one of them already - okay, maybe Karn), get to my synth and play the lead lines to the track. I'm dressed in a white suit, pleated trousers and a bolero jacket, have my hair in some sort of shade of blonde with a pony tail, I am bare chested, and looking every bit like the pop star I deserve to be. I'm not too sure if I pissed off the rest of the band by straying from our usual 'black uniform', but at that point I just wanted to feel good, enjoy the gig, and get laid, hehe.

We had three backing singers that night, affectionately called 'The Country Roads' singers as they looked so fucking countrified, sexless and boring, lol! One of them, at least, (Suzanne) was hot sauce and far sexier than any of the others in the band... well, in my opinion she was - some of the others may have disagreed with me on that point as I'm pretty certain Jimbo was trying to juice up her sister, Catherine?. Jim was always flirting with her, I thought she looked a bit of a tart (in a prim way), but was guessing she was Hamilton's local 'bike' and probably had a vaginal grip like a dying man's handshake! Yeah, just like punching smoke! The sad thing was that the girls were in the band not just to expand the vocal arrangements, but to add a bit of glamorous, sex-appeal... something they, especially the two sisters, singularly failed to do. The rest of the band expected them to be flashing flesh and making the guys in the audience drool - but their idea of being revealing seemed to be a skirt that showed off their knees and making sure that at all times, their chests were masked in any kind of clothing that left everything to the imagination... it was just as well they could sing, a bit!

Jim and Derek had went for the usual look, 10cc guy and glam rock style, ala 'The Sweet', while the rest of the band were in black and looking hot and tidy at least - great stuff when you make the effort! As for the gig itself - would you fucking believe it, there was a problem with the desk or the PA almost from the first note. It turned out to be one the 'DI' boxes (direct inject), so the bass, I think, was not going to be in stereo and sounded a bit one sided and heavy. Luckily Jim managed to sort the sound out fairly swiftly, and somehow it all went really well. My only concern about the gig was that the crowd looked a bit taken aback by what they were seeing... perhaps they were expecting a country band, after all! (He he) No fucking way were the audience getting 'Rhinestone Cowboy' style - we dress to shock and we play to win!

What a gig - we were fucking brilliant! Everyone seemed to love it. I even gave some autographs to some fawning females near the loos - someone even touched my hair and screamed, "I touched him, I touched him!" Fucking yes, now this is what stardom is all about. I wanted it badly and more than ever - I know it's superficial, I know it's crass, but you are only young once and you have to take what you can get... and enjoy what you have, for tomorrow may never come at all!

This is the end result of years of hard work,

rehearsing, inventing your look, then reinventing your look and sound many times to hone it to musical and visual perfection. I looked good, Jonn Harton looked good, the girls looked good - fuck it, even Jim and Dek looked okay, playing the straight men (no, not that we were gay! Fucking grow up, you homophobes!)

Looking good, sounding good, and knowing your audience - a simple recipe, right? Fucking harder than 'Alchemy'. I had started out dyeing my hair black, but just looked like a negative-reality inversion of an imposter trying to be me! Then I made the mistake of trying to bleach it and the fucking hair turned bright green - for fuck's sake, I had to go to the psycho bakery full of retarded football junkies with alcohol issues looking like that. These cunts fucking beat me and laughed at me... okay, so I guess that maybe I deserved that one. Eventually the green grew out, and next I went for a mousy-brown with blonde highlights, looking good this time and was a hit in the night clubs with girls and guys falling over themselves to be beside me - I looked fucking brilliant! Sexy, slim and ready to take the world of pop on - how the fuck could anything go wrong? Oh, yes ...wait - the world is full of delusional people who will do all they can to fuck with you, control you, use you, hurt you, and then throw you in the trash when they are done.

I remember I was in a music shop in Glasgow (it might have been Virgin or something similar, it was in Union Street anyway - so figure it out, if you are old enough) ...it was the one 'The Skids' had gigged at on the roof, trying to copy The Beatles 'Rooftop Gig'. Anyway, I was in there and this punk girl just keeps looking at me. Now, me personally, I did not get off on punk bitches wearing bin liners for dresses and razor blades for earrings, but she came up to me with an intense stare.

She said "I've seen you before, did you play some concerts in town? You play synths, right?"

I felt a bit famous and said, "Yeah, you're right - that's me!"

Then she said, "Oh, yeah, that's right - you're the ugly one!"

Fucking punk bitch, she was goading me and slapped me down hard. Lesson learnt there, for me.

1998 – Northampton

I'm watching CoConi playing in the finals of a local band contest, taking place in a dingy pub full of drunks and tarts, thinking "For fuck's sake, what are they doing?" Had they followed any of my advice at all? No, they looked like a 70s rock band - no appeal and no idea what they were doing. They played the same songs I had heard a week before, but now seemed to lack the energy that they had previously managed to inject into their repertoire of songs.

At that point I decided that they were not going to listen to my advice or get any further, destined to just melt into the landscape like so many other bands. They had a good bunch of songs that could be re-done and made less rocky, CoCo was fit, looked good, and had a great voice, while the other guys were okay and would probably not last for long after a signing or deal. They were just not up to par, but CoCo could not see it and I'm sure Alison was pushing them in the wrong direction - getting them gigs in any dive for forty pounds a night... is not how you do it, but perhaps they were short on money, so who am I to judge? But one thing I do know - what they were doing was no way to get noticed. This was all going south and my dreams of scoring some heavy money from my advice and guidance as a way of accumulating some decent cash to allow me to leave the UK were slowly sliding away from me. Funnily enough, I got a mention in a local magazine article about CoConi when she did some modelling shots for it - they had somehow got me confused with a member of Kajagoogoo... I didn't want to ask which one they thought I was (hehe), fucking ace or what?

I was so fucking mad at having to walk away from them, but I know they would've driven me insane with their lack of knowledge and no fucking clues about how to become famous. Youngers always think they know better, right?

Glasgow – Old Springburn 1977

I never really went out much as a teenager - sure, I had a job and 'friends', but preferred my own company... much as I do now. My brothers were of a differing breed and thought I was 'weird', purely down to my taste in music which, by that time, was Steve Harley and Cockney Rebel whilst they were more Deep Purple and Status Quo kinda guys - Oh, there was one band they liked that I secretly liked too... Thin Lizzy, 'The Boys Are Back In Town'! Fucking brilliant! I would never admit it to them, of course.

My older brother, Harry, would call me an 'alien' and a 'poofter' at times, but I now know he was kind of proud of me for not being a typical Glaswegian 'NED'. I was quiet but capable of defending myself if the need arose. I remember, one evening, some guy was shouting at me, calling me a 'dick' and 'fanny', and was with three other guys at the same time - so, I'm thinking "Bravado is easy when you're in a team, you cunt"! Uncharacteristically, I shout out, "Fuck off, you prick - go and fuck yourself!" The next thing I know, he's running at me full steam and intent on fucking me up big style! But something inside of me stayed calm and I waited until he was about two feet from me - and I then launch myself into a 'Kung Fu' kick, and it catches this cunt square on the right side of his face! My shoes were covered in 'Segs' at the time, (little metal studs to help preserve your soles from wearing too thin) ...getting kicked with these would result in 'FUBAR'! (Fucked up beyond all recognition.)

A few days later I get home from work and my sister, Wendy, says, "Don't go into the living room - I have a new fella, and he's bit shy!" So, I say, "No problem," and go to my room. About thirty minutes later I am gagging for a 'cuppa' and nip up to the kitchen, which is off the living room. I slip in, make tea and when I'm coming out, and make my apologies - unable to resist having a quick look at her new beau. I nearly spat my tea out! Sitting with my sister on the sofa is the guy I had kicked in the face (while defending myself). He's looking over at me and one side of his face is hideously black and blue - I let out a "Fucking hell!" and Wendy says, "Yeah, some bastards mugged him and gave him a kicking!" I nod at him and ask, "Really? Fucking rough out there at times, mate - right?" He looks away and I go back to my room feeling a bit guilty for enjoying such a salacious moment. The moral of the story being - don't be a twat!

I've recounted many times when violence was prevalent in Glasgow, my family life, school days, and work - but, to be fair, there were times I really cherished living in Glasgow and something I truly miss about the place... the openness of people and the connectivity that lots of people share with each other. You can't be an arse in Scotland, they won't let you get away with it - even if you are Sean Connery or Billy Connolly, and they still treat you as if you were just one of them. The minute you try and raise yourself above them all, they will remind you exactly who you are and where you come from in about two seconds flat. That's what I love about the place - there's no subterfuge, it's either a handshake or a punch in the face, and that's the kind of people I can deal with.

2015 – Leicestershire

I currently live and work in a village, it's a nice little place, a bit boring and predictable, perhaps, but a million miles from Glasgow. The place is full of pretend gangsters, weekend poseurs, and teenage 'hard men' who trawl the local pubs - but, all in all, its paradise compared to the1970s place I grew up in. It's made me a bit soft and sometimes I even sound like a 'Sassenach', but I know deep down I am Scottish, born and bred! I don't mean that in a nationalistic sense at all, I am no 'Nationalist' and don't give a hootenanny to Football teams or Rugby teams - I have no connection with them or even want to understand them. I also have no interest in Andy Murray and all his tennis achievements. My affinity is with music and the people of The Far East who are arguably the nicest, most peaceful people on this rotten apple called 'Earth', but deep down I am still a Scot.

I have two cats (Tokyo and Sarai), a pretty Filipino lady called Britt who puts up with more than she should have to from me at times as I hurtle through my fifties to what is, hopefully, 'The Best Years of Our Lives'. I know I still have a long journey ahead of me and, hopefully, can write about some more of my life - past and present alike.

CoConi... wow, well, what a fucking surprise - seven years on and still no recording deal! To be fair, 'CoCo' looks very different, like a merged version of Kate Bush in a butterfly themed, wedding dress as if becoming a soft version of Siouxsie Sioux - a look that I think could work for her. She is still peddling the same batch of songs and the newer ones seem softer, with more thought devoted to the words and music, but I think she needs to let Alison go and find her own way as I know there is something more there. I had even heard that she was taking bookings for people's houses! What the fuck is that all about? No idea if that would work, but I don't think many recording executives would be chasing someone who did that - playing to your fan base on a one to one basis in their living room. Maybe I'm missing something in this? Time will tell, but I fear CoCo has missed her chance with fame... and the way the music business is going, she would be quicker selling her soul to The Devil.

The European Tour I was substituting on keyboards for started in Stockholm, and before the gig I get the chance to walk around this beautiful city. Man, Swedish women are fucking hot ...and very fit indeed! It's a scorching summer's day in July and most of these blonde beauties are topless, lying on the grass, soaking up some radiation. It's so different from the UK in so many ways, they seem to be more open and their minds are a bit freer. The riverside is fucking stunning, and I am pleasantly surprised by the beauty of this city - it is even more majestic than Paris (and I love Paris, for personal reasons, and would have no problem living there), but Stockholm seems more sophisticated by far. I toy with the idea of buying somewhere to live here when I am rich and famous.

How the hell did I get from being a malnourished sewer rat from Springburn to travelling the world with all these possibilities in front of me? An answer to that question would elude me for now as I simply enjoyed the cities of Europe. My heart takes me back to different times and makes me ask why some people are born into shit, and face dire situations with no means of escape unless something drastic happens in their lives that will catapult them out of misery, and into a world that they have never known before.

I was eating regularly and eating healthily too - gone were the days of finding food to eat or living on pot noodles and cans of tuna fish, even 'crisp sandwiches ' were a dinner favourite... yes, that's right, when you are poor, a packet of crisp in-between bread is a feast not to be sniffed at.

The gigs were all going brilliantly - Helsinki next, then Oslo, then Berlin, with a few, strange, minor places, in-between, then back to London, then Sheffield, and finally finishing in Birmingham. I had a few run-ins with the dickhead singer and he had stated how he "...can't wait till the other guy is back out of hospital," and I can be 'let go' - the arrogant cunt! He needed twatted there and then, but I needed the money and I needed fame even more ...and time was running out for 'Mr Soft'.

Luckily for me I get to be in the band for another eight months on their American/UK tour, having a fucking ball of a time - money, women, travelling, modest fame... what more could a guy want? A fast car? I remember one night the band were rehearsing and they had these electronic drums that I fancied trying out, and, unbeknownst to me, in America they let the crowds in really fucking early. Anyway, I ask if I can have a go on the drums and they say yes. So, I sit there and start pounding them hard, and one of the bastards in the band opens the curtains so that the crowd thinks the gig's starting early, while I'm sitting there looking like a right dick on the drums with all these yanks clapping and whooping me. Golden memories!

I caused a bit of a stir in Leicester once, when I met one of the band at a Chinese Restaurant in King Street, just round the corner from the gig we were doing at the 'De Montfort'. Anyway, I turn up in an blue suit, accessorised with one red shoe and one white (such a Poseur), and perfectly dyed, blonde hair (before it fell out, yes), when the other guy turns up in a white suit and looks fucking cool. He brings two Japanese girls with him and says, "This one's yours," fucking brilliant, hehe. The whole restaurant could not take their eyes off us - and, no, the Japanese girls were not twins and named 'Fook Mi' and Fook Yu', ha-ha.

I remember, years later, when I ended up staying in Leicester, one job I had was in a Supermarket doing the server stuff in the computer room and this girl was going on about how she saw this band years ago and she caught a tambourine. I said, "No fucking way, I played that gig and I threw that tambourine - I signed it with a kiss!" She said, "Fuck me, small world - right?" I went out with her for a long time and she was a great girl - so, thanks, Jill, for entertaining my cock on those long, cold, winter nights. She was a lovely girl, but had pussy lips you could hang-glide with. I always joked she should put a curtain rail up for them - she thought I was really funny and never, ever, took offence over it. Jill was a great laugh - she was Irish, so maybe that accounted for that side of her. On one occasion, I remember she was naked, on top of me, and she decided to move onto my face... but, fuck me, her 'inner lips' nearly suffocated me, they were like bacon rashers - my gag reflex kicked in and she had to run and get me some water. Great days, ha-ha!

Los Angeles - Relax and Swing

Being in L.A. for a couple of months had made me wind swept and interesting, I was meeting some great people, going to some great gigs, and even better parties I went to one of Suzanne's friend's parties, and it was full of gays, lesbians and swingers - not that I knew that at first, I was just enjoying it all. The first hint that something was 'different' was when I saw two ladies making out on a couch in from of me, they were really kissing deeply and I was so transfixed that I just stood there and watched. They kept looking at me and winking, I knew they wanted me to join in with them, but I already had a great sandwich to munch, hehe, so they just smiled and went back to snogging each other's tonsils out - I guessed they would be eating lettuce soon enough.

Most people were naked in the pool, and it felt like a rock star party. I presumed most of them were stoned as well, a very affluent party with many beautiful people there. I felt a bit like a 'Hobbit', but I did not have to worry as they were all very friendly and loved it because I was Scottish.

I met someone later in the night who was recalling to everyone their 'Ayhuasca' experience and I listened intently. Apparently there is a ritual carried out by a Peruvian 'shaman' that involved taking a ritual hallucinogenic called 'Ayhuasca', technically called Dimethyl Tryptamine (DMT), this occurs naturally in plants and even the human body produces it in small amounts. After listening to this, I was fascinated and asked if there was another ritual pending - he said, "Yes, next week - but you have to be invited by someone who has already went through it!" Fucking great, this guy says he will sponsor me and says I need to give the Shaman a hundred dollars at the end of the ceremony - I said, "Cool." I get to this big house a week later and there are twelve of us there, including this spooky looking, old guy who genuinely looks like he's just stepped out of the jungle. There are twelve mattresses and twelve red buckets all neatly placed together - What the fuck am I thinking? I am later informed that when I drink this potion, made from plants and a few other extracts, I will be out of it for up to eight hours ...and will probably be violently sick. I just think, "No problem, I've had worse dates!" (hehe)

He starts this ritual and is mumbling things, talking to the corners of the very large room and the ceiling. There is a strange smell, and I notice that outside there is deep glow which turns out to be a fire with a huge pot on it and someone stirring it. Suddenly, the guys brings this liquid into the room - it smells fucking awful, like bile, and looks like sick chocolate. The 'shaman' goes around the room and gives everyone a cup of this sludge and tells us all to wait and to drink it only on his command, and to drink it down in one gulp. Everyone looks tense and a little afraid, and, I must admit, at this point I was ready for bolting out the door... but something stopped me. It tasted like shit and was much too hot - I had to gag a few times to swallow it all, but swallow it I did, just as everyone else had done. So, now I feel a bit weird and sick, but fight the urge to 'Hughie' (vomit) into the waiting red bucket. I start laughing and have no idea why! A girl beside me is crying and lies down on her mattress. Others are either silent or in some state of discomfort, and I feel my head burning like there is the hottest chilli ever grown lodged in my head. Suddenly, it explodes like a supernova and I fall down on the floor - the next thing I know, I am floating along a tunnel of light which is gently rotating as I move forward in a weightless tube. Then, I see writing on the inner walls of the tunnel and think I recognise it as I hear myself laughing again and suddenly feel a light coming from ahead of me, like a translucent glow - it wasn't menacing, but gentle and inviting. As I drifted further, I now know the written words are Sanskrit, but I am unable to decipher them. I see a shape form in front of me, a gentle shape, very much like an out of focus body, but shimmering with some sort of energy. I feel very scared and hear my voice ask, "What are you?" A beautiful, melodic voice whispers in my mind, "Go to the next level, you are ready." Now I ask, "Who are you?" The voice repeats, "Go to the next level." I say, "What do you mean?" But now I feel I'm moving backwards along this tunnel of light and I see the shape in front of me melt into nothingness, to become part of the colours all around me.

I remember throwing up for about fifteen minutes, not daring to move from the safety of the lip of the bucket - the smell is torturous and I am aware of others throwing up all around me. I lie down and fall asleep for the next six hours. I had followed the instructions given by the guy who sponsored me to the ritual - not eating meat for a week and only drinking water... he had said this might help with the vomiting being less harsh. Well, he was fucking wrong!

To this day, it still feels so real and substantial, but in the tunnel it felt very non-Corporeal. The being of light that spoke to me filled me with peace and wonderment - I mean, I knew it was a hallucination that was the only logical conclusion, right? I am not religious, but I am aware of the spiritual connection we all have between each other, all the things we share on the Earth and the Universe - we are all made of 'Star Stuff', infinite and never ending... so here I go, onto the 'next level'

CHAPTER TWELVE

BEING BOILED

Catterick Army Barracks, 1963

The child was screaming at the top of its tiny lungs, screaming for a pain it did not or could not understand, falling over onto the floor, it's left arm and parts of its back were stripped of silk like skin by the scalding water that had just rained down on bare flesh - flesh that by now looked like an undercooked piece of a Ham joint 'Being Boiled' in a pot.

Its' Mother was also screaming, and picking up a lump of mercifully unconscious infant that had just been hideously scarred - running with the child in her arms to the Army Hospital which was close by, almost blacking out with grief and fearing the worst.

I'm fifty three now and my arm and a good (bad) portion of my back has been scarred all of my life as a result of the 'accident' that happened in that kitchen, back so long ago in the early sixties - an ugly, visible reminder of what boiling liquid can do to soft flesh... and perhaps the psychological damage it can inflict on the mind of someone so young.

Call me a fucking, twisted, cunt, but I have never believed the story of 'that day' - and the more I asked for clarification about it, as I was in my teens, the more confusing the memory of events that was relayed to me by my Mum and Dad. It was as if the story had morphed over the years and had fresh embellishments added to it, making it almost impossible to find a beginning and an end.

Dad was in the Army and he was stationed at Catterick Barracks (which is still there, I believe), where we lived in a house either given to us or subsidised to some extent by the 'MOD'.

I was supposed to have pulled down a kettle of freshly boiled water onto myself, and accepted that version until I was about sixteen or seventeen - then I started to question how a barely two year old child could stand upright for long enough, and exert the necessary strength needed, to pull a heavy kettle filled with water (probably with a combined weight in excess of a kilo) off the work surface and onto itself.

The top of the kitchen work surface was probably not even within reach, and the kettle's cable was probably not dangling far enough over the edge to grab in any case. Ever since the Internet came into being, I have searched for 'kettles - during the 1960s' ...and, yes, there were some electric ones available - but mainly to those affluent enough to afford them. In all my life with my family, growing up in the 60s, 70s, and early 80s, we have never had 'another' electric kettle.

A dark side of me wonders if my parents were fighting (as they were always doing), and perhaps I was the accidental victim in one of their acts of violence towards each other. I suppose I'll never know the real truth behind my scarring - something that occasionally affected me while I was in my teens, trying to understand girls, and find one to love... as any normal, young guy was trying to do at that time in their life.

Some women were fucking evil to me about my arm, some laughed, and some said, "Oh, you're so brave to walk around like that!" "Fuck off, you thick bastards and leave me alone!" I would say to myself, thinking I would be on my own for a long, long time... because who would want to be with someone who had such an ugliness about them? It was even beginning to affect my mind and made me more withdrawn than ever.

I found solace in listening to music and reading great books that I would get on loan from the local library. I was interested in Freud, Jung, Aristotle, Thales, and Zen to name but a few, trying to expand my mind and knowledge of the world around me. I wondered what the other side of the world was like, what people were doing and were their lives different to mine. Eventually I realised that I had to overcome this thing that was eating my fucking self-esteem away and embrace it as a part of me - and if people did not like me, or women did not want to be with me because of it, then they could all fuck off!

I felt so lost in my teenage years, something I know a lot of us felt during the 70s - a sense of emptiness and perhaps despair about the future... and what the hell was it all about? Born to this world, rushed into education, learning to read and write, then moving up to more education - I think there were only two teachers that ever taught me anything useful in my entire life... my Primary school, English Teacher, and my Secondary school, Music teacher. The rest of them were not fucking interested in teaching any students anything fucking useful at all, it was just a pay packet to them at the end of the week... as I guess it is with most jobs and most careers.

My secondary school was horrendous and had a bad reputation for gang violence. Kids from differing parts of the surrounding areas, such as Springburn, Milton, and Possil Park, all mingled to apply hate and scorn on each other - something I never understood at all, and still don't to this day... to fight over something as trivial as a post code was beyond lunacy, but indicative of the illogical need for borders and boundaries that gave these idiots identity.

My first day at 'Colston Secondary' was short, I was late getting there as I had to walk an extra four miles from where I lived to get there - no money for bus fares back then. It was get to fucking school and out the door for all of us - no breakfast or perhaps a slice of dry bread. We had something called 'Dinner Tickets', a little brown card with the school days printed onto it, clicked by some 'Dinner Monitor' whenever you used it for your 'free meal' - something I was very glad of, but never understood the stigma that came with owning one. Kids with dinner tickets were teased and bullied, called scabs and tramps by the more fortunate ones on a daily basis - something made all the more obvious by the Teachers making us stand in a separate queue while we were waiting to get served... and, yes, the ones that paid, got served first.

I was ten minutes late as I got to Colston Secondary for my first day. As I walked through the huge gates, an older lad came up to me and said "Give me your fucking money!" I was a bit stunned and nearly crying, saying "I don't have any," - then he went through my pockets, took my dinner ticket and proceeded to stab me in the abdomen with a compass (minus the pencil). It went into the fleshy part near my navel and started to bleed profusely - by that time a School Monitor had found me and took me to the School Nurse who put a plaster on it and told me to go home... yes, that's what she fucking did!

A different era and a different way of dealing with things - certainly in Glasgow, at least.

My older brother had already been there for a couple of years and was known as one of the school hard men. When he found out what had happened, what this mindless thug had done, he apparently tracked him down and introduced the guy's head to one of the toilet sinks until he was nearly unconscious, warning him of the consequences of any further antagonism towards me - all hail for big brothers, yay!

Glasgow –Old Springburn 1977

I would usually be in my room listening to Steve Harley or Pilot, writing poems or verses that I thought I could make into songs - if only I could play an instrument. My Dad played guitar and never worked at a real job in his life, he sort of survived by playing in local pubs and working men's clubs near 'The Barrows' in the city centre. I never aspired to the guitar and I put it down to hating my Dad for being the violent nutter he was and I never, ever asked him about music - ever.

The new place we had moved to on 'Balgaryhill' was less run down than the tenements of 'Old Springburn', and some neighbours had cars and obviously a bit more money than some other people. One of my neighbours was a nice guy called Alan West, and I got to know him and a few other guys in the street - Johnny Kay and Alan Sloan (Radio

Clyde DJ - Billy Sloan's younger sibling). We would hang out in the street, talking bollocks about this and that, and chase girls... but I wanted something more. One day while I was in Alan West's house, I saw this 'Bontempi Organ' sitting near his bed and I said, "Does it work?" and he answered, "Yeah, but its fucking shite! I hate it, but I can play a few things on it."

He put a record on and started to play along with it on the Bontempi, and, fuck me, he was playing, note for note, 'Magic Fly' by Space, which was just in the charts (okay, it was not the same sounds, but, fuck, it was the same notes, and I was fascinated by it). Anyway, I asked him if I could borrow it and he said, "Sure, no bother... but can you give me a loan of your Steve Harley albums?" Right away, I said, "Fucking yes!"

So, over the next few weeks I listened to some stuff and finally I managed to pick some things up - soon playing along with Space, Abba, and even Cockney Rebel. This is fucking brilliant, I had found something that my brain wanted to learn more of and I found it easy to locate the notes on the keyboard - although by now I was getting bored with the thing. The 'Bontempi' was limited, it had three sounds - pipes, organ, and a weird, string sound like you were sucking air through a reed instrument instead of blowing through it, ha-ha.

As I watched 'Top of the Pops' I would look at the keyboards and wonder what they were playing.

Luckily, on some album covers, they would list the name of instruments used for the tracks - I started to see names such as 'Moog' and 'Arp', so then deduced that perhaps I should visit a music shop to see if they had anything similar. What a dreamer - no fucking money, but big ideas and an insatiable desire to play along with my favourite tracks... but using the right sounds. At that point, I just wanted to stay in my room and play along with my '45s' (vinyl single records) and revel in imagining I am in a band and playing alongside of them onstage (a rather technical version of using a cricket bat or a hair brush in front of the mirror).

For fuck's sake, I realised, it had taken me till the beginning of 1978 to get to the only fucking music shop in Glasgow that had anything remotely looking like the keyboards I had seen on TV. These heavenly instruments, I had learned, were called 'Synthesisers' and were electronics that shaped simple wave forms, such as Sine waves, Sawtooth, and Pulse waves to create unimagined sounds. This shop (the one I have already mentioned far too many times in this book) had around five differing synths in the downstairs department and the cunt shop assistants would not let you down to see them if they thought you did not have any money, let alone the talent to actually play one.

On one rare occasion this bloke let me in and I was fucking amazed, as I looked like a dick who obviously had no money, but let me in he did and I stood there with my jaw agape at all of these magical things in front of me. He suggested that I try 'The Moog' - I held a note down and this huge sound came out of nowhere, it was just fucking brilliant, it went on and on for what seemed like ten minutes, changing tones and frequencies. I nearly pissed myself with joy - I wanted one and looked for the price tag... then saw a figure that did not compute in my tenement mind. Twelve hundred pounds (£1,200) for a Mini Moog, a sum that was unattainable for most people in my situation.

I went home with my tail between my legs, knowing it was out of my league and that I would be using the 'Bontempi' for years to come, if not forever. I felt totally crushed and questioned how the fuck could people afford those things? It never occurred to me that people could make enough money to buy such expensive things... I mean, fuck me, this was Glasgow - weren't we all poor? I always thought people with money lived elsewhere in the world and not in Scotland. I had just gotten a job, under duress, as my Mum had said, "No job and you're out the door!" - a rather obnoxious threat from a parent, I must say, but one I took heed of as I did not want to be out on the street, as she kindly kept reminding me that it was where I would end up if I did not get my finger out.

I wandered into a factory type of building and they asked if I had any qualifications, and I said, "Fuck me, what are they?" Then they asked to see my school grades - okay, now I get it! I show him the grades - all As and couple of Bs, and a distinction for 'Catering' and 'Music' (fucking surprise or what?). The interviewer said, "Okay, catering, that's good - maybe we can train you up. Start on Monday!" "Fuck me," I muttered as I left 'Scars Bakery' on Maryhill Road, "I've got a job!" My Mum was, of course, delighted and was soon asking for money off me every week for my keep - I asked her, "Fuck me, did you have kids to make a profit in life, then?" In reply to which she smacked me hard around the head - "You're not too big for a smack, you cheeky bastard." So. Every week, she took eight pounds (£8) from my hard earned ten pounds (£10), only leaving me with two pounds (£2) - so that was it... I had started saving up for my much wanted 'Mini Moog', the only thing I was focussed on in my life.

'Your life is like a schedule,

How true this fucking line from an early 'Human League' song is. What the fuck is life all about? Money? Taxes? Grief? I just want to fucking live and do what I want - is that too much to ask? Apparently it is, and in this fucked up world of hidden slavery, we are going nowhere fast with less and less free time to be 'free'. I now know this shuts down the right side of our brains, kills imagination, and, in turn, dumbs us down into drones in the hive of debt servitude. Where are all the revolutionaries? 'No More Heroes' anymore? And 'If I only could, I'd make a deal with

God' - but there is no God, no one's going to 'save us'... it's up to us. Why are we a nation of 'sheople'? We moan about taxes and the government screwing us on a daily basis, and yet we do nothing about it. We are the majority - if fifty million people turn round and say "Fuck your Council Tax, we're not fucking paying it," then what the fuck can they do to fifty million of us? Put us all in jail? I don't fucking think so. But what they cleverly do is separate us and divide our communities so we are no longer a united, coherent force - they demonise the most vulnerable of our society (the elderly and those who depend on benefits), and use scape-goats such as immigrants, (yes, sure, they have some effect on our services, but it's all smoke and mirrors to distract you from the real fucking criminals). Now there are hardly any more unions, and the ones that are left are either uninterested in resisting, have no power, or not enough numbers to stand fast and say, "I'm mad as hell, and I'm not going to fucking take this anymore!"

'I see a bad moon a-rising,

Glasgow –Old Springburn 1974

My older brother has just hit me with a poker across my back for the third time as I was shouting, "Sorry, sorry!" He was hitting me because he had sent me to a local shop with saved up 'Cigarette Coupons'. He didn't smoke as he had no money (much the same as everyone else), but it was just another way to get money. People who bought 'tens' and 'twenties' packs of cigarettes got a coupon in them, and if you saved up enough of them, there was this shop in the city that you could exchange them for goods such as irons, vacuum cleaners, a dinner set, etc. It was all a con to make you buy more and more 'cancer sticks' and up their sales - in fact, I think my Mum worked in the tobacco factory in Duke Street (before we were born) as one of her first jobs. I believe it was called 'W.D. Wills' and was a rather ominous looking building that was an icon to lung disease.

We would scavenge for these coupons, much the same way as empty pop bottles (with a return value of two pence or so). We would find them in empty packs, sometimes on stairways, lying in the street, and often in the communal bins in the backyard. On this occasion my brother had managed to gather about a hundred coupons, worth a princely sum of two pounds - the shop keepers took them as cash against goods and set their own monetary value on them as they too would want to cash them in for something from the 'Embassy Store' in West Regent Street.

My brother had decided that he wanted a 'Mars Bar' and some other sweets, but the stigma of going into the shops to trade them over for goods was something he did not want to endure... and, so, threatened me to take them in. I, of course, was as ashamed as he was to trade these things in for sweets and, I don't know why, but I came back with a bottle of milk which promptly got me the beating he thought

I deserved. My brother was an evil cunt sometimes, and back then he was the one left to look after us while my Mum was out working all the hours she could to pay the rent and feed us.

I got him back a few weeks later, though. We had this, old, vinyl sofa-chair, and he would come in and jump over the arm of it into a sitting position (as it was angled the wrong way in the room, due to lack of space). One day I shoved a strategically placed screwdriver into the foam cushioning underneath... and I was waiting for him to come in and do his usual, stupid, jump into it. Indeed, on arrival, he did exactly as was expected... but, fuck me, the screwdriver had shifted with his weight and it came out angled, taking a fair bit of skin off the inside of his thigh - ha-ha, served the evil bastard right for beating me up. Fuck me, revenge at ten years of age - surely not right in any way, shape, or form of justice? Or not, as the case may be.

My brother even put me in hospital on one occasion. He wouldn't let me in the house when Mum was out working, and he had the keys. I demanded that he let me in as I was very hungry, but he was with his mates and told me to "Fuck off!" It made me think what a cunt he was. I was about five feet away and, I don't know why, picked up this old, heavy, 'Ever Ready' battery thing (you know, the ones with four connections on it) and I threw it at him, hitting him on the ankle. He screamed and ran at me, then kicked me right in the balls - it really fucking hurt too. They ballooned into a haggis-shaped, bag of pain, making me curse him as I went down. I know I was in hospital for a few days and had a severe limp for weeks - thanks very much, you bastard... and remembered revenge is sweet.

Glasgow-New Springburn 1978/79

At some point my brain pointed out that I could play along with the newly, 'hire-purchase', financed Minimoog, to my collection of '45s' with my eyes closed. I was playing along with Cockney Rebel, Bryan Ferry, Kraftwerk, and a few others, when I thought about trying to play something of my own creation. Synths were a bit basic back then - although powerful, they were only monophonic (one note at a time) and had no 'user settings' or 'internal memory locations'...everything was done by hand tweaking all the various 'Oscillators' and 'Wave Forms' manually to attain the sounds. It was great, as you never knew if it was going to be the same sound twice, and there was always a new nuance when you set the sounds up again - fucking brilliant! So that was it - I started writing my own basic tracks and quickly realised that I needed someone else with a synth to play other parts, and also needed to get one of those new gizmos called a 'drum machine' (they were basic as fuck, but I did not want a live, skins drummer at that point - after all, what was the point in getting another skull involved?).

I still think to this day that synthesisers saved me from a life of misery, and got me out of a vicious circle that many Glaswegians never get out of as they are not exposed to anything but drinking, football, sectarianism and poverty - what fucking chance do we have? So, Bob Moog, little did you know that one day you would help save my life and expand my mind with your wonderful invention. It helped me focus, learn, and yearn for more, made me seek out other people like myself, and move in different circles - all the while expanding that lump of grey matter in my head to go beyond the boundaries of my own ignorance and enforced way of life. I was like the apes in the classic movie, '2001, A Space Odyssey', I had touched the Mono(synth)lith, which represented the age of man, and had been imparted with original thought... and finally my I.Q. was moving ever so slowly to triple digits - and all because of music and a synthesiser. What the fuck was going on?

Skelleftea, Sweden,

My first time in Sweden and I am going to meet Noi in a city called Skelleftea (pronounced 'she left her' apparently). I'm sitting on the plane in Arlanda Airport in Stockholm, and the plane has fucking propellers - whoa, whoa, wait a fucking minute... I like jet engines, they go faster and are more reliable, right? Next thing I know, there is some sort of crane with a guy on it, spraying pink goo all over the fuselage and the wings of the plane. "For fuck's sake," I'm thinking, "What the fuck is this all about?"

I ask one of the cabin crew about the pink goo, and she curtly says, "Oh, that's the anti-freeze to stop the ice from forming on the wings and rest of the plane!" Okay, now I'm fucking scared and want to get off this flying, tin can, but she assures me its okay, they have been doing this for decades and have never had any accidents on the way up north. Skelleftea is quite near the 'Arctic Circle' and the temperatures can drop to minus forty (-40) she informs me with some pride. It just makes me think, "Why do people live there again? Do they have fucking igloos or what? Husky transport perhaps? Tennis rackets on the bottom of their shoes?" The stewardess thinks I am hilarious, being really funny, and has no idea I am being totally serious for a change, ha-ha.

I am totally blown away with the beauty and majesty of Sweden, all the mountains and lakes, and a landscape that could house twenty African nations with ease - the place is huge and stunningly beautiful, I am awe struck. We land a few hours later at Skelleftea airport, one small runway and a terminal the size of your average bus station, and there's fucking snow everywhere - there is no colour, absolutely everything is whited out apart from the cars and the bus. I eagerly meet Noi, who has been there for a while now, and we get on the bus to head off to the city - I'm hoping it's not made of ice and there are no fucking Reindeers lurking on every corner to be used as taxis!

Fuck me, it's a very modern city, a very beautiful city with no high buildings (maybe, at most, some are six stories high), nice shops, and big, wide streets. We stop and make our way to the 'Best Western Hotel', dying to get into the warmth again. I am happy to be with her for a few days, and to meet her sister and family too (who are all here for the Mushroom and Berry picking season via Thailand). Migrant workers can apparently make lots of money in Sweden doing this, enough to send their kids to school for another year, or even buy a car or truck.

Swedish guys appear to be drunk all the time and are mostly swigging out of bottles in the street - I am, of course, stereotyping here and I mean no offence to any of them as I found them all to be very nice guys... but they had one thing about them I did not like, they have no qualms about stealing someone else's girlfriend from right from under their nose. It was a trait I found in a few of the men I met there, and a trait that makes me kind of mad at them for being so slyly dishonest.

I go on a 'Skidoo' run and enjoy it immensely, darting through the snow on this powerful, 'Yamaha', motorised, ski sled thing was sheer brilliance... and even fucking better when you were drunk on warm Swedish Vodka. I fell off a few times, going over minor bumps, and they all stopped to laugh at me now and then - bastards! We camped up north, stopped at

Being Boiled

a cabin restaurant, and later watched the northern lights - it was fucking ace, and I lay on my back, outside, looking up for about an hour before they told me to come in as my core temperature would be dropping dangerously low and I would soon become unconscious and die. Spoil-sports, eh!

There are lots of Thais here for the cherry/ mushrooms pickings, and the ones who already stay here and sponsor them to come over have great parties - I almost feel as though I am back In Bangkok and look forward to being at 'The Temple Of Dawn' again at sunrise. I tried skiing and nearly broke my fucking neck going over a ski jump and landing like a drunk trying to mount the stairs in the dark - what a fucking muppet I looked like! I was getting heckled by Swedish guys, laughing at me. One night we were all at a festival in the city centre, under a huge marquee - there were about six bands, all playing one after the other, and it was pulsing, fucking great. The Swedish cunts said, "You can't beat Sweden for music," to which I replied, "Yeah, but it's all fucking UK songs, you thick fuck!" Ha-ha, fucking brilliant comeback - and the look on their faces was classic.

All in all, I had a wonderful time with Noi, her sister, Tuk, her brothers and their wives - they were all a great laugh to be with. The fuckers dressed me up as 'Buddha' one day, and I went along with it as they all rubbed my tummy for luck. At one point there were about ten of us sleeping in a hotel room only meant for two - man, it was so fucking hot and sweaty, I nearly went out for a minus forty degree walk to cool off. We were warned not to go out into the forests at night as there were still wild Bears and Wolves that came across from Finland via Russia at times, and they were very dangerous indeed. I wondered what the Wolves and Bears would think about 'messing' with a Scottish person.

I got back to the airport where we said our goodbyes, and I told them I would come to Bangkok soon to see them all. They were staying in Sweden for six months of hard work in the forests, and I really hoped they didn't get eaten by anything nasty! So, here I go, back on the plane covered in pink goo (which looks like a flying condom, I might add), and heading back to Stockholm, then back to London to pick up my car, and then back to my boring life of work and toil as a debt slave to the British Government and Banks.

'The Look of Love' - Glasgow, 1979

I started listening to 'Tubeway Army' and loved 'Are Friends Electric'', a brilliant track performed by a cool looking dude, and at this point I dye my hair black and sort of vicariously live like him as much as I could. I have the Synth, I have the hair, the black eye liner, and I can sing his songs. I'm on the bus, coming home from town after buying (I think) a newly released single by Mr. Numan, called 'Complex'. I'm on the top deck, which is a part of the bus you do not usually want to go as all the 'NEDS' and drunks went up there - I remember a warning given out by Billy Connolly, "Never go upstairs and never wear a Duffel/Parka coat with a hood, as the drunks would use it to puke into, leaving you with a messy hairdo at some point." Bastards! Anyway, I was on the top deck and wearing a black, leather, box jacket, a black shirt, black slim-fit jeans, and black Chelsea Boots with a Cuban heel... and, of course, black hair, nail varnish, etc. I notice this girl sitting opposite in the reflection of the window, and she seems to be looking at me - fucking hell, what do I do now? She smiles when she realises I can see her reflection, and I turn around and say "Hello." She says the same back and then inquires if I am a 'Numanoid'? "A what?" I ask. This girl explains, "Oh, it's what Gary Numan Fans are being called now." I feel a bit of a dick and say, "Well, I guess I am one of them," and my face goes a bit red - then she says "But I am too. I love the music, it's so different from all the other stuff in the charts, don't you agree?" I am just happy that a member of the fairer sex is actually talking to me, then I think she is only talking to me because I look like her idol - which, if you think about it, is fucking bizarre! But why the fuck should I care?

Her name is Diane, and she is bloody beautiful, with a cute smile and a breathy voice. She has Blondish hair with beautiful eyes and is a very nice shape. As the bus gets nearer Possil Park, she says, "This is my stop," and gets up to go downstairs and get off the bus. I freeze and I don't want her to go, but I can't seem to say that or ask her for a telephone number, etc. Before I know it, she has gone and is walking down Saracen Street - I look at her walk away as the bus moves off, and she turns to me and smiles. "What a fucking idiot," I think to myself, "I meet someone nice and I blow it!" If I'd been brave enough I would have gotten off at the next stop, but I assumed she would have thought of me as some kind of nutter if I had perhaps carried that thought out.

I am painfully shy at eighteen and have never had a real girlfriend. I did stupid things like snog the local girl that everyone had already 'had', or went out with girls that hung around with gangs to look cool. I remember one girl called Frances, (sorry, Mum, another Catholic), and she was kinda pretty and cutesy with reddish hair, and she lived near 'Morrin Street'. Anyway, I would walk and talk with her sometimes, and she would kiss me and we would be groping each other in a shop front alcove until it was time to go home. One day, and this is the reason I hate Beans, I could not wait for a snog, so I went up to her house and her Dad said she was eating her dinner and would be out shortly, so I waited in the street for her eager lips to come out to play. Ten minutes later she is down, then we walk around the corner and lock lips - but, fuck me, she has eaten about twelve cans of Beans and her mouth is coated with the sauce. The smell and taste is fucking overwhelmingly awful - I nearly throw up in her mouth, but manage to suppress it. Frances stops tonguing me ten minutes later and I think, "That was fucking gross! I've been less sick eating old chips out of a litter bin! ...Or getting a kiss off my Toothless Granny!"

I'm sorry, I know it was a crass thing to do, but I had to dump her - no way am I eating beans by proxy ever again or tomato sauce for that matter, and to this day, yup, I will not touch either. Thanks for that, Frances!

I desperately start getting on the same bus for weeks with the sole intent of meeting Diane again, but three weeks have passed and I have not seen her. I tell my friend, who seems to sympathise with my situation as he is a geek like me and would only get to meet someone in some sort of, random, blind chance, fluke-like, event which regularly occurs with every coming of the Blue Moon and when pigs fly!

'Gary Numan and Tubeway Army' have announced their UK tour starting in, fucking wait for it, the 'Glasgow Apollo'. Fucking yes! I get a ticket and my sister, Wendy, is coming as well (my brothers think Numan's a poofter). I am standing in the rather long queue to get into the 'gig' and there's this girl a few feet in front of me, and yay - it's Diane! I shout, "Hi!" and she looks round, smiles at me, and genuinely seems pleased to see me. Diane comes over and tells me she is excited about the concert, I say, "Me too - I am learning to play 'Are Friends Electric'!" She seems impressed that I can do that and I ask her if she wants to come round to the house and hear me play, to which she says, "Yes, that would be great, Tam."

Two weeks later, I have a girlfriend called Diane... and we are inseparable. Fuck me, but she works in an office building not two hundred yards from the Bakery I am working at - how I didn't see her there is beyond me!

We did get engaged a year or so later and I loved her so much that I wanted to be with her all the time. We would fight, of course, as all couples did - but sometimes it would be worse than others and we would not talk for days or weeks, and I feared we would split up for good. We actually did split up at one point and, a few months later, we got back together and it was all hunky dory again. I asked if we were still engaged and she told me, "Well, no, as you took the ring back!" I simply said, "Oh" - what I didn't tell her was that I had given her up as lost and had then given the ring to my Mum... and there was no way I was getting it off my Mum's finger without the use of a mask and a gun.

So, Diane and I got engaged twice, with a brand new ring and a new engagement party with pissed off guests from the first time around buying less expensive presents this time, ha-ha! Now we were together again, and nothing was going to split us up ever again - little did I know my Moog Synth had other ideas!

Leicester, 1986

Hazel was a lovely girl I had met in a place of work, she was a bit dippy and was a geeky looking Salvation Army Officer that looked cute in her uniform. Once, when I met her in town, she tried to get me to go into a meeting - I said, "No, I don't believe in imaginary Gods!" (Although, I do believe in imaginary friends.)

We were diametrically opposed, philosophically speaking, but she was lusting after me - maybe her sex genes just switched on, I don't know, but she was nice to be with despite being a bit plain and bookish (in an endearing way), and she was a great kisser who could snog for the Olympics! I was always the gentleman, of course, and I never, ever made her feel uncomfortable, and never tried to seduce or sex her up in any way as she was nothing less than a virgin at twenty one. A lot of our time together was spent just enjoying those kisses and being subjected to her over-indulgence in fictional biblical characters that frankly bored me to tears (for fuck's sake, why do they get hooked into this shit at such an early age?).

Her Mum was a divorced, battle axe who had a face like a fucking fat bulldog chewing a Wasp off a Nettle leaf that had been pissed on! I did not like her much - she was as bitter as lemons and a new convert to Feminism (Fem-Nazis), hated guys, and everything guys were. Unsurprisingly, she hated me, but put up with me because of Hazel, I assume. I frequently wanted to slap her, but don't really know why - just had one of those faces that looked like it needed it :-)

One day Hazel came to my flat, just off the Narborough Road, she had come straight from the Salvation Army Mission meeting, just across from the 'Hay Market' shopping mall in 'Charles Street'. Anyway, I let her in and, fuck me, she looks really fucking hot and sexy in her little uniform. As she sits and crosses her legs, I get a flash of suspenders (the proper, hold up ones), and my cock starts to twitch. Now, I must admit, up until this point, Hazel had not turned me on in any way - sure, she was a great kisser, but had no sex appeal whatsoever. If you can imagine 'Olive' from 'On The Buses' (the seventies comedy show still running in endless loops on ITV3), you will get the idea of how sexless she was (not that she looked like Olive in any way, I must point out - lol).

So, she is sitting there and I am looking at her in an entirely different light. She tells me to kiss her, so I do, and then she looks at me and says, "I'm a Virgin!" to which I nodded in agreement, 'of course you are'. Hazel then takes me to the bedroom and jumps upon me, fully dressed, and we snog and roll about for a while. Then she commands me to go to the 'Western Pub', near the Bridge, at the bottom of Briton Street, and get some condoms! I am back in four seconds flat and have my cock firmly planted, deep inside of her (she still has her uniform on, and it just adds to the naughtiness of the moment).

I make love to her in all the positions I know from

the cheap porn tapes you get from the video store. I have her on her knees and I'm fucking her hard from behind when I suddenly feel this blinding pain in the tip of my nob - I have missed the opening and hit her squarely on the bone somehow. Hazel has not noticed I have screamed like a Banshee and stopped thrusting like Thomas the Tank Engine as she is wrapped in ecstasy (hehe, of course). I look down and my cock is trickling blood into the condom, so I gasp and run to the loo to dowse it in cold water (maybe overdid it, huh?). I take a good ten minutes cooling it down and making sure there is no more bleeding - now all too aware that hitting a bone with the tip of your penis is bloody sore! I go back to see if Hazel is alright and, ha-ha, fucking hell, she is still on the bed with her bum up and has not even noticed I have gone! Since she still seems to be operating at a high working temperature, I slip back in and continue thrusting and shunting for another fifteen minutes, then collapse onto the bed with her and cuddle up for a few hours before starting all over again.

And the moral of this particular story? Well, if your love life is on the wane, buy her a Salvation Army uniform and do a bit of fantasy role play, or try and find a real Sally Ally girl (as the old saying goes 'the quiet ones are the dirtiest', and I can personally vouch for that!).

I lost touch with her after six months or so as I had to return to Glasgow for a family meltdown, and the last I had heard she was slagging me off in a Leicester pub, calling me a Scots git! Ah, well - I'm sorry if I broke your hymen... and your heart, my dear. Sometimes I think of her on a Sunday when I hear brass bands and sermons on street corners... and sometimes I smile to myself when I think that I introduced her to a very different kind of 'Rock' to worship (I can feel all the Fem-Nazis fuming at me right now, hehe).

CHAPTER THIRTEEN

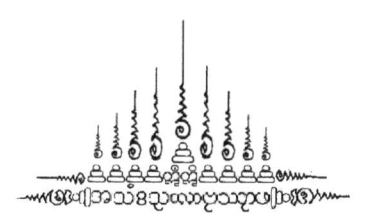

COMPUTER LOVE

A nod to personal computers and *'The Antikythera Mechani*sm'

Another lonely night,
```
01100011  01101111  01101101  01110000
01110101  01110100  01100101  01110010
00100000  01101100  01101111  01110110
01100101
```

Lots of people often assume I have been working with computers all my life - boy, are they wrong! Okay, to really explain how I got into computers for a living, we need to go back to 1987. I was still pinning my hopes on getting a record deal in a 'band' and had just come back from a brief sojourn in England. I had previously and regrettably sold my existing music gear - my beloved Moog Source, Poly Moog, Mini Moog and a few other toys I had gathered over the years. So here am I with a girl from England in tow and had we had just gotten a new flat on the Balgary Hill area of Springburn (yeah, bandit country).

Now, Sue was a lovely, sweet girl I had met in Mansfield, just a few miles north of Nottingham, where I was living in a rented house with my reprobate brothers and girlfriend. I had met Sue at a pub in town a few nights earlier where she just about sucked my tonsils out my throat and ripped the hairs from my chest with her bare hands. I remember the sex we used to have, it was almost always in the street, up against a wall, or over a park bench. Exciting, yes! Preferred, no! We would do it every night - even in the bloody rain and snow, and only ever three times at her parents' house or where I was living. Anyway, somehow I managed to ask her to come to Glasgow with me, and that was that! Something I would later learn to regret.

I don't know what it is, but everyone I have ever been with has always benefited from being with me and never myself - something I could never work out. Sue managed to get a great job in the 'House Of Fraser' financial department in Glasgow city centre, and here was me - still looking for something to do before my funds ran out and I had to go begging to the wicked 'social' department and all which that entails. Well, bless her little heart, she says to me, "Can I buy you something to cheer you up? Seeing as I have a good job and all!" "Fucking yes, you can", I said to myself! She then says, "Okay, but nothing more than a grand!" ...Wow, a grand! This woman is fucking great!

So, here I am, browsing round fucking McCormack's once again, looking for a suitable bit of kit when I spy this new digital 'Kawai K1' bundled with something called an 'Alesis' Midi Recorder (fuck knows what it was, but it would change my life shortly). I got home and immediately plugged this new toy in, played some old tunes from it, and it was great - a bit cold-sounding and harsh (well, that's digital for you), but nice enough and would do me just fine. Now the other part of the gear was a mystery to me as I tried to figure it out without any help from the reading material. Typical guy - we don't need to read instructions... but later on I learned that in order to get the most out of new tech, it's best to RTFM (more routinely called READ THE FUCKING MANUAL). This package had come with things called 'midi cable' and after I had figured out where to insert them on the Synth and the Alesis midi thing, I was just about mentally knackered. This was all new to me, new technology, no simple analogue gear - now we have buttons with menus and sub menus and a little window to see it all in, algorithms for sounds and effects. Fuck me, this is a challenge.

Being Boiled

Okay, all hooked up, what am I forgetting? Using headphones for now, (no amp yet, but it's on its way). Right, all set - here we go. The fucking Alesis thing is blinking lights at me and wants me to 'press record'... I'm thinking "Record what? There's no fucking tape, you piece of plastic shit!"

Anyway, I press 'record' and play something - and this midi thing starts a metronome sound. I play a few bars and then stop - the Alesis thing stops too, then I press 'play' and, fuck me, it plays back the very thing I had just played (including the timing error, hehe). This is fucking brilliant! I can see the potential - it's like a reel to reel recorder thing without tape, but has internal storage of some sort, and after reading the manual again it says I can 'multi-track'! Oh, now this is all making sense to my out of touch brain. To be fair, it was one of the first of its kind and I had been out the music loop for about a year at this point.

So, I can 'multi-track' eight (8) parts and play them back (polyphony allowing), providing up to twenty eight (28) note polyphony - the Alesis steals notes if I go over that amount. Okay, good, I understand, got it now... I can see that one day this is going to be fucking immense! But I somehow feel it will take a little bit of the 'soul' out of playing music and can envisage a future of just pressing buttons to robotically play previously recorded parts! The actual potential for this is massive! I have recorded nearly a whole album of music and figured how to take a 'line out' to the analogue tape deck to make a 'master tape', and it's only taken me one week to complete this - that's from the drums to the keyboard parts and lead... okay, so, no guitar and vocals, but the technology is looking interesting.

I met up with Jonn Harton and Jim McKenna a few months after this and subsequently got involved with them doing more stuff. I think by that time I had mastered the Midi recorder side of things, but it was still a bit away from using it in a live situation as it felt mechanical and was not tried and tested to such a point I trusted it to work reliably.

'White Heat' - a new band and a new direction, with some very good material. My favourite riff was 'The Company of Women', and a rehash of 'I Don't Believe in Love'. We did actually do a gig somewhere in Glasgow, I think near the 'STV' studios, and went straight back into the classic situation our last band, VIVA, had found itself in - no-one in the audience was ready for what we had played... they all stared in confused silence. We were at least two or three years ahead of similar things and feeble minds were just not ready for it - we were the 'Leonardo Da Vinci's and Aristotle's of music', much too advanced for simple minds.(no pun intended)

No-one willing to take a chance on us, we were too off the wall, not mainstream enough, I guess, and certainly not everyone's cup of digital tea. Lots of 'awake' people at the gig complemented us on what we were trying to accomplish, but the 'Hoi Polloi' of the ordinary masses just did not get it one fucking little bit! Lots of people are low frequency and will always be on that level of existence, never moving forward and always only assimilating whatever fodder is the offer of the day. Un-fucking-believable!

I'd felt lost and a bit weird after splitting up from the previous band, we had so much going for us at that point and it seemed it was only a matter of time before we were all media stars... but some things never happen for whatever reason.

Sue was lovely - she was a top whore in bed, but had unfortunate, giant, ugly, flappy, pussy lips (again) that always made me think of gammon rashers (ha-ha), but not as tasty... but she was good fun and buying me a Synthesizer and other gear was an unexpected pleasure from her. Eventually Sue had been offered another job back down in England, something to do with 'Harrods Financial Services', and she was making noises that she would be leaving soon and did I want to come with her? I was well pissed off! With no offer of work for myself yet, struggling to get back into the music stuff, as well as trying to learn computers back in the eighties with no training and no internet to guide me... I felt fucked up in my head again.

I told Sue that evening, "Okay, if you have the job, I will come with you to wherever it was."

She said, "It's in Leeds!"

I groaned and replied, "Oh, fuck! Not there - it's a shit hole... worse than Glasgow."

So, in the end, we decided we would move to Leicester on a temporary basis (as it was easier for me to find work there) and she would commute to Leeds until I had something and could transfer up. I eventually got a job in Sainsbury's as a Bakery Manager for the time being (although later I was their Systems Data Manager).

I felt bad about leaving 'White Heat' as it was a great little package - the songs were good, but the project needed a more solid direction and the 'ahead of the times' curse was still haunting us... we were constant victims of circumstances beyond our control and I felt it would never be our time as we always outpaced the current trend in chart music. In the end, I knew I had to go, and I thought moving back to England would help me at least get back on some sort of even keel... and, to be honest, my family were doing my head in again.

So this is how I had got into computers. I knew the Alesis midi thing was a step in the right direction, and a few months later I was the proud owner of an 'Atari 520' computer, only purchased because it had MIDI ports built into it, (Musical Instrument Digital Interface), meaning I could hook up my synths to this computer, load up a bit of software (I think it was called 'Pro 24'), and it was essentially a twenty four (24) track fucking recording suite. Altogether it cost me around nine hundred pounds (£900), which was a lot of money in the late eighties.

I had it all sussed, was busy recording stuff in this computer, playing it back, and then recording it onto tape - fuck me, I was writing my own albums in the house... this is fucking brilliant! But more than a year later the Atari stopped working - it would switch on, but it would behave erratically and I was lost without it. I called Atari and they said it would need to come back to them, costing about four to five hundred pounds (£400 to £500) to repair it. I was livid - these were still new things in the tech world and the prices were hilariously fucking unreachable. So I asked the guy how much the schematics were and he said fifteen pounds (£15), but I really had to know what I was doing with it and needed some sort of engineering degree before even attempting it or I could make it worse. I could hear his scornful laughter under his breath as he talked to me, smart arsed cunt that he was!

Anyway, the schematics arrive for the Atari 520 and I have a look at this huge document and map of circuit boards etc. I list the most common problems on another troubleshooting sheet, and the one that hit out the most obviously to me was a little resistor thing that looked burned and misshapen. Next, I track down the offending part at a local electronics shop and bought myself a little soldering iron. I sat there for an hour or so getting this tiny thing out of the circuit board, then put the new one in and solder it into place - it took me a few tries and a nasty burn to my finger, but I managed it. Now, the moment of truth... I turned the Atari on and, fuck me sideways, it worked! Fucking hell, I fixed a computer and I did it without the degree and the training, maybe I'm a natural? Maybe I'll look into it in more detail later, perhaps I can get some decent training or a degree and get a half decent job?

I did eventually have loads of training, paid for expensive courses and exams, and got some professional credentials that served me well into the 90's and beyond, but technology moves on so fast and there is not enough time or money to sit more courses when you are working daily, so everything is on 'catch up' and 'hands on' - something that can demand a difficult and different learning curve every few months.

Well, here I am - my first 'real' computer job, starting in the late 80's and going into the early nineties, sorting out Home Computers (PCs) running 'Windows 3', having already cut my teeth on the Atari and Amiga operating systems as well as 'Windows' 1, 2, and 2.11 operating systems a few years earlier while I was learning it all from the expensive training courses. Frankly, I found it easy to assimilate and the information just flowed effortlessly into my cerebral cortex and neural pathways, filling my empty mind with new knowledge... not knowing that in a few years' time it would prove to be an annoyance dealing with people who had no or a limited understanding of the computers they were using in their everyday lives.

I mean, for logics sake, I have heard Teachers at

many schools and colleges state that they can't teach their lesson if the computer does not work - they are so disconnected from their own brains now that it's fucking scary! These 'Educators' now have no 'Plan B' and simply shut down as their intelligence has been so dumbed down to a GCSE level or less - paradoxically new students/teenagers born in the early millennium are now starting to show signs that they have no idea how to use a computer or even comprehend why you would want one! They have been conditioned into the 'touch' world of tablets and smart phones so that any form of thought process has become obsolete and even a hindrance to them. This phenomena reminds me of that classic film based on H.G. Wells, 'The Time Machine', where the traveller goes so far into the future he finds that over the eons 'humans' have lost the ability to learn and retain knowledge. People in that era are mindless and need constant guidance, but with no-one there left to guide them and as all the people who maintained the machines eventually died out too, the skills to keep everything running was somehow lost. Is this going to be the shape of things to come?

Personally, I think the more technology progresses, the dumber we become. It's inevitable that we will get to such a point, where we will probably be able to control things by a neuron implant connected to the world wide web that talks to all the gadgets we so heavily depend on - so that with just a mere thought that transmutes to something the implant can beam out on the web to our devices and gadgets, we will be able to control them without the need to touch them. This theory is not even beyond today's science and will probably become the norm very soon... assuming we have not annihilated ourselves in the interim with all the nonsense that is transpiring around the planet Earth just now.

What a connected world that would be... but with disconnected people unable or unwilling to engage real people on the street or sitting next to you. If you are thinking that would not happen, just take a look around you right now - how many people are sitting next to you, texting or emailing, and have no interaction with their environment... be it at the doctors or supermarket or coffee houses? We are all going the same way.

I would rather text than call someone I don't really want to deal with - it's becoming the 'norm', people texting each other in the same fucking room! Remote communication now seems to be socially preferable - rather than to vocalize their thoughts into the spoken word. Just take, for example, computer games that are so real and so violent that they can program your mind and de-sensitize you to accept violence to such a level that you lose your empathy to the 'real violence' going on around the world today. I really worry for us all as we seem to be losing our humanity more and more each day - I love technology, but there is another dimension to how it's integrated into our lives and it's not the way I envisioned it when I used to watch 'Tomorrow's World' on our TV, back in the days of my youth.

People seem to have become more nasty and vitriolic online, using fake personas and hiding behind the mask to intimidate and bully others they have never and will never meet - I am skipping past the obvious impact the web has on positive learning etc. and focusing on the human psyche's ability to bend things to their will and use them for nefarious purposes, to hurt people on a whole new level. Why would we do such things? Internet 'Trolls' who, for the sheer pleasure of it, hurt and damage everyone they come into contact with and can turn any topic toxic and poison it with their insidious thoughts, just for the fun of it!

We've probably all done it at some point or another, been on a chat site and pretended to be more than we are with a little white lie misrepresenting yourself - and there's no real harm in a little fantasy role play now and then (according to Freud, anyway), or accidentally browsing some porn just to see what's out there hehe. We are only human and we are flawed, but we must remember to keep perspective and maintain the roots to our own humanity and, as Ayn Rand, was once quoted as saying,

> *"He/She is free to evade reality, he/she is free to unfocus his/her mind and stumble blindly down any road he/she pleases, but not free to avoid the abyss he/she refuses to see."*

Computer Love

Technology does not stand still and computers do make some things obsolete, including people, and this is wrong on many levels. The day we elevate the machine above humanity is the day we lose our way. Old does not mean obsolete, people will always be people and there are many skills we should keep alive for the times when the technology does not work or some disastrous Sun activity sends us back to the Stone Age. We do not want to end up being the 'Eloy' from that H.G. Wells Novel! We have too much to lose! I love computers, but I love all the things we achieve as a collective race of people - all the good things... all the right things.

Artificial Intelligence is here and now, in just a few years we will have Androids of some sorts to carry out menial tasks that humans get bored with... and that's great, but we must not throw people away! Perhaps in the future we can all have a droid that we send to work for us by proxy and still get paid? Who knows?

I am here for the full tour, the full duration of my life and I want to live it before the disease of old age robs me of my faculties and turns me to dust. I have always been a bit misanthropic and usually do not like to talk to adults between the ages of eighteen to thirty five as I think they have no significant life experience. To date I have only met a handful of people who do not bore me to tears or make me lose the will to live when speaking to me - am I claiming to be better than them? No, of course not! It's just my mind is wired in a different way and I have to hide it every day and pretend to be someone else to other people as they would never understand the real person who inhabits their 3D world.

It turns out that Sue and I were only meant to be together for about a year. We had a house in Leicester where I stayed and she commuted to Leeds, but the inevitable happened and she met someone else. Typically, she did not have the courage to tell me outright, and strung me along until I found out what she was really doing behind my back, which disappointed me immensely. But I am used to being knocked down... and flesh is only flesh. In truth, the meeting of our minds was minimal as her path of desire was a very different one from mine - to procreate and add more woes to the population of non-entities that there are already just too many of.

Sex is not everything, and once you get past the pussy, ass, and tits thing, if there is no connection between each other's minds, a void so vast that you cannot find any crossing point that will allow you to meet and meld, there is nothing. A lot of people never get out of this sex cycle. Hey, I'm not saying sex is crap... I love sex, but my idea of sex is probably a bit more advanced or sophisticated than most people's, to say the least.

I really do not operate on a basic level anymore and my libido does not command my cock now - perhaps in a computer sense I have been upgraded and my software is not compatible with software that is still running in 'basic' (hehe!). I know what an arse some of you are probably thinking of me... but some of you will totally understand exactly what I am saying here. (And you know just who you are!)

I have always been fascinated by the Antikythera mechanism ever since its discovery by sponge divers in 1900, dating back at least two thousand years. This has now been classed as the world's first computer, a computational device that could see into the future and map out the phases of the moon and five other known planets discovered in that time. It could also predict lunar eclipses and solar eclipses, and over the years it has been x-rayed, digitized and put into 3D render - in addition to which many working models based on the design have been made over the last few years.

The Antikythera mechanism is an ancient, analogue computer designed to predict astronomical positions and eclipses for calendric and astrological purposes, as well as the Olympiads (the cycles of the ancient Olympic Games). Found housed in a '340mm × 180mm × 90mm' wooden box, the device is a complex clockwork mechanism composed of at least thirty, meshing, bronze gears. Its remains were found as eighty two separate fragments, of which only seven contain any gears or significant inscriptions, are approximately 140mm in diameter and originally had 223 teeth.

The artefact was recovered in 1900–1901 from the Antikythera shipwreck off the Greek island of Antikythera. Believed to have been designed and constructed by Greek scientists, the instrument has been dated somewhere between 150 and 100 BC, or, according to a more recent view, at 205 BC. After the knowledge of this technology was lost at some point in Antiquity, technological artefacts approaching its complexity and workmanship did not appear again until the development of mechanical, astronomical clocks in Europe during the fourteenth century.

All known fragments of the Antikythera mechanism are kept at the National Archaeological Museum of Athens

This is an incredible device and it makes me wonder what happened that this knowledge was somehow lost or forgotten and the mechanics of it did not reappear till the 14th century - where would Humankind be now if we had not lost the technology so long ago? Would we have been centuries ahead now? Would all the things we currently have now been available in the first millennia? We will never know now.

One thing I like to muse over is that perhaps we have had significant technology in the past - has our civilization risen and fallen many times before? Have we lost our way and previous knowledge, only to rediscover it all over again? And, if so, what is the lesson we are not learning in keeping that knowledge? So many questions, but perhaps only one stark and obvious answer - we, as a race, get to a certain point and somehow manage to destroy ourselves, losing everything, and it takes many eons for the survivors' to rise up and start all over again... to learn and perhaps rebuild along a different path each time. What can we do this time to make sure we do not turn our world to ashes again? Fuck me, I'm starting to sound like Erik Von Daniken here.

I was recently on holiday on the island of Lanzarote and, although I was very tempted to take my tablet, I made a firm decision and did not take any technology with me (okay - except my phone, but only used it to read a new chapter of my friend's book). I wanted a distraction free vacation with nothing to think about except feeding myself and communing with nature (and, no... I'm no hippie).

I admit that for the first two days I went cold turkey (or should that be cold circuit?) and felt separated from everything, but eventually I used my five senses to navigate the place I was in and I enjoyed it very much. I spoke to people, I joined in with things, I even managed to enjoy the naïve evening entertainment, and met some really nice people - namely Shereen and her lovely mum, Lydia, who managed to make me smile... and that's a hard thing to do hehe.

Computers are tools and nothing more, we must learn to walk away at times and connect on a real level with real things, to get involved with real situations and help others more. It's too easy to get distracted and forget everything else, so I have promised myself not to have my tablet in my hand every five minutes or have my smartphone in my pocket all the time. Switch them off now and then and re-discover yourself - the computers tablets and phones will be there tomorrow... can you say the same thing about yourself?

I freely admit I am where I am today because of technology, starting with synthesizers, drum machines, and eventually basic computers - all things that shaped my life and helped me crawl out of the abyss of ignorance... and it all started the day I bought the 'Moog synthesizer'. If I had not had bought that object and opened my mind to technical possibilities, I would probably be one of those 'over fifties' who have been left behind in the wake of all the new gadgets and technical advances that I would perhaps be less aware of. In fact, maybe I would have been less aware of many things and taken a completely different path, perhaps a better path? I will never know now, but the path I have been on for the last thirty odd years has been mostly good to me, apart from some annoying human units whom I did not sync with and who managed to disrupt my life on too many occasions.

I have managed to get most of this chapter done without too much swearing, and it has a feeling of the real me injected into it, but don't worry I am sure the cussing will return again in other parts of the book,

The only funny thing I can add to this chapter, I think, is spawned from the reference to my recent holiday and remembering being in the spa almost every day, and especially the Jacuzzi (which sounds like Jack's Uzi, Jonn, lol - personal joke).

Everything stops for tea!

Years ago, when I was around seventeen and had my first holiday somewhere abroad (I think it was Majorca), the Hotel had a bubbling pool that perhaps ten people could squeeze into. It wasn't quite a Jacuzzi, but was very similar, and my lovely girlfriend was in it along with a few others. I had just finished a late breakfast and was going to join her, but my eyes were fascinated by the immense choice of teas on offer, I had never seen anything like it, so I stuffed some differing flavours into my shorts so I could have them later on in the room. Somehow, between liberating the makings of the world's second most popular drink in the world, and getting into the pseudo Jacuzzi, I had forgotten to take the tea bags out of my shorts... and, as I got into the water, they started to seep out until I had this burgeoning, brown cloud swirling around my nether regions. "Fuck me!" I said unconsciously and saw about nine people looking over at me, seeing this growing, darkening, brown coloured cloud emanating from my shorts, growing in volume and darkening in tone. Unsurprisingly, everyone else immediately jumped out the little pool, shocked and horrified by the assumption that I had just emptied my bowels!

The last thing I remember was my Glaswegian girlfriend saying to me, "You are such a fucking tramp," and to this very day I never told anyone it was teabags!

Fucking hell, if that's not classic Scottish... I don't know what is.

CHAPTER FOURTEEN

TIMELESS FLIGHT

The Hill and Hibiscus Flowers

We were sitting, gently passing time and pondering the huge climb ahead of us and wondering, "How can we ever succeed where no man has succeeded before us?"

We asked each other many questions and discovered many new and exciting answers and we felt like pioneers already.

The sun was high in the cloudless, royal blue sky and was punching relentlessly into the back of our heads so that soon we could no longer speak but only sit in silence, gazing in hope at the forbidding monument before us. It was the big, red smell, as it drifted in divine yet ominous wafts into our distant homesteads that first drew us towards the Hill.

And it was the Great White Bush with the voice of Age and Wisdom that encouraged us to stay and to fight.

"Sit beside me," said the White Bush, "and we shall talk of Miracles and ... Water."

"Will we find the water we need to save the thirsty plant-life of our homesteads here, O Great White Bush?" we asked in hope.

And he said to us: "The water of which you speak is at the top of the Hill. There is enough water to give new life to all your dying plant-friends; water precious enough to give them all life such as is enjoyed only by the Giant Red Flowers that dominate the Hill. But no man has ever before reached out his hand far enough to cup and retrieve the water. You must see, your quest is impossible."

"But we are pioneers," we spoke. "We have the strength of youth to fight the Hill and to retrieve the water that will restore plant-life in our homesteads."

"You are youthful, yes; but your hope and juvenile determination are not enough to overcome the big, red smell of the monumental Hill. It will beat you off before you are within reaching distance of the water, for it has a far greater strength, that of Philosophy. And in a battle against the wisdom of maturity, what help will your youthful hope be to you?"

And at this we were angry as only insulted young men can be angry and we fought the old Bush with words of faith. The Bush continued to teach but we were no longer listening. Our hungry minds were fixed on the Hill.

We set out then into the throbbing heat and were at once blinded by the red, red glow and nauseated into a daze by the big, red smell. We clutched each other's hands and we bowed our heads and charged with faith in our hearts and, for an instant, we believed we could make it and gather the water and save the dying world we had left behind.

Halfway up the Hill we rested semi-consciously and talked of our Wind of Change before it became a raging hurricane. Then, without warning, a great wind came unto the Hill and swept us in one human ball into the air and down the Hill. We tumbled helplessly to the bottom and came to rest beside the Great White Bush.

We were again angry and agreed instantly to recommence our quest.

But the Great White Bush spoke to us saying: "You are in pursuit of an illusion, my young and determined friends. The big, red smell will prevent you at all costs from collecting the Water for your suffering plant-friends."

"But", said one of us, "I'm a ratepayer, I can pull a few strings."

And the Bush asked: "What makes you say such a wild and innocent thing?"

"My Father told me this."

"But listen, you again are in pursuit of an illusion."

And he could see our strange and sudden stupefaction at his words of Age and Wisdom and he then said: "I have seen the land of Burns through the eyes of Rimbaud; I have seen calm and unutterable peace such as you'll never know; I have seen all your dreams and heard all your schemes and I tell you, you'll see when you grow."

And he then said: "I have talked with your fathers who have told me of the old times, good times. And I have told them that there are no old times. When they are gone they are dead. There are only new times, now times. And in now times the red smell is big and sweet, but to you it is frightening. But you are so young ...

"And I want you to know that maybe one day the big, red smell will be blown away by another Wind of Change and the Hill will dissipate and leave you with water and peace ... like a Miracle. But again the wind will become a raging hurricane and the strange, red smell will return, sweeter than ever before.

And again you will search for the final answer, the Great Illusion you so constantly pursue.

"You must learn," said the Bush, "that the pain of disillusion is greater still than the pain of hate."

And he repeated: "You are in pursuit of an illusion."

Then he reached to the earth beside him and handed us an Hibiscus flower and told us: "Inhale the sweet, red odour. Be my best friends, go now, please."

We were young and could not speak. We returned solemnly and slightly wise to our homesteads believing the answer must surely lie elsewhere. The Hill looked peaceful, at least.

THE END

"The author and Publisher wish to thank Steve Harley for his kind permission in allowing the use of this piece (copyright Steve Harley 1975)"

I fucking hate liars, and I fucking hate cunts that indulge in subterfuge - you know, these bastards that want you to believe one thing while they are actually saying something else, usually to avoid having to deal with the fall out of actually telling the truth. They sometimes disguise it as 'not wanting to hurt someone's feelings' - so apparently people will lie to save you any kind of embarrassment and any pain the truth may cause you!

Of course most human beings are multifaceted and tell a myriad of complex lies every day to make themselves feel better and to sometimes simply 'fit in'. This is the 'White Lie Syndrome'...

"Does my arse look big in these trousers, darling?" she might ask.

"No, baby, you look great!" A husband would answer his partner's question so as to keep the peace.

It has always fascinated me how many lies people actually get involved in every day, and I like to watch and study as they squirm their way through another one. Most are sycophants, pretending to like someone for whatever reasons they validate it with.

After a promotion? ...then lick the boss's arse and hope no one notices

Trying to get into girls knickers? ...pretend you like the same music as her.

People will say anything to anyone, just to be liked, to be loved, to be in control... but I fucking hate it!

My childhood was a nightmare and my parents were part of that nightmare - pretending to love each other and pretending to love their kids as well. If you have read the previous chapters you will see the shite that my siblings and I had to endure - and I know this is a global disease that perhaps everyone has been involved in at some point in their lives.

I have been honest since my early twenties, much to other people's annoyance, including my family, friends, and work colleagues over the years. I can't count on my fingers and toes how many times I have come to blows with people, verbally or physically, about 'lies'.

Society is based on lies. The Government lies to us every day, while banks and media outlets lie to us profusely for their own reasons. I am not going to get into much about politics and religion in this chapter as I am more interested in telling you why I fucking hate liars - yes, it has to do with my upbringing and my Dad being the number one lying bastard to all of us, especially to my Mum.

I strive to be the best person I can be and to do things in an open and honest way. I may be from the gutter, but I have integrity - that has been tested many times over and has never crumbled... it has made me possess fewer friends, but at least I can sleep at night.

One of my major hates in the world of lies is someone trying to use subterfuge and playing me for a pawn in whatever game of lies they have created or whatever predicament they have managed to get themselves involved in. I pity the people who try to get me to be part of it all and try to get me on their side of the argument - sorry, but it's not going to happen.

I do not care who you are and how close a 'friend' we are now or have been in the past - if you try that with me, I will call you on it and I do not fucking care if you get caught out, end up hurt, or find yourself covered in the fallout of it all. I will not and never will change my position on how I want to get through life.

Some people have asked me, "So, you don't lie at all?" And I actually never do. If I am asked a direct question, I will answer it honestly. If I suspect that answering an obviously loaded question will cause so much pain and suffering, I will simply refuse to answer - I have not lied, but I have not told the truth in the purest sense of the word. This action hurts me, but I am not a complete idiot - to know the difference between maintaining a principle at the expense of causing immense pain. If I do not answer, it's only because I have deemed that by answering directly and truthfully it will cause violence and someone will get hurt through my actions... so, I will simply walk away and not get involved except under the most exceptional circumstances.

I work with some lovely people, namely Ann Marie, Troods, Shaz, Mandip, Tim, Gerry, Ian, Helen, Chris and too many more to mention here but who are as close as I can get to calling friends in England as I don't really have that many 'real' people around me, people that I trust or rely on every day to make me smile or just make my day a little bit easier, so thanks guys you have made me smile and stay far longer that I would have normally.

My poor Mum used to put up with so many lies from my Dad time and time again, over many years. He was usually out shagging other women during the day, as he was often seen with them in and around Springburn or in Glasgow city centre by various friends of my Mum, and he would never 'tell her the truth'... making her think that her friends were lying. He would usually kick the crap out of her for having a go at him (always a major sign of a guilty conscience) and we were too young to understand any of it. We never understood why we were placed in such an abusive situation or why my Mum never had the courage or strength to walk away and leave him.

In retrospect, I would have understood if she had put us all into care to get away from such a violent cunt - perhaps then she would have found true love and real happiness... and, paradoxically, perhaps we would have been better off being adopted out and maybe have been much happier and luckier in life too.

I was always jealous of my cousins, Danny and Elaine, they had my Mum's sister for their mother, my sweet Aunty Betty, and my 'solid as a rock', Uncle Danny, as their father. To me and to my siblings, they were a perfect family, loved and looked after - they always had nice clothes and always had birthday parties and happy Christmases. We never ever had a birthday card or a party - it means nothing to me now, but this hurt so much in the 1960s and 70s.

Years later, when I lived in England with my Aunt Betty and Uncle Danny, they would tell me bit and pieces of my Mum and Dad's life, and how my Dad had an equally twisted father who would mistreat him and his two brothers and sister, David, Rab, and Margaret, all whom had kids to pass their own brand of misery onto.

I seemed to want to distance myself from all of them, never blaming them for who they were, but more for what they didn't do to change the cycle of shit they seemed to have been caught in and were now passing onto their own kids - all of whom seem to be under educated to one degree or another. Okay, so, yes - I am from the same stock, but I think I managed to evolve and to self-manage myself to such a point there was a profound paradigm shift. I became 'persona non grata' after I left my miserable life, and after many years I feel like a complete stranger to my siblings and my parents, who still seem to think I am the same person who left the boiling pot in the 80s.

I was at Colston secondary school during the early 1970s and was more or less the same as everyone else at that time in the school - I never really thought about my future or a career path. Other kids may have had more concerned parents and a better chance to be something or do something else in life, but the 'Scott' family were cursed to failure at school and doomed to making a meagre living in life - this being one of the reasons I have never had kids of my own... and although my life took a completely different path, I still took the firm decision not to have them. Perhaps, in retrospect, I did this to catch up on things I had missed in my own childhood.

I know a lot of you reading this probably had a similar upbringing and perhaps find this painful to read as it brings back too many unpleasant memories - but, believe me, it's best to face up to them and move on... or they will haunt you forever, already adding weight to some psychological damage that never really healed within you. I truly hope some of you managed to better yourselves as I believe I did.

How did I cope with it all? I think getting out of the house at an early age really helped, and then moving away altogether definitely helped. It took many years, but I managed to put the past behind me and make peace with the demons that haunted me. Now I do not blame my parents for the crap life anymore - I know they too were victims of circumstance. Poverty, having four kids, both of my parents having dreams of their own and never being able to get anywhere near them, then getting angrier and more lost as the years went by and transferring that pain and anger of a life never realised onto their own kids until they too became part of the cycle of lies and violence - that's the reality of it.

I imagine my brothers and sister will read this and a part of them will hate it and probably hate me a bit for writing it. Perhaps they will try to deny any of it or certain parts of it really happened, but my feelings are that they have hid it or just got on with life and put it down to 'it's Glasgow - we all lived like this, right?' The answer to that would be a resounding 'No!'

I know Harry, my elder brother, has never once been able to say he loves Mum or Dad, either to himself or to them. I can still see and hear the pain in his voice. When I had a talk with him about the past, he seemed deeply upset and I felt a little guilty for taking him down memory lane - sorry, bro.

My younger brother, David, is more verbal about the past and calls my Dad a 'fuck nugget' and my Mum 'a pain in the arse' - it's his way of dealing with the past. I know he was more drawn to my Uncle Danny as he would not stand for any nonsense and would put David in his place or tell him off - this evolved into a deep respect which my brother still reminisces about to this day.

As we hurtle towards oblivion we only have a short, finite time to be the best we can be, from whatever beginnings we hailed from and to whatever end awaits us. So, for me, being the best I can be is important to me... for me! Sure, I enjoy many things around me and detest many more. I am in my early fifties, reasonably healthy, reasonably happy, and looking forward to doing some more travelling before any care worker has to wipe my arse and tuck me into bed at night.

Life has been long and hard, and I have journeyed through it the best way I can. I was never disrespectful to the older generation before me, but of course I was young and thought I knew all the answers and how could anyone older relate to things that they did not understand - Punk music! Fashion! Girls! Parties! But, as I grew older, I started to understand that the advice of some of the older people I knew years ago was so spot on and so profoundly, annoyingly correct. Being so young and arrogant blinds you to the meaning of the words, even though you understand them as they are spoken to you, and I now find myself saying the same things to the youth of today I meet. I feel philosophical and very knowledgeable, but I know they will be the same as the younger me was and nothing I say will make sense until they reach that point in their lives where mind and heart meet and everything becomes clear.

This is one of the reasons I do not lie, play silly mind games, or indulge in fancy semantics - I say what I mean and make it as clear and open as I possibly can be so that there is no room for misinterpretation. My friend, Jonn, in Glasgow is one of the few people I know who is as truthful and open as I am and for that I am grateful - I know he will not pander to anything and certainly not massage any egos as I would never do.

I need the truth as much as it helps or hurts me -

it's the only way I can be certain that everything in my life is as real as it can be. I choose not to believe in any Gods because no one can prove the existence of one to me. I am not disrespectful to any religion as we are all free to follow whatever we want to believe in - but, by the same token, if you can't prove it exist... it means nothing to me and is not the truth, so therefore does not add value to my life.

Life is complicated and shitty enough without compounding it with lies, subterfuge and fucking other people's heads up with even more crap - so, come on, guys, keep it real... and you will only be the best you can be.

I don't know why it is, but the further south you go in the UK, the worse the people are - not all of them, of course. I don't want to generalise, but I have been here a long time and, in my personal experience of dealing with southerners, in every place I have lived, there arc too many cunts who like to lie and talk bollocks.

I'm not having a go at all southerners, before you all go off on a witch hunt or start trolling the Internet to burn me, it's just my personal view of lots of individuals I have met. It makes it hard work to get on with people who are constantly full of shit and infecting every conversation they get involved in with lies and subterfuge.

Northerners generally do not do this, and you can count on a northerner being straight with you to the point of point blank honesty that may hurt you or put you in your place. I am trying not to be too biased here, but it's obvious that there is a difference between the two regions - people as far as, say, Manchester will have the same northern qualities and not bullshit you too much.

I find it kind of sad, and try not to let it get to me too much, but some cunts I just can't ignore and I have to be Scottish with them to get them to be straight with me and to stop fucking me about - they don't like it and they especially don't like being outed as a lying bastard! So, remember, be careful as this can go tits up and work against you - but, for me, I stick to my guns and do not let anyone try this shit on me... even it means them never speaking to me again! No fucking great loss to me!

Maybe it's due to my humble beginnings and all the stress of being poor and from a poor area, but it makes you more honest and you learn a lot about life really quickly.

In reference to Steve Harley's 'The Hill and the Hibiscus Flowers' at the beginning of this chapter, it took me all my teenage years to finally work out what the fuck it was about. When we are young, we think we know all the answers and older people are just burned out, smelly, old fucks who don't know anything - right? Wrong! Learning from your elders is, in fact, the only way you will ever learn anything of any value pertaining to yourself - well, any elder who has anything worthwhile to speak about the trials and tribulations of life and living it decade by decade. My life would have certainly been a lot different if I had only listened to my Mum about marriage for example, and although I listened to her about it, in my young, fucked up mind, I would only think, "Yeah, but it'll be different for me - what the fuck do you know?" What a young and arrogant arse I was in my early twenties, to think that I knew better than someone who had been married for almost thirty years - what the fuck do old people know about young people and what we want... it's a different world from where and when they were born, right?

I was so wrong about so many things, so many times, and only since my late thirties did something switch on in my brain and I would hear a voice in my head asking myself questions. Two marriages down and numerous girlfriends later, all of a sudden I realised that I should be learning to expand my mind and my life, and not thinking from my cock like so many guys do! It was time to be alone, time to think about me and what I wanted from my life that I had never thought about having before!

Thankfully I had not spawned any brats, as that would have been a tragedy, and my life would have spiralled downwards to the abyss that some Youngers fall into. Looking back over the years, at all the women and marriages, I am still amazed that I managed to keep kids out of the equation. Yes, yes, of course kids are okay for some people and I am sure they get a lot of enjoyment from them, but I wanted something more in my life - to learn to explore my own mind and my path. Travelling really opened my mind, and as new cultures and new experiences came to me, the more philosophical I became... and I liked it!

I began seeing the world through different eyes and not just the 'Eat - Fuck - Sleep' cycle that a lot of us live our lives by. The little guy that was me in Glasgow all of those years ago has long since changed, and when I look back at my life it's like a fucking bad dream that surely did not happen! If I'd had the intellect back then, there is no knowing how my life would have been changed today. I estimate that by the time I am seventy I may know enough about life to actually enjoy it and make something really special of myself - but, of course, the Grim Reaper will be on my tail and my health will probably be letting me down. I don't have any regrets about not getting to this level sooner, it's better to have gotten this far at all than to still be in the quagmire of misery I was given at the start of my life.

I look around at kids today and potentially a lot of them have the ability to learn more about life and to get as much out of it as they can - to discover what their path is and to help themselves and others understand the need to dig deeper into your inner self and free themselves from the cycle of Born, Live, Die. There is so much more about life than just 'going through the motions' or following the 'path frequently travelled' - free your mind, and for fuck's sake throw the TV out the window... you will not find your life in that box full of subvertisements. Don't consume everything like a virus.

Sadly a lot of kids I see today are as lost as I ever was and it will take them till near the end of their lives to discover what life is... and you probably only have one chance at it. Don't squander the days on Earth watching shit TV shows or playing console games or you will never understand what you have been truly missing - the chance to become part of everything, everywhere, and with everyone ...no barriers, no boundaries, no limits!

You are the Sun, The Moon, The Planets and the Universe! But we just tend to live like rats in a cage, fighting, preying on each other, ready to kill and to die for something we do not understand or even desire.

Fuck religions - you will not find the answer to life there. Run up the hill of life, discover things on the way, listen to wiser people, and learn the true value of yourself. Find a place in your life cycle and learn to live - it's time to wake up!

The Hill looks peaceful, at least.

Hairless Ape, my arse!

Lost my hair in my early forties, no one else in my family has lost theirs so I can only assume it's a throwback from a distant gene from another bald fucker in my family tree - so, thanks for that!

However, my body tries to make up for the loss by granting me extra hair on my back, knees, arse and chest. This drives me bloody crazy and I have had to shave it down a bit every few weeks. I usually accomplish this in the bath with the help of one of those rechargeable, body shaving things - so I generally get the hair off my shoulders, knees, and most of my arse.

Well, at one point I had to ask this lady (she knows who she is) to help me out in the arse department - and I asked her to give me a good shave there. Now, when you say 'arse' to anyone's partner who speaks English, they usually agree it's the arse cheeks and shave you there accordingly - I like a smooth bum, what can I say?

Anyway, I asked this lady to do it for me and I innocently say... "Hi, Babes, can you shave my arse for me?"

But in her minimal understanding of English, she interprets this a little differently. As I am bent over, arse up (the best way to shave it - obviously) she sticks this charged up hair trimmer right on my fucking chocolate starfish causing me to scream like a pig being spit roasted!

It felt like a thousand tiny teeth rimming me and was as painful as terminal 'haemorrhoids' dipped in 'scotch bonnet' chillies and doused with concentrated lemon juice! It was so mind-bogglingly painful that it took a whole week for the pain to subdue. I no longer ask her to shave my bum anymore... and she still bursts into fits of laughter when I say "I'm just off to shave my arse!"

CHAPTER FIFTEEN

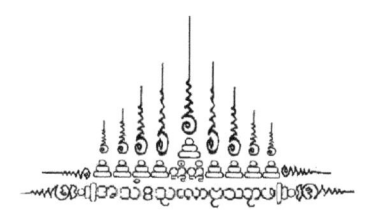

GHOSTS

It's been along time since I moved away for the sake of health, sanity and my future. A part of me is sad that I had to do that, but Glasgow prepared me for life on the road, gave me a good grounding and a full dose of humility to take with me on my travels... of which there were many - some good, some bad, but life's a journey, not a destination! So, I still have no idea what life really has in store for me and that's the only thing that makes me feel alive sometimes. It's not money, it's not my car, it's not my life now, but the fact that it's not over and anything is possible. I expect something to reach out to me soon, good or bad, I have no idea which, but so much of my life has revolved and evolved around equal measure of pain and happiness... and it has made me who I am - resilient, resourceful and grateful for the opportunities that have come to me and those still to come.

I often go back to Glasgow and catch up with my two brothers, Harry and David, my sister, Wendy, and my parents. At first it was fucking weird living away from Glasgow, I felt very vulnerable and often nearly came back, but the little 'voice' in my head would talk me out of it and so I stayed with my Aunt Betty and Uncle Danny. They were very supportive and never once took money off me when I eventually got myself a job. My Aunt's Scottish and has been in England, a very, very long time, where she has been happy with her chosen life away from Glasgow too, and I can never thank them enough for all they did for me. My Uncle sadly passed away many years ago now, but my Aunt Betty is still as active as ever and, at eighty plus, still going to line dancing!

Sometimes I drive around Glasgow and try to take it all back in. I park the car at Charing Cross and walk along Sauchiehall Street, passing the big dance hall that used to be called Tiffany's - the place where I did some 'paid' disco dancing as a warm up act and nearly got gang raped by a bunch of brute-ugly, fucking nurses with arms like 'Popeye the Sailor'. Standing at the door, I can see myself inside, a ghost of myself so long ago, so eager, so bright and with no idea where my life was going to go. I did not think I would be standing here thirty eight years later, remembering all the great times I had in this dance hall - all the girls I knew and loved... I wonder what happened to them? How many of them escaped or how many found peace with what they had... I will never know. Moving away in the early 80s, when all we had to keep in touch with was paper and a pen or a public call box, I lost touch with everyone and everything up to a point - but memories are forever, and I can still recall their faces, the kisses, hugs, and all the great times we had beyond the doors I am standing before now.

I walk a few yards along the road to the very first disco I ever went to, named 'Shuffles'. Some Glaswegians would often call it a 'Ned' palace, and it was, but only upstairs, whereas downstairs was where all the 'Poseurs' went to dance - the cool looking ones were having a ball, our kind of music and our kind of people. If a 'Ned' happened to come downstairs (they looked sort of like rockers - flared denims, with Kung-fu jumpers, and a set of brogue shoes), they soon turned tail and went back upstairs, just being so out of place.

We were 'The Tomorrow People', the future! Hey, I had a 'man bag' back in 1976 - it was trendy to buy a khaki, gas mask bag from the 'Army Surplus Store', and most 'Poseurs' had one. I had a change of shirt, a small bottle of 'Irn Bru', a comb (but more than likely a Denman hair brush), and would have a bar of chocolate for some much needed energy during the long night of sweaty dancing. I look at the flight of stairs leading up to the entrance and remember all the times I waited in the queue with a girl - Jan, Ann, Sophie, Patricia, and many more. I see the corner I would stand in to 'snog' them while trying to cop a feel of their boobs or feel them rubbing my 'fun stick'. I feel a tear well up in my eyes when I think back to all those days and nights of my youth.

Sauchiehall Street looks different now, there seem to be more and more eating places and shops in general - it feels different too. There seems to be a lack of energy about it, and it has the feel of an ordinary street, just like any one in any other city. I always got a buzz from walking down this street - such a shame it has become homogenised and 'diverse', losing its soul and identity. As I walk a bit further, I turn down Hope Street, which eventually goes down to Glasgow Central Station. I don't feel any connection with this street, but the train station is perhaps where I would cut through to Union Street, on my way to the infamous 'Dizzy Corner' (which, if I remember correctly, was the corner before 'Boots the Chemist'), where most people arranged a date with someone and got stood up. When your date didn't turn up, this was called a 'Dizzy' in Glasgow parlance - most people would walk by it and say to a guy or girl, "Aww, did you get a Dizzy?" (The bastards - ha-ha). It happened to me twice and I still don't know why they did not turn up - I was left standing around like a dick with a bunch of flowers that usually ended up in a bin a few hours later and me riding the bus home for another five knuckle shuffle. I mean, WTF was wrong with women back then?

Central Station was another meeting place, but it was always full of drunks and 'Lobby Dossers' (tramps) begging for wine money. This is a grand old place with a posh hotel ensconced within the Station - I remember that someone once told me that Laurel and Hardy had stayed here while on their tour of Great Britain many years ago, and Danny Kaye too. I wonder how many more famous figures of yesteryear have graced its bedrooms and met the people of Glasgow, who are, by default, one of the friendliest and most helpful people on the planet - something a lot of southerners seem to have lost... if they ever fucking had it at all!

Argyle Street! It, too, has sadly lost its way and has become one of those tired shopping experiences you see in any modern city, whereas before it had its own vibrancy and its own life. 'Sloan's Bar', on the corner of Buchanan Street - what a fucking great place that was back in the 70s and 80s... as was 'The Mars Bar' on Howard Street, just off St. Enoch Square (later forced to change its name to 'The Countdown' after Mars instigated legal action to stop them using the name of their chocolate bar product). This was a little venue where many Scottish bands played before answering the call to fame and fortune - I seem to remember 'Simple Minds' and 'Skroo' (I think one of the guys from Simple Minds played for them, and one of them became the front-man for

H20 too), Altered Images, The Zones, The Berlin Blondes, The Zips, The Cuban Heels, Owen Paul and The Venigmas - all of whom has their moment in the sun. The Mars Bar was a great place to hang about - we were definitely underage, but that just added to the fun... we just used to dance around anyway! I remember 'Ken Dodds' (Mods) would hang out there too, and remember seeing the funniest thing near there. I was walking along the street when a mod came flying down on his scooter with about 40 mirrors on it (never fucking understood the mirrors part, how many do you fucking need?), anyway, the 70s Mods were still at odds with Rockers (Heavy Metal dudes) - the ones that drove big fucking motor bikes (yeah, those guys). I see the Mod pull up beside the Rocker at the traffic lights and then give him the finger before he shot off as fast as he could on his 125cc scooter - hopeless! The 500cc bike caught up with him in seconds and, as I turned the corner, I saw the Rocker throwing the scooter into a big skip at the side of the road and kicking the Mod up the arse - haha, served the cunt right! Brilliant!

Howard Street was usually full of drunk women or 'Hen Party' women who would drag the 'Bride-to-be' around all the pubs, banging and crashing on pots and pans. They would stop you and you would have to give up some cash before the 'Bride-to-be' would kiss you on the lips - not bad for fifty pence... I just wished they would shave before they came out.

George Square - this was where all the late buses

would be waiting for the disco crowds to come out. I think the last bus was at 3am. Waiting in or around the square was brilliant, there were about a thousand or more people waiting for buses and we would all mingle together - a great way to meet new and interesting people. Most times there were cat-fights amongst the girls, and the odd fight between idiots. One of my best friends John Starrs got stabbed here, after a night out at 'Shuffles', some dick stabbed him in the stomach and ruined the night - he was okay, but after that I never really saw him much and I am sure his family emigrated to the USA sometime after. George Square also feels different now - they have a fucking 'Ferris Wheel' thing and large screens reminiscent of Piccadilly Circus and Times Square. Once again, I feel slightly sad, although it certainly looks better, cleaner and has a more contrived look about it - but it could be anywhere, any other big, British city. I look across to what used to be 'The Copthorne Hotel' and the place where I proposed to my second wife in the early nineties... no, it's not a fucking hobby!

I pluck up courage to drive back to my old primary school and the area where I was brought up on Keppochill Road. I feel slightly apprehensive, it's been a long time since I have been here and I am not sure if I am ready to face more ghosts from the past. I'm standing outside my old school, I remember running away the first day my Mum took me there only to be dragged back with no mercy so my Mum could get off to work. The place looks the very same except that it seems smaller, but perhaps that's because I'm an adult now and not seeing it through a kid's eyes. I feel empty and perhaps it's too long to think back and remember it all. I have vague memories of being bullied, or running around the playground chasing girls and looking up Claire Sweeney's skirt, and then remember a girl called Rhona Anderson screaming and hitting me near the school wall - I still have no idea why. Maybe she was just a crazy bitch or had just started on the rag, who knows?

Around the corner from the school is a large piece of spare ground that was usually covered in reddish ash. I look over to where the Tenement used to stand and I can see all the places I would play, and sit, and wait hungrily for my Mum to come home so we could eat. Sometimes she would not get home until seven or eight pm - pulling an extra shift at work so she could perhaps buy some eggs this week. I feel sick and disgusted with these, all too lucid, flashbacks where so much pain and sorrow was meted out on a daily basis - and yet, we overcame... I overcame. My brothers and sister still live in the area and my Mum and younger brother still live on the same fucking street! I often wonder if I had been braver and stayed, would my life have improved? The answer is, of course, yes, but not as much as it improved by moving away and dealing with life on my own fucking terms!

Glasgow gave me everything I needed to survive, but it could never give me an antidote for the misery

I went through, that we all went through as a family. Paradoxically, it was simultaneously the best and worst times in the seventies, and only getting far worse as we turned the corner and into the Eighties.

There's an ugly looking building at the end of the street, a gathering place of worship for sectarian violence - it still looks the same, Union Jack flying and high, barbed wire, fences... some things never change, and it's one part of Glasgow I do not miss, never understood and never want to!

Keppochill Road still looks the same - dirty and unkempt. The surrounding streets have the odd spattering of new build tenements and there is now a dual carriageway where most of Springburn Road used to be. Walking up towards the shopping centre, nearing 'The Bells' Bar', there is still a sinister atmosphere around this area. It looks dated and could still be the place I knew and avoided all those many years ago. This is where the last sighting (so I believe) of Bible John was apparently - cornered in a tenement house near 'Kay Street Baths', cornered and shot. I remember it had all of Springburn talking about it for weeks and how most people saw him, saying, "Yeah, he ran right by me and he looked like the devil!" (Scottish people love to embellish a story ;-) ...but, as it turned out, this was not Bible John, and I finally found an extract from a Glasgow newspaper explaining what was really going on when I was so young.

The Kay Street Siege - 15 July 1969

An extract from the 'Evening Times'...

Five plain-clothes officers went to an attic flat in Kelvinbridge to interview James Griffiths, 34, in connection with the murder (Rachel Ross). They were unable to gain entry, and Griffiths, who was said to be pathologically afraid of prison, began shooting, injuring one policeman and firing at anyone who appeared in the street. Still shooting, he raced to a car in Great Western Road, and wounded a number of people. Retrieving a cartridge belt from the boot, he returned to the flat, where the siege continued. By now, the police had bullet-proof shields and had been joined by a marksman with a high-powered rifle. But just as they were preparing to use tear-gas, Griffiths escaped, commandeered a car at gunpoint, and took police on a three-mile pursuit to Possil. Griffiths ran into the Round Toll Bar, where he fired some more shots, asked for a drink, changed his mind, and then made off in a stolen lorry, before ending up in a tenement flat in Springburn's Kay Street. There, he fired into a children's' playground and exchanged gunfire with police, his bullets ricocheting wildly and forcing local people to cower on shop floors. It fell to Chief Superintendent Calum Finlayson and Detective Sergeant Ian Smith, both armed with revolvers, to end the siege. Finlayson later recalled: "It was a warm day and I was perspiring and excited, but I was not afraid. I knew that Griffiths had a rifle and sawn-off shotgun and I knew the devastating effect of the latter." I said, "If he gets us on the stairhead, he'll blow our heads off."

Finlayson opened the letterbox and could hear Griffiths shooting. Then he noticed the gunman's shadow. Finlayson decided to fire and try to disarm him. He raised the revolver to the letter-box and took aim at the mans shoulder. He fired, but then heard Griffiths shoot back at the door. The officers feared their bullet had missed, but it hadn't - it had found its way from Griffiths shoulder to his heart.

It was the first time that a wanted man had been shot by Scottish Police. In all, Griffiths had fired more than one hundred shots, injuring thirteen people. One, a news vendor, died of his injuries. The following day's coverage of the siege contrasted with the optimistic stories about the launch of 'Apollo 11', which was taking Neil Armstrong, Buzz Aldrin, and Michael Collins to the moon.

Funny story, I remember taking my younger brother to Kay Street Baths in the 70s - I must have been about eleven or so, and my brother, David, about seven. We were in the shallow end of the pool and he said, "I need to pee!" I said, "Just do it in the water!" I looked away and then looked back - he had his trunks down to his knees and was peeing away merrily (haha), I about turned and moved away from the daft fucker!

I walked up towards Balgray Hill, the place we eventually managed to escape to, going from five in a bed in a 'Tenement, Single End' to having our own beds and bedrooms - it was still one of the best moments of my youth. Galloway Street still looms ominously at the top of the hill, and I stopped to reflect back on the night my older brother and his friend Ricky almost died at the hands of some fucking evil maniacs who are hopefully all dead and buried or locked and up rotting away somewhere that they fucking deserve to be. I see the street's been renamed to 'Lenzie Terrace' - what the fuck? ...a shit hole is still a shit hole, and changing the name does not make it any nicer! What the fuck was someone thinking about? But I see Chinese, Sudanese, and Afghanis walking around this area now, and perhaps peace has finally come to this part of town where I spent my teenage years in fear of the roaming street gangs and stabbings that occurred more often than I care to fucking remember. Perhaps Springburn is diverse enough now that people have learned to live with one another, or perhaps it's just as violent and rotten as it always has been, but with more exotic victims to choose from. I decide I do not want to stay around and find out, so I start my walk back to 'Old Springburn' (hoping my car is still there).

I will always remember on one visit to Glasgow, a few years back, when I was with my brothers, who had managed to convince me to go to a club/pub on Hawthorn Street, a place called 'The Ashfield'. I would never normally go into a place like this as it was a fucking dive, filled with criminals and scum from Possil Park and Springburn, but my siblings had convinced me 'that was years ago, and it's all changed now'. So, I went along with them. Going in felt like going into a fucking boxing ring, I was waiting for someone to knock me out - that's the feeling this place gave off. Right enough, it was full of hard faced men drinking their sorrows (and wages away). We were in there for almost ten minutes when a fight broke out between two fucking ugly Neanderthals. I just looked at my brothers and they said, "But it's usually okay" (famous last words) - Taxi!

I know in my heart I did the right thing, but there's something that has always bothered me - did I make a mistake and miss growing up around my family? I still feel I did the right thing as I look around Springburn - in my objective opinion, it has not moved on much since the early 80s and my family are still living in the past (psychologically, at least). My sister has a bought house in Springburn, actually on the site of Forest Hall, which was a 'Poorhouse' with about two thousand inmates. I used to go past these place sometimes and it really gave me the creeps, it had a stone wall all around it, which is still there as part of the new housing estate. I did some digging on the net and came across this to anyone who is interested in local history.

Source : Wikipedia

BARNHILL gave its name to the poorhouse which was built there in 1853. In the year 1810 a mental asylum had been built in Parliament Road and in 1843 was transferred to its present site at Gartnavel. The vacated building in Parliament Road was, in the same year, taken over as the city poorhouse, which in turn was transferred and amalgamated with Barnhill Poorhouse in 1905. Strict discipline was observed in Barnhill. Able bodied inmates were required to make up 350 bundles of firewood per day and stonebreakers were expected to break 5cwt. of whin metal per day. Any inmate not producing the stated amount was put on a bread and water diet in solitary confinement for 12 hours. Disorderly conduct such as swearing or breaking of rules, resulted in being put on a diet, excluding milk and buttermilk, for a period of three days.

In 1945 Barnhill was renamed Foresthall House and Hospital, and the place can be aptly described as a village within a city.(I used to walk by this place and here strange stories of zombies and psychos,I could not walk by it quick enough ,this was one seriously scary looking place , I don't know anyone who ever played on the grass near the front , which resembled a little park , quite an open space that lead up the main buildings, urban myths have always been a part of Glasgow culture and whether these stories were real or made up to terrify youngsters I don't think anyone will ever know the answer to that question, but what a way to treat disadvantaged people, I only hope any long term residents found the happiness they were long denied and some sort of eventual peace.

I will never truly know what kind of person I would've turned into had I stayed, but one thing's for certain - leaving when I did I saved myself about ten years of insanity, and for not living like that I am forever grateful! I guess my views have changed over time, I feel like an outsider - not Scottish, but not English either... perhaps both, or neither? A stranger in a very strange land. Perhaps I am beyond connecting with so much of my past to make an honest evaluation of it anymore - after all, I have spent most of my life trying to forget it and sometimes it feels like parts of it never really happened, seeming more like a newspaper story about someone else's pathetic struggles with early life. Perhaps some things are best left in the past, and in the past is where they should remain...

This used to be my playground

CHAPTER SIXTEEN

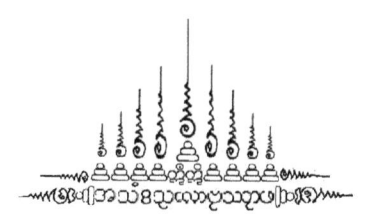

STARBURST

"Captain, deflector shields have just come on There's an object travelling at warp six on an intercept course"

"Go to yellow alert!" I say calmly, "and take evasive manoeuvres!"

"Aye, Captain," the Helmsman replies, "Captain, the object has changed course and is still heading towards us... and has increased speed to warp eight point two!"

"Go to red alert!" I say loudly, "Phaser crews stand by!"

"Unidentified vessel is now going sub-light, Captain, but still resuming intercept course."

"Communications officer, hail them," I state firmly.

The sultry, but efficient, Communications Officer sends out a standard hail and then replies, "No response, Captain."

"Open hailing frequencies," I command

She almost immediately replies, "Hailing frequencies open!"

"Unidentified vessel, this is Captain James T Scott of the Federation Star Ship 'Europa', please identify yourself and your intentions - we are on a mission of exploration and pose no threat, but we are capable of defensive action if necessary."

"The ship is firing its primary weapon, Captain, some sort of ionised, plasma energy burst," the Science Officer reports, "Impact in twenty seconds. All hands brace for impact - shields to maximum!"

The mighty Star Ship rocks and shudders to the explosion and immense impact that strains the defence shields which surround the outside of the ship. "Shields holding at eighty seven percent!" he adds.

"Return fire, Mr. Harton!"

"Phasers firing, Captain - direct hit to their port bow and engines! They're hurt and are warping out of range."

After a brief pause, I state, "Go to yellow alert, all decks report to the Science Officer any casualties and damage!" (Cue 'Star Trek' intro Theme)

"Is all that we see or seem, but a dream within a dream?" (Edgar Allen Poe)

"Tam, Tam, TAM!!! Wake up!"

"What? Eh? O-fucking-kay!"

I'm having a brilliant, lucid dream and she has to wake me up!

"Let the cats in - it's raining!"

"For fuck's sake, lazy bitch!" I mumble quietly, so she does not hear.

I get up and let the cats in, give them some food and wonder if I will be able to step back onto the bridge of my Star Ship in a few minutes and carry on with the adventure - but, no! I love her very much, but she does take me out of fantasy land much too often. I started reading 'Science Fiction' in my youth and was very drawn to Philip K Dick, Brian Aldiss, Asimov, and Arthur C Clarke to name but a few. These stories would be my gateway out of hell, and my life, for a few hours where I would dream of being out in the star filled Galaxies, discovering new life and civilisations, to boldly go... (Better stop there, eh?)

I am, of course, a 'Trekker' or 'Trekkie', as it was the only 'Sci-Fi' programme that made any sense to me. 'Lost in Space' was okay, but too many gimmicky situations and orange faced aliens for me, if you know what I mean. 'Star Trek' was more cognitive and appealed to my sense of wonder more than any other, and I am sure it influenced my song writing and Synth playing in later life. I often would play big soundscapes and name the tracks after Stars and Constellations, not realising that 'Tangerine Dream' were doing it years before me - fuckers!

I believe Science Fiction helped expand my mind and look critically at everything. I questioned everything I was ever taught at school, much to the disdain of my 'Teachers' who would often try to shut me down and get me back on the path they were leading me down. Religious Education was one of the classes where the 'Teachers' really hated me being in as I would ask, "What do you mean, God created everything? How? And where did God come from? What was before God?" All were questions that none of them knew the answers to. "Why are you teaching this stuff if you don't even know the answers?" I would ask, "It's like teaching maths and saying we do not know how to add or subtract!" Most illogical!

Of course, I would be asked to stand out in the corridor as their feeble minds were not programmed at University to deal with such questions. Even the ones who took a Theology Degree had no answers to these questions, even now, and I often have some brilliant times pulling their belief structure apart if they ever engage me in conversation (or try to evangelise).

Jehovah's Witnesses (called JoJo's in Scotland, for some reason), from time to time, would knock on my door in Glasgow and always left crying. I would invite them in and they would ask me, "Do you believe in God?" I would say, "Well, if God is demonstrable, then I would be prepared to accept that there is one - but I still would not worship one who stood by to let all this cruelty be inflicted on us!" They, of course, could not demonstrate their God to me, but always pointed to the usual rhetoric and say, "Look all around you - the trees, the majestic beauty of life, the blue skies, the grass, and all the creatures he has blessed upon you!" "Oh, for fuck's sake! Here we go," I would say to myself, "Creationist dribble with nothing but a book to go on!" I wondered if the followers of Christ ever realised that it was supposedly set in the Middle East and that John, David, Paul, etc. (I forget the rest), are not Hebrew names - kinda says it all to me.

I would ask, "Who created God?"

They would reply, "No-one, he is infinite and always has been."

"How do you know? Can you prove it? Did he come from nothing? How is that possible? And if he came from nothing, what was the nothing he came from - was it a something? And if it was a something, where did that come from?"

And, yes, after some more standard responses about faith (the best 'get out' clause ever!), they would wander off and try another house - but strangely never returned to my door in the coming weeks, months, years... which was a shame, really, as I loved our little existential 'chats'.

I think that as you go through life, the more detached you become from accepted beliefs - unless you have been heavily indoctrinated into your particular 'faith'. A lot of people are 'awake', and a lot of people see religion as a control mechanism for the weak minded who like to be led and told 'it's okay when you die, there is something else - all you have to do is grovel all your life and give us your money, attendance and obedience... and we will look after you all!' Fucking retards in my honest opinion! And what a bunch of hypocritical leeches the Churches themselves are - religion has been the biggest cause of wars and suffering on this sicko planet for centuries! I'm not saying that they are all 'fucked in the head' or 'delusional', but a lot are, and they are the dangerous ones - they pose a threat to your very lives, much as politicians pose a threat to freedom and sovereignty.

"Religion is the opium of the people (Masses)" (Karl Marx)

Glasgow - July, 2015 Maryhill

I get out my car after a seven hour drive to meet ex-band member, Jonn Harton. He comes out to greet me and he looks tired, but looks good - and it's great to see him. He has kindly offered me a place to stay during my short visit, and I think we stayed up till 5am talking about the band, the past adventures, and the times when we had all moved on in life. We talk about how fucked up the world has become and compare it to the World Wars, the 70's and 80's, and we both agree that there is something afoot ...and whatever it is, it's not going to be beneficial to any humans that are not on the 'elite' list. We talk about technology and come to the conclusion that we have been guided or helped in some way from where we were to where we are now - some of the leaps in computer tech (particularly the 'discovery' of 'solid state technology' in the post-war era) is almost beyond fucking comprehension!

Jim then turns up and we discuss these issues some more... and, bizarrely, we are all of the same opinion - proving that over the last thirty years we are more or less of the same mind-set. We even rip apart the fucking SNP, who we believe will be the end of Scotland if they ever get their way - let's not forget that they were politically aligned with Hitler's Germany during the war and wanted the same options for our nation ...and still do! If you don't fucking believe me, do some research of your own and stand back in horror as the truth hits you where it hurts! Scottish Nationalist Party or more to the point Socialist Nationalist Party, National Socialism (Nazism for short).

Capitalism isn't any better, but it's not fascism (not quite), and in the end is no better as fucking greedy corporations infest everything, everywhere, like a virus and sucks the life and money out of everything till it's dead and can give no more - we need something else, people, I have no idea what ...yet! I never even fucking vote for any of these cunts! I always go to the voting station, register I am there, then pretend to vote and take my ballot paper home - it has to be counted as a non-vote as I registered being there but did not cast it, not a lost vote in any sense! If only we all did this! We need a vote for 'none of the above' - we have to show them we do not want any of them and we want change now!

Perhaps we could have a Parliament of Common People - Teachers, Nurses, Firemen, Postmen, Midwives, Carers, and general workers - they could run the country for a couple of years and then refresh them with another run of common people who know what we want, as they are 'us' ...they were not born into some aristocracy or spoon fed by a private nanny and tutored at Eton! Oh, and we really need to get rid of those fucking 'Lords', who are only interested in preserving their elites and indulgences! Spend a few minutes thinking about our 'Democracy' which is code for socialism and how it works, why you participate in it, and why it consistently fails to meet the needs of all the people without whom it could not exist - and that in itself will have made the price of this book worthwhile to you!

Glasgow - 1977, Nightshift, Scars Bakery

Here I am, at work on nights, slaving for a fucking pittance, working with Neanderthals and hairless apes who can only see getting through the next day till pay day, where the cycle of drinking and violence starts and ends as the money runs out. They were a rough bunch, but at times they were profoundly funny. I still remember how they would set me up and get me into trouble with the management. One time they asked me to turn on the washing machine, and I said, "Oh, but it's broken!" They said, "Nah, it's fixed now - can you wash these bowls?" So, I would put these massive bowls in, switch it on, manually spin it round to the water jets at the back, and spin it round till all the compartments were drenched and had washed all the things inside the machine. I turned it round and lying inside one of the cages was... the Factory Manager, 'Tommy Moore' - he was inside the bloody thing and had been trying to fix the jets and told the Bakers not to use the machine till he was out of it. The bastards had set me up to soak him - fuck me, did he go ballistic! There was no way was I 'grassing them up', though, as they would have stuck me in the oven or doughnut fryer!

As with all places, no-one liked the boss - he was a bit of a 'brown noser' to the owners and we all hated him for it, especially as he would grass us up at the drop of a hat. What a cunt! One day, he said, "Tam, you're with me today. I'll teach you how to pipe pancakes onto the hotplate." So, being the trainee, I was with him on this big hotplate, knowing that the bakers were all laughing at me for being with him - they would whistle and make odd noises to make me laugh while I was beside him and I had to bite my tongue. Well, after about an hour of this piping shit, he grabs a bottle of 'Irn Bru' and says, "You want some?" I was just about to take it when I see some Baker gesture from behind the manager, mouthing 'no', so I reply "No, its okay, I'll get some water." He puts the bottle to his lips and starts gulping it down, then I hear muffled laughing and Bakers moving away from me - I thought, "What the fuck?" Then the manager spits out the 'Irn Bru' and everyone is laughing their heads off - the manager with 'Irn Bru' slithering out his lips and all over his chin looks at me and grabs me. "I'm going to make you suffer, you cunt!" he shouted at me.

It turns out about five Bakers had pissed into the 'Irn Bru' bottle (which looks like piss, anyway). I couldn't tell him it wasn't me as they would all have kicked the crap out of me. I think, in truth, he knew it was them, but took it out on me to save face (too fucking late to save that, dude!)

Another time on nightshift, they said, "See that fucker over there, (Andy Denim) the cunt's got a car, (yes, they were jealous that he had a car), go out and let his tyres down or we will fuck you up!" So, a very scared me went out, laid on the ground and was in the middle of letting his tyres down when I hear a voice. I looked up to see a steel toe-capped boot hit me in the face - the cunts had went and told him what I was doing, and he had ran over to sort me out... either way I was getting a kicking, it was never a question of when, it was always a question of who!

Live and Let die!

At fifty four there's a lot I still want to do in life - I want to finish this book and perhaps get another album of tunes or songs out before I shuffle off this mortal coil. My journey through life has been tough, but I know other people have a greater struggle and I am thankful for the small heights I have managed to attain through sheer determination and hard work. I can only feel a sense of pride to have gotten so far and lived as long, and I mention this because I have been having really bad headaches and, being a guy, I just put it down to being tired or a strained neck muscle. Finally someone tells me to have this looked into... so I do.

Anyway, off I toddle to the Doctors, and it's probably been ten years since I was here last ...and was not looking forward to talking to the twats. I hate the way they start the conversation off, "So, what seems to the trouble"? Oh, fucking brilliant, he wants me to self-diagnose myself and do half the fucking work for him! Cheeky bastard! He should give me fifty quid for doing half of his job! Lee Evans puts it brilliantly, "A licence to practice medicine? I want one who's doing it for real"!

Anyhow, it transpires the headaches are due to high blood pressure (185 over 125 - text book healthy is 120 over 80), so this is well into stroke and heart attack domain! Cheerfully, he is surprised that I haven't had one yet, puts me on drugs right

Being Boiled

away and a diet that would starve a fucking rabbit to death! And that brings me to where I am now - I've never smoked, done drugs, ate reasonably healthily after my teen years ...and now I get this shitty news! In the end, I guess something is going to get you, whether you have any vices or not! Right now I'm wishing I could rewind and do all the bad stuff, just like a proper 'Rock Star' - all of it, Cocaine, Heroin, Smoke, eat rich food, and drink to excess as I would end up in the same situation! For fuck's sake, who did I piss off in life that Karma came looking for me wearing big, tackety boots? Life really is a bitch!

By now I've had my head filled with what happens if I snuff it anytime soon - I have no significant assets to leave anyone, no property (the first two fucking marriages sorted that out for me), and definitely no money, so all someone gets is my shitty pension, a rather nice collection of Synthesisers, and a nippy Audi TT (oh, yeah, and some bad 80's clothing I've never had the heart to throw away ...and, let's face it, if I sent them away to a poorer country, right now someone would be walking about the Serengeti Plains looking like Nick fucking Rhodes from 'Duran Duran', ha-ha). So, not being into all these fucking robbing bastard, funeral home cunts with their fucking two grand coffin and a three fucking grand service ... my theory is - no bastarding way, thank you for fuck all!

Being an Atheist, anyway, I would much prefer just being driven to the Crematorium in the back of a transit van and being toasted in a cardboard coffin (currently a bargain at a hundred pounds - £100 - on the internet) ... maybe just one of my 'friends' saying something amusing as the door closes for 'The Burn' - something from a 'Carry On' film would be quite fitting, like "Frying Tonight' (Carry on Screaming, I believe, ha-ha), or perhaps someone could say "To boldly go where no man has gone before," or "Make is so!" or even, "Resistance is futile!", but I definitely want the end theme from the movie 'Star Man' playing as I crackle and pop! ...or maybe play 'Disco Inferno' at the very least - I'll leave it up to you Jonn and Jim, but in the name of all that's holy, don't let anyone else choose... they'll pick something from 'The Carpenters' for fucks sake! *'Why do birds suddenly appear, every time, you are near...'* or 'We've Only Just begun' or 'Solitaire' or 'Goodbye to Love' ...I think you get the jist!

Okay, so that just leaves the ashes to sort out after the main event - fucking great stuff, I've never smoked in my entire life and now I could be the entire contents of all the cigarette ashtrays from outside a pub emptied into a midsize jar - how about that? At first, I thought perhaps I could be put in a blender and mixed into a zombie smoother, but after a few lesser entertaining ideas, I settled on having my ashes poured into a mega-'fuck off'-firework and set off on Hogmany from the top of Lennoxtown Castle... the place where I was spat out into this wonderful life!

Right, so, I'm on two lots of pills for blood pressure

and something else, had an 'ECG' where the male nurse hooked me up to a twelve point scanner - and it came out flat line! So, I gave him a sideways glance and asked, "Problem? He said, "That's weird, I'll try it again." He does indeed do it again... and again, and it's all flat lined. The man looked puzzled, so I wittily said, "Am I already dead?" It seemed he didn't appreciate the humour and went off to get another nurse to sort it... and confirm I was actually alive, I assume. As it turned out, he had one of the wires on the wrong ankle and the circuit was not complete - ha-ha, what a dick!

Shuffles Disco, Glasgow, 1977 - 'Night Fever'

I've never really been ill since my early years, but tonight was different. As usual, I was dancing like there was no tomorrow and enjoying the attention of all the 'poseurs' who thought I was a cool dancer. I never drank or took drugs or had any kind of vice (yawn), and here I am talking to these cracking and absolutely fuckable twins, almost at the point where we are all going home together for some numpties (or at least into the ladies for a 'five knuckle shuffle' and some flossing) when I apparently blacked out - just fell in a heap on the floor and was out for about fifteen minutes. I woke up in the ladies loo with the twins fanning me and putting cold water on my face - I was well pissed off, but that was the only time I ever felt ill... till a few weeks ago.

I said my farewells to the twins and walked eight miles home in the pissing rain as I had no money left and was chilled to the fucking core. I think I got home around 2am and was due in at work at 6am. I've never been one for calling in sick or bunking off, as I was not made 'that way', and anyway, the bastards would not give out sick pay - they'd just dock you a day's wages. It was so primitive back then, so it was not worth the aggro.

The doctor's advice, the next afternoon, was "You're burning the candle at both ends!" I confusedly said, "Eh?" He explained that I was doing too much and not resting in-between or sleeping enough and my body was exhausted - so I had to slow down. I promptly came back with, "Fucking whoa - I'll sleep when I'm fucking dead, pal!" To which he replied, "It's your choice!" The fucking cunt, I'm sixteen and he's telling me I can't hack it and need to slow down - well, fuck that... and to this day I have never slowed down for anyone or anything, but it seems I need to pay attention to the doctors this time or this book will be a few chapters short and may well be renamed as 'The End'. Fuckers!

Music is my raison d'etre and I always toyed with the idea of a reunion. I was inspired by watching a great little bit of TV directed by Martin Clunes called 'Hunting Venus', which was about a fictional band called the 'Venus Hunters' - whoa, wait a minute, fuck it, ok this is what I found on Google, so here goes...

Source : Wikipedia

Hunting Venus is a British television comedy-drama starring Martin Clunes and Neil Morrissey as former members of a 1980s new romantic pop group. The one-off drama was broadcast on ITV on 31 March 1999, and was produced by Buffalo Pictures for Yorkshire Television.

The plot follows former pop-star turned con artist Simon Delaney (Clunes) is kidnapped by two fans of his eighties band the Venus Hunters, and blackmailed to re-form the band for one final performance, live on television.

It features cameos from a number of new romantic pop stars, including Simon Le Bon (with his wife Jasmine Le Bon), Tony Hadley, Gary Numan, and Phil Oakey. Jools Holland also appears, as himself, and also wrote the song "Starburst", The Venus Hunters' biggest hit.

It's difficult to get hold of this TV show anywhere, commercially, and the only copy I have seen of it is on 'YouTube' (hooray!). The video quality is abysmal, obviously taken from a VHS tape, so second generation, and it did not help that the tape had probably been used about three hundred times to record some other shit on it, making the audio-track sound worse than 'The Billy Sloan Band'! Anyway, it inspired me to want to do this with a non-fictional band, a fucking real, live band, and in my warped head, it would start with me going to Glasgow (or wherever), trying to track everyone down and then convincing them that we should get back together for a one time only event a-la 'The Venus Hunters'. Hey, this is a plan!

John Healey; Drums, Percussions

"The feeling has gone only you and I

So, if I was getting the band back together, ideally I would start with the drummer, John Healey, as he was the first drummer in a band called 'Zoneheim'. So here I go, dredging the Internet and thinking of all the ways to search for him - I try typing 'cunt' into Google... but it does not help as I am immediately hit with thousands of pages, (who'd have thought?). Anyway, I finally track him down to a place in Glasgow called Drumchapel and he is living deep in the middle of a scheme (a housing project for chavs). I knock on his door and this fat, bald, bastard opens the door and I say, "Hi, is John there?" and he looks me over a bit and says, "Yeah - that's me, what do you want?" I reply, "It's me, its Tam!" And he says, "Who the fuck are you?" Realising my mistake, I correct myself and say "It's me, it's Tommy - Remember? We played in band called Zoneheim!!" And then the penny drops, "For fuck's sake! Tommy - Yeah, I remember you now - come on in!"

I sit down in the living room and wait for him to bring me in a cup of coffee, then he says to me, "So what brings you here, after thirty years?"

I said, "It's been hard tracking you down, I live near London and have lost all of my contacts from up north... lost touch with a lot of things and people - but I had this crazy idea of getting the band back together for one last gig!"

He doesn't look too impressed and says, "I don't know, it's been a long time since I picked up sticks ...and I look like shit now. Anyway, you cunts kicked me out the band because of Angela, and it fucked me up big time! All you had to do was let me stay in the band and keep seeing Angela and I would have sorted all the rest out and been brand new! So it's a big, fat, fuck off from me, Tommy!"

I was helpless to ask the next question - I had to know...

"Did you marry Angela?"

His face twisted a bit and he nodded, "Yeah, and had five kids... then the fucking cow left me for some other bastard with more money and I got stuck with the kids - and all my dreams were crushed and I ended up with nothing, Tommy. I mean, I was a great wee drummer, right? I was fucking spot on with my timing, like... right?"

I had to agree and say, "Yes, you were great actually - I'm sorry you never got a chance to do more with your skills and got shafted by the love of your life... but that's a chance we all take. I've been married three times (no kids, thank fuck), and have been let down and kicked in the teeth so many times I've got no teeth left to kick... and promised myself I'd never get into that position again!" "Yeah, you're fucking right there, Tommy. I wish I had the guts to know myself like that and not be so fucking stupid!" he replied and paused thoughtfully, "Okay. Okay, I'll do it - if you can organise anything, I'll do it, Tommy. This is my last chance to feel good about everything, right? At least I'll have something to remember... even if it is too late in life."

So I said, "That's great, I'll be in touch when I find the others!"

Then I said my goodbyes, turned my collar up and walked off into the cold night air.

Derek Fairlie; Drums, Percussion, Backing vocals?

Alright, fellas, let's go!"

The next member was Derek. Now he was the replacement drummer for Healey, when we outed him from the band. Derek was easy to find, I knew he lived in Largs and I managed to track him down fairly (he he) quickly, knocked on his door and his wife Suzanne answered the door.

"Tommy?" she says.

"Yeah," I said, "it's me. Is Derek around?"

Smiling, she stood back and said, "Yeah, come in - come in. It's great to see you - Oh, he'll be chuffed to see you." A moment later she is still smiling, looks upstairs and screams, "Derek! Come down here, there's someone to see you!"

Derek comes down the stairs - he looks slightly bigger and has a shock of grey, waist length hair. He almost shouts in surprise, "My God! Tommy!" He shakes my hand firmly, gripping it tightly, "What brings you here?"

"Well," I explained, "We're getting back together, the band, I mean - a one time only gig."

He smiles and says without hesitating, "Yes, let's do it!"

"Brilliant," I replied, "I did ask John Healey if he would be interested - because he was the first drummer we had before you, Dek... so it might turn out we have two drummers for this get together. Is that okay?"

"Eh, I don't know, Tommy, I wouldn't want to share any stage with another drummer. Well, I have quite a large drum kit, if you know what I mean, and I'm a bit of a selfish bastard when it comes to sharing the limelight and all that!"

I just nodded and said, "Oh, yes, of course, I quite understand, Dek - but I think it would be a nice thing to do."

"Okay... okay," he agrees, "I'm in, and we'll work

around it somehow - it would just be great to get together again!"

Then I ask him, "Any Idea where Jim, Jonn, and Lynnette are?"

He gives a smile back and nods, "Well, funny you should say that, but Jonn's been online with a book he had written years ago and a pile of other stuff he's been involved in. I always wanted to get together with him and chew the fat, but I never took the opportunity to contact him... but I do have an email address for him. Oh, and remember we did the Andy Scott cover, 'Invisible'?"

"Yeah," I say and nod in agreement.

"Fucking great track, right? You and Jonn nailed it... and I really appreciated it very much."

I gave a little smile, "Perhaps we can do it live - when we get back together... it would be great to play it live!"

But then he goes quiet and speaks in a confessional tone that make me feel like a fucking priest.

"I did something really bad - I bought some master tapes years ago, right from under Harton's nose... and he found out I had them. I got a bit scared he would sue me, so I burned them in the garden and he hasn't spoken to me since!"

"Fuck, it's been thirty years, man - let bygones be bygones. I'm sure Jonn is more than capable of letting the past go as much as any of us are able to - we all do things we regret... but they don't define us forever, Dek. Get a fucking grip, man! We all have a past, but we don't have to live up to it. What's more important is now - let's go looking for Jim and the others, eh?" I ask him.

"Brilliant," he says, "Yeah - let's go!"

Jim McKenna; Synths, Piano, Bass Synth, all things weird.

"Light my fire".

So, we are in the car together and go off looking for Jim McKenna, who the last I had heard of was working in the 'Royal Scottish Academy of Music and Drama', fixing synthesisers and anything with resistors and capacitors involved in them. I get to the front desk with Derek and we ask if Mr McKenna is still working here, and the lady on the desk says, "Who? Oh, you mean, Jim? Yes, he is - who shall I say is calling?"

"Tell him it's Tommy and Derek from 1985"

To which she says, "Do you mean you're both time travellers?"

"Yeah, ha-ha – good one! Now... call Jim, you comedienne!"

I thought for one moment we would have to break Jim out of a Mental Institution much the same way the A Team had to break out Murdoch when they needed him for a job, I was sure Jim would be the one person who would be the hardest to track down!

McKenna comes down the stairs with a big grin on his face, rushes up to us, and we are all standing in a group hug.

Jim tells us both, "Fuck's sake, guys, I knew this was going to happen - there've been weird things happening all week around my aura... and just the other day I was listening to 'Let the Rain Come Down'... and I haven't listened to it for ten years or more! This is so meant to be!"

Then I explain things to Jim...

"Get the band back together?" Jim screams, "Are you fucking crazy? It's been thirty years - who wants to listen to has-beens... especially a bunch of minor celebrities?"

I raise a hand and stop him.

"Dude, have you not seen 'The Venus Hunters'? What about some show called 'Bands Reunited'? It's the time of getting bands back together, we still have a fan base out there and, who knows, we might just enjoy it?"

"Okay. Okay, yes - it might just work at that, but we need the main man on board and we all know what a difficult person he can be... and he's still a Prima Donna (I believe…. I believe …. I believe)

Jim lets us know what he has been doing in the intervening years and we listen intently - Jim's tales are always great to listen to, and he is a great talker... I miss that part of him and being in a band with the man. It's then I realise I was privileged to have known him so long ago.

"This is going great," I say out aloud, "Only one more guy to sort and we have a band (of sorts). I wonder how the old scrote is doing... and if he is a day walker yet?"

Jonn Harton; Guitar, Vocals, Lyrics, Synths, Samplers, Witty Repartee

"Oh Lordy, oh Lordy"!

We all turn up at Jonn's address and knock on the door, not knowing what to expect - Is he fat? Is he bald (like me)? Can he still play guitar? Azig, azig, ahhh! He opens the door and is beaming a luminous smile. "Fuck me, it's one o'clock in the afternoon and the fucker's awake," I say to my inner self, "and he looks good - still slim, still has all his own hair... mother fucker! I did not expect him to look that good, and to be honest, Jim looked the same except for a little Kangaroo pouch. I, of course, was bald and a little bit beefier... but also wiser and more of a sound designer these days, a bit (dare I say) like Eno. Perhaps I could change my name to 'Tam, Peter, George, St. John le Baptiste de la Salle, Scott'? But I digress.

Jonn is pleasant, open and very warm to the idea of a get together - he seems relaxed and chilled, as he always was, and I am impressed there is no ego or any awkwardness between him and Derek after the Tape fiasco of yesteryear. He shows us his book 'Revolutionaries' and is clearly proud of that achievement, and rightly so, and it makes a part of me wonder if perhaps I could write something of my own? Perhaps one day I will give it a go?

I ask Jonn where Lynette is, but he just waves his hand and says, "She could be dead for all I know!"

It's only then do I realise that they are not together anymore. They were good together, but cracks appear on even the best relationships... and nothing lasts forever - I am living testament to that in my journey through love and life.

Fucking yes, yes, yes! Jonn is clearly in and all we have to do now is sort out some instruments (I still have all of mine and I'm fairly sure Jimbo can get a hold of some cool analogue gear). We have a band again!

Now, the next part I cannot write as I really want this to happen - let's just say I am honoured to have met and played with guys of such character, good or bad. We all managed, under the direct talents of Mr Harton, to create something special and unique - certainly in Glasgow, if not Scotland, and for that I am damn proud, and hats off to the brains of it all for pulling us all together and making some fine tunes and songs that still sound fresh and edgy.

But for today only, we are 'The Venus Hunters'!

Tam Scott; Synths, Vocals, Sampler, and Japanesque looks and sounds

"So, I'm down to this"....

EPILOGUE

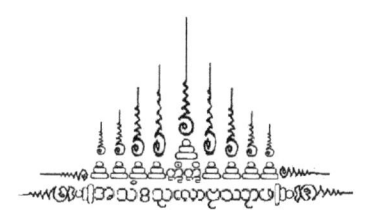

I'm the king of rock 'n' roll completely

The six o'clock alarm wakes me as usual with its monotonous din and I open my eyes, even though I have been awake most of the night looking at images projected onto my closed eyelids, wondering and worrying about the future... and missing my past self - How fucking crazy is that? After all, it's taken me all these years to find inner peace and some sort of stable environment, but here I am wishing I was back in the past? What the fuck is that all about?

Surely I don't miss the pain and the family feuds, lack of money and no direction, crazy bitch wives and even crazier situations that drove me to the brink of insanity and beyond!

Reflection is never an easy thing, all those unanswered questions you pose to yourself - did I do the right thing? Should I have stayed put in my life and perhaps everything would have worked out for the better in its own way, good or bad? Do I have 'No Regrets" as the Midge Ure song implies, or do I have many? The answer is, of course, yes - I have many regrets and my main one is not spending time with my now very ill Mum who may well have passed on before this book ever reaches a publisher.

I always thought I had failed her as a son, running away to make a better life and abandoning her to a life of misery with my 'Dad' who, to this day, treats her like a piece of shit. When I visit her and hear him speak to her in that way I want to knock his brown ugly teeth down his vile fucking throat. But my Mum seems to be very proud of me and says "I wish you were not so far away but I am happy you have found a better way in life". My brothers and sister stood their ground, never ventured out into the world much, and seemed more at home in Glasgow where they made it work for them But, for me, I felt Glasgow was eating me alive and I would be dragged down into the quagmire of hopelessness, drinking and drugs that consume the low achievers which certain parts of the city seems to spawn into existence.

I never went on to buy my Mum a house or an expensive gift, took her on holiday, or tell her that I love her (except in the past six years or so) and she has started to do the same - she said to me last year, "I love you Tam!" and I burst into tears and hugged her to my chest for what seemed like an eternity. She was never an emotional person or overly caring - I guess it's a Tenement thing or being married to a selfish violent cunt that makes you 'that way'.

My Dad does not have much time left to live as years of smoking have taken its toll on his breathing and he is now paying the consequences. He smokes forty to fifty a day, every day, his little flat stinks as his lungs must stink with the filth of tar and thousands of other carcinogens engrained into his very being... was it worth it? I wonder if he has any regrets, but somehow I doubt it.

I was recently visiting my Mum as it may be the last time I get to see her and my dad was sitting near the window, smoking and drinking with my younger brother, and I heard him say he never cared about any of us - I just exploded! Yes, we fucking know you don't care about any of us, we all knew from the age of six that you were not 'A Dad', we get it, you cunt - Hannibal Lecter would have been a better Dad than you, and even Darth Vader would have been more caring than you! Because of your selfish sex acts many years ago, we all have to deal with a life that we did not wish for or want. But here we are, and in the face of adversity we have made it work without any assistance from your 'Fatherly influence'.

Anger is quite rightly viewed as a negative emotion, but it also has its own form of release by flushing it out of your system - paradoxically you get angry to expel the poison from your system. How I envy computers, and wish I could simply get someone to turn me off and then on again - simply flushing my memory of all the bad sectors.

Many people reading this will identify with every word I have said, perhaps have even been in the very same situation and purged it out of your system by now. I know people around the world have it worse than we do, but back then we never knew about the world, the world we knew was just out the front door or hiding in a closet to avoid a drunken beating or worse!

I try to replay the happy things over in my mind and rebuild them into little sections of movie clips (the only way I can explain it) in my mind's eye, letting me relive some portion of it - my first kiss, my first pay packet, the joy of sex, and even the marriages that failed have some lighter moments that I like to remember... little snippets of joy that mean nothing to anyone except me. If people see me smiling to myself, they must think I am quite the madman. If 'happiness' was a drug, I would be taking it every day... as we all would.

'Star Trek - The Original Series', as we 'Trekkies' like it to be known, began with the first (untelevised at the time) pilot. 'The Menagerie' was something I always understood from my early teens, and I would have been perfectly at ease with someone such as the "Talosians" manipulating my mind and life experiences, loving anyone I could imagine or going anyplace, anytime, anywhere... I mean, that's all we want - right? A life with no struggles and heartache or pain, no death or suffering? Or is it as 'Kirk' once said to 'The Companion' in the episode 'Metamorphosis'? There, he was essentially making the point that taking away all obstacles in life is no life, and without the challenges we would wither and die.

In the sickest sense of the word 'life', does pain and suffering map out a learning curve or does it destroy us all in the end? How on Earth can pain and suffering make people better? That is a question I have no answer for, I'm afraid, and is perhaps best left to Philosophers.

The curse of political correctness will surely be the end of free speech as we know it, fucking social Marxism at its very worst and calculated to do exactly that, to silence us, make everyone a victim and to invent some new ones, these feminist, social justice warriors are all deluded, feminist issues were solved in the early eighties, what are they bleating on about now? A wage gap? , for fucks sake it's illegal to pay anyone in the UK less for doing the same job , the only way women get paid less is because they make different life choices.

Now we have a 'far left' movement called social justice warriors , this is where other groups of people will happily be an apologist for everyone else and blame the 'far right' for so many injustices, stop picking on us all, black lives matter! Of course they do but so does everyone's else's lives matter , now they shout transgender people have the right to be seen as men or women ,ok I and want to be recognised as a moose.

The world is getting weirder by the minute and I am sick of all the crap people make up, the world has real issues and real problems so stop making shit up, I think people are leaving universities dumber than when they went in these days,

A few things to 'Google' will soon have you making your own opinions and researching into this subject a little more, so first thing to search for is trigglypuff, have fun with this one and make your own mind up.

So where am I now? Well, I am in my mid-fifties and reasonably healthy apart from a blood pressure issue that is more or less stress related to the crazy job I have and all its up and downs. It's essentially a great job, but is let down with a few people who really should not be there, you know the types - the arse lickers and sycophants, work weasels and especially the younger fucks who are far too arrogant and think 'they' know all the answers.

I am now waiting for the passing on of my Mum and Dad, at the same time, trying to re-evaluate my life - putting everything into perspective to try and rationalise what else in my life I want or could accomplish. I know I really want to do a bit more travelling and experiencing some more cultures before I make excuses about my age and health to become a stay at home, middle ages dude. I also want to write another book based more on being in bands and the music business surrounding it.

I still think I have another album in me, a grand Synth blockbuster on the scale of 'Jarre', 'Tangerine Dream', or 'Tomita' and would relish doing it along with my former band mates. I want to leave a musical legacy as well as my written words, it will be out there till the end of the Earth - there is no need to lie in the ground and just become dust, you can 'live' forever in one form or another. I am in an exciting part of my life, fluxing in-between a state of completion and my own metamorphosis to another part of my journey in life.

I have lived my life as best as I can and rose to the top, as far as I am concerned, from zero to hero in my own experiences. I really hope, and think about this often, that all the underdogs from my generation somehow managed to find their own way to the top and are proud of what they have achieved.

To all those kindred spirits, I salute you and leave these timeless words as a mantra for all our lives... 'Don't let the bastards ever get you down'!

ABOUT THE AUTHOR

Tam is a 1980s' musician-recording artist and has been on several TV and radio shows and has recorded and toured extensively with named bands worldwide as well as having commercial success with prominent Glasgow bands of the day in the early eighties.(you all know who you are)

He has also recorded a successful series of relaxation, meditation Cds' that have appeared on numerous Health magazines in the late 1990s' as well as writing a piece of music for a successful 1980s' US drama show.

I would like to thank each one of you for purchasing my first novel and I would be very happy if it entertained you by reading it as much as it entertained me by writing it, I can only hope that this will inspire me to carry on writing another book in the near future.

Sincere best wishes,

Tam

SOURCES & CREDITS

Japan (Ghosts; From The Album- Tin Drum, released-1981)

Alkazar (Crying at the Discotheque; From The Album- Casino 2000-released 2000)

Sister Sledge (I Wonder why, he's The Greatest Dancer; From The Album- We Are Family-released 1979)

Dream Academy (Life In A Northern Town; From The Album- The Dream Academy released 1985)

Duran Duran (Save a Prayer; From The Album –Rio- released -1982)

David Bowie (Space Oddity; From The Album - David Bowie-released 1967)

Murray Head (One Night in Bangkok; From The Album-Chess-released 1984)

Gary Numan (Complex; From The Album- The Pleasure Principle-released 1979)

Tubeway Army (Tubeway Army; From The Album – Replicas-released 1979)

The Blue Nile (Tinsel Town in the Rain; From The Album – A Walk Across The Roof Tops-released 1984)

H20 (I Dream To Sleep ; From The Album – Faith – released 1983)

The Human League (Being Boiled; Empire State Human; From The Album – Reproduction-released 1979)

Kraftwerk (Computer Love; From The Album Computer World-released 1981)

The Venus Hunters (Starburst; From The Album – Hunting Venus-released-1999)

'The Hill and The Hibiscus Flowers' from the album 'Timeless Flight' By Steve Harley & Cockney Rebel

"The author and Publisher wish to thank Steve Harley for his kind permission in allowing the use of this piece (copyright Steve Harley 1975)"

Google;

Wikipedia;

The Evening Times

The People of Glasgow

Bing

Lightning Source UK Ltd.
Milton Keynes UK
UKHW010854010219
336564UK00006B/405/P